DAMIAN FARROW & JUSTIN KEMP

realised early on that they'd never make it as elite sportsmen
so they opted for real jobs and became sports scientists. Their first
book, *Run Like You Stole Something*, was published in 2003.

Dr Damian Farrow (Ph.D., M.App.Sc., B.Ed.), above left, is the
Skill Acquisition Specialist at the Australian Institute of Sport,
working with a variety of AIS sports and consulting to professional
teams in football codes.

Justin Kemp (M.Sc., B.Ed.), above right, is the Exercise Physiologist
at the Australian Catholic University in Melbourne. He is also a Ph.D.
scholar at Victoria University. He hosts 'Run Like You Stole
Something', a sports science show which he started with Farrow in
1996 on Melbourne's 3RRR. The show can be heard live (9–10 am)
every Saturday morning on 102.7 FM or at www.rrr.org.au

WHY

DICK ^Fosbury^ FLOPPED

AND ANSWERS TO OTHER
BIG SPORTING QUESTIONS

DAMIAN FARROW & JUSTIN KEMP

ALLEN&UNWIN

The authors acknowledge the support of their respective employers, the Australian Sports Commission/Australian Institute of Sport and the Australian Catholic University, and the assistance provided by staff members of both organisations. Thanks also for the continued support of 3RRR 102.7FM.

First published in 2006

Allen & Unwin
83 Alexander Street
Crows Nest NSW 2065
Australia

Phone: (61 2) 8425 0100
Fax: (61 2) 9906 2218
Email: info@allenandunwin.com
Web: www.allenandunwin.com

National Library of Australia
Cataloguing-in-Publication entry:

Farrow, Damian, 1970- .

Why Dick Fosbury flopped (and answers to other big sporting questions).

Includes index.
ISBN 1 74114 494 9.

1. Sports - Miscellanea. 2. Sports sciences. I. Kemp, Justin, 1969- . II. Title.

796

Edited by Karen Ward
Text design by Andrew Cunningham
Typesetting by Studio Pazzo
Printed in Australia by Griffin Press
10 9 8 7 6 5 4 3 2 1

A poll taken in Britain asked 43,000 people to rank their favourite screen scientists. Dr Bunsen Honeydew and his tragic assistant Beaker of *The Muppets* came out on top with 33 per cent of the vote. Spock from Star Trek was runner-up with 15 per cent, and The Doctor from *Dr Who* gained 13 per cent. Sadly, no sports scientists made the Top Ten. But then again, a white lab coat looks so much cooler on a scientist than a pair of tracksuit pants.

CONTENTS

THE WARM UP

The history of sporting endeavours can be traced back almost to our very origins. Throughout evolution, humans have become stronger and faster, and our posture has really picked up. Sport, too, has undergone its own evolution. Once upon a time, people packed a cut lunch when travelling a mile by foot, but it wasn't long before that distance was being covered in under four minutes. Once confined to the sporting arena, the baseballs, Frisbees, javelins and the like of today must almost carry a passport due to the immense distances that they can now travel. It took an Australian with a brain the size of a small planet to end sport's longest-ever winning streak and displace the *America's Cup* from Yankee soil. And by turning the world upside down, humans suddenly reached all-new heights – and that's why Dick Fosbury flopped.

Why Dick Fosbury Flopped steps back in time to chart the evolution of the sporting techniques and technologies that lie behind the jaw-dropping feats that amaze us as sports fans. Often ethe athletes themselves are amazed at what they achieve. Some of sports most famous innovations evolved by chance, others by experimentation at training, and others by planned scientific research. Who would have guessed at the impact that a few scrapes and scratches (soon to evolve into dimples) would have on the flight of a golf ball?

DEFINITION
Sports science
The study and application of scientific principles and techniques to enhance sports performance

---

But this book doesn't just address the incredible – and often bizarre – sporting histories that make today's athletes better than ever before. It also explains the scientific secrets underpinning the great sporting revolutions that have led the rare athlete to Olympic gold or to become the Champion of the World.

But never fear, sports fan, though you may watch in awe the unfathomable feats of skill achieved by sport's elite, there is no need to feel overwhelmed or jealous. Just remember the words of Joseph Heller in his famous book, *Catch 22*. He wrote, 'Like Olympic medals and tennis trophies, all they signified was that the owner had done something of no benefit to anyone, more capably than everyone else.'

So read on to discover the science behind the record breakers, the legends and quirky tales of the most famous of techniques, and the evolution of the weird and wonderful equipment used through a history of sport. You'll get a stitch just reading about them.

Did you know?

In scientific terms, a 'stitch' is referred to as 'exercise-related transient abdominal pain'. Unfortunately scientists have invested more brain power in thinking up its cool medical name than in actually working out what causes it.

To compare the state of play across generations can be a frustrating business; invariably, comparisons will be made between players of the modern era relative to those of yesteryear. This chapter reviews the evolution of the sporting techniques that helped make past and present champions great, starting with perhaps the most famous of all – the technique that revolutionised the sport of high jump – the Fosbury Flop.

The footballing paradox: Even at the peak of their careers, players of yesteryear already looked like players of yesteryear.

THEY DON'T PLAY LIKE THEY USED TO

1

The evolution of
sporting techniques

RECORD BREAKER
Dick Fosbury – the Fosbury Flop

A gangly 21-year-old high jumper named Dick Fosbury had trouble mastering the standard high jump technique of his day – the *straddle*. So instead of persisting with the common modus operandi of leaping facing the bar and swinging first one leg and then the other over the bar in a scissoring motion, he transformed his style to something that vaguely resembled a twisting somersault. His new technique had him staring skyward as he dramatically arched his back over the bar, finishing his jump by landing on his shoulders. The *Fosbury Flop* was born. With his new style, Fosbury could only manage a third placing at the 1968 United States Olympic trials, but that was enough to book him a ticket to the Mexico Olympic Games. Unveiling his method to the world, Dick Fosbury caused a sensation by winning the gold medal with a new Olympic record of 2.24 metres, revolutionising the sport of high jumping along the way.

WHY DICK FLOPPED

Before the Flop, many other styles of high jumping had been developed (see Fig. 1.1). The first was the *scissors*, so named because the athlete's legs performed a scissor-like action as they crossed the bar. Next came the innovatively dubbed *modified scissors* or *back layout* style.

The Brill bend

Fifteen-year-old Canadian Debbie Brill claims to have developed the Flop technique independently of Fosbury – reports of the *Brill bend* date back to 1966.

However, the requirement to land on one's back coupled with the absence of foam mats ensured a short-lived development. A similar style that involved the athlete rotating sideways as he rose to the bar became known as the *Eastern cut-off* due to its popularity among jumpers in the eastern United States. However, the flexibility demands meant the technique was rarely achieved with maximum efficiency. Not to be outdone by his east coast adversaries, a Californian jumper then developed the *Western roll*, so named because it was created on the west coast of the United States. The *straddle* then became the style of choice for the world's high jumping elite, where the athlete essentially lay face down along the length of the bar as they traversed it.

In 1954, Dick Browning reportedly somersaulted over the bar at a height of 2.28 metres: the world record at the time was 2.12 metres. In 1962, Gary Chamberlain pushed the envelope when he cleared 2.23 metres by performing a back handspring with a backflip; a height that was only centimetres below the world record of the time. Both techniques were outlawed. But a 'legal' revolution took place at the 1968 Olympic Games when Dick Fosbury 'flopped' over the bar backwards, his face to the heavens (see Fig. 1.2).

One constant amongst all these innovations was the search for maximal jumping height through the refinement of a number of key factors. The maximum height that a jumper can clear is the direct result of two main factors: (a) the vertical velocity achieved at the end of the take-off phase, and (b) the height of the jumper's centre of mass at take-off.

At the moment that the foot leaves the ground during take-off, the height of the jumper's centre of mass is usually somewhere between 68 per cent and 73 per cent of their standing height. This means that taller athletes already have an advantage – hence, elite-level high jumpers all stand tall. The vertical velocity achieved at take-off will then determine how much higher the athlete's centre of mass will rise through the airborne phase of the jump. The speed of the limbs, the strength of the jumping leg, and the coordination and timing of the jumping action all influence take-off height and velocity.

The bar height that an athlete can clear is greatly affected by the way in which the body is positioned as it crosses the bar. The difference between the maximum height reached by the centre of mass and that of the height of the crossbar is termed the 'clearance height'. This feature is what cemented Fosbury's place in high jump history. Dick Fosbury's technique through the air involved movements that positioned his body parts in a way that allowed his physical body to pass over the bar whilst his centre of mass actually passed through or even under the bar. This gave him extra height to his jump for a given take-off velocity.

Get on your high horse
The 1900 Olympic Games included an event called the Equestrian High Jump.

The flipside to the Flop

Revisiting the biomechanical evolution of the high jump, one can see how the issue of clearance height was paramount. In the original scissors technique (usually performed by most kids at school sports days), the athlete's upper body remained upright, meaning that a clearance height of 25–30 centimetres above the bar was needed for a successful attempt. Compared to future jumping styles, this was far from optimal, but at least the jumper landed on their feet.

But by rotating backward or sideways in rising to the bar, the modified scissors allowed the athlete to arrive in a clearance position in which the distance of 25–30 centimetres was greatly reduced. Theoretically, the Eastern cut-off allowed the jumper to reduce the distance between the height of their centre of mass and that of the bar to a mere 2–5 centimetres (and perhaps even zero). However, the demands that this style placed on flexibility and gymnastic ability meant that the athletes who used this technique rarely achieved clearance heights of less than 15–20 centimetres.

Similarly, the Western roll, which required the athlete to cross the bar with the knee of the take-off leg tucked in against the chest, reduced the critical difference value to approximately 15 centimetres.

The straddle technique ensured the athlete rose to a clearance position 'lying' face down along the bar's length. When the body was stretched out, the centre of mass may have been only 10 centimetres above the bar. However, if the body was wrapped around the bar, the distance could be reduced by as much as 5–10 centimetres. Hence, prior to the arrival of the Flop, it was the preferred technique.

Couch carnage
After seeing Fosbury on TV, many young athletes started switching their technique to the Flop style. This resulted in parents writing to Fosbury, complaining that he was responsible for ruining their furniture as the children flopped over the back of couches in the family home.

DEFINITION
Centre of mass
The point that represents the average position of all the body parts (often referred to as the *centre of gravity*). It is usually located somewhere between the lower abdomen and lower back or pelvis, though it is normally lower in females than males.

FIG.1.1 THE EVOLUTION OF
HIGH JUMP TECHNIQUES

Style		Clearance height (cm)	Development
Scissors 		25-30	Early 19th century First and still popular with beginners
Modified scissors 		15-20	
Eastern cut-off 		15-20	M.F. Sweeney, 1895 Popular in eastern USA
Western roll 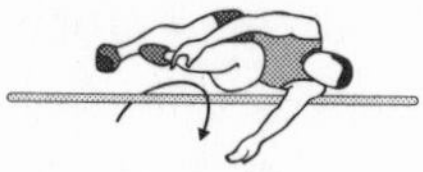		15	M.F. Horine, 1912 California
Straddle 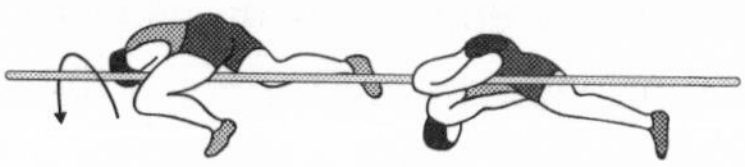		10	Russia Late 1950s, early 1960s
Fosbury Flop 		0 or below	Dick Fosbury 1965-68

Do the Flop

The Fosbury Flop required a clearance position in which the athlete was arched backward over the bar. Such a position afforded the possibility for the centre of mass to actually move outside the body, thereby theoretically allowing it to pass through or under the bar as the jumper passed over it.

Essentially, the Fosbury Flop relies on the biomechanical theory of 'action and reaction'. Once in the air, the maximum height that a jumper's centre of mass will reach cannot be altered; however, Fosbury's style made it possible to move certain body parts in one direction (action) thereby causing other body parts to move in the opposite direction in compensation (reaction). The athlete's head and shoulders first cross the bar, followed by the torso, characterised by the familiar arching of the back that typifies the Fosbury Flop. This arching acts to move the centre of mass outside of the body, and perhaps even pass below the bar as the jumper's physical body passes over it.

Once the torso and hips have cleared the bar, the legs are now in danger of dislodging the bar. The action of extending the knees to raise the legs (to now clear the bar) causes a concomitant reaction in the athlete's upper body, thereby un-arching the torso and dropping the hips. This technique also allows the centre of mass to shift along the body, again avoiding the need for it to directly cross over the bar, and hence, maximises the jumping height for a given amount of take-off velocity and height. With the Fosbury Flop, timing is everything. If the body un-arches too early, the jumper will 'sit' on the bar. If the body un-arches too late, the legs (particularly the calves) will clip the bar, dislodging it. Dick Fosbury got his timing right in Mexico City in 1968.

Dick Fosbury failed to make the 1972 Olympic team and although achieving gold and a new Olympic record at the 1968 Olympics, he never once set a world record. However, his innovative style still stands as high jump's dominant technique. He was inducted into the US National Track & Field Hall of Fame in 1981 and into the US Olympic Hall of Fame in 1992.

FIG. 1.2 THE FOSBURY FLOP

World record

The current men's high jump world record of 2.45 metres was set in 1993 by Cuba's Javier Sotomayor, while the women's world record holder, Stefka Kostadinova of Bulgaria, jumped 2.09 metres in 1987.

Weather prediction

After observing meteorological data that Montreal frequently experienced rain in summer, the coach of Polish high jumper Jacek Wszola made him train under a garden hose to simulate wet weather conditions. During the high jump final at the 1976 Olympics, the heavens opened up over Montreal. Wszola captured the gold medal, and when asked at what point he knew he could win, he replied, 'When it started to rain.'

SKI JUMPING –
'V' IS FOR VICTORY

Legend has it that in 1860, Norwegian Sondre Norheim (the father of ski jumping) skied off a rock to soar 30 metres, heralding the birth of the sport. Two years later, the first official ski jumping competition took place in Trysil, Norway. Modern ski jumping sees competitors airborne in the order of 6.3 seconds, whilst flying a distance of 186.7 metres; these were the *mean* statistics for the 1994 Ski Jumping World Championships.

The form at take-off is suggested as the most crucial factor in successful ski jumping. At take-off, the skier is attempting to increase both their vertical lift and their horizontal velocity, simultaneously. The ski jumping take-off involves moving very rapidly from a crouched position into an extended body position at and after the ramp's edge. The ski jumper performs this movement in 0.25 to 0.30 seconds, over a distance of about 7 metres, extending both the hips and knees in order to maximise their horizontal and vertical velocities. The velocity of knee extension is reported to be the highest correlating factor to the distance jumped. Bend and stretch, reach for the sky.

The take-off movement is also important in providing angular momentum to allow the skier to assume the flight position as quickly as possible. The flight posture of the ski jumper will impact on the final distance achieved. Firstly, they need to minimise the drag so that they are slowed down as little as possible. At the same time, they need to maximise the lift forces, so that the oncoming airflow 'holds them up' as much as possible, increasing flight time.

But the score in ski jumping competitions is not all about how far you travel down the hill: only 50 per cent of the score is attributable to the distance jumped; 25 per cent is given for technique during flight and 25 per cent for the landing technique. A perfect jump results in 60 style points and 60 or more points for distance.

The positioning of one's body parts and skis whilst airborne, in order to attain maximal flight distance, has changed greatly over the years: techniques included the *Superman style* (where jumpers assumed *Superman*'s flying position with arms outstretched), the *parallel style* (where the skis were held parallel during flight), and the now-ubiquitous

V *style* (where the two ski tips are spread apart to form a 'V' shape). In fact, Norway held a longstanding Olympic ski jumping winning streak until 1956, when two Finnish jumpers performed the more aerodynamically sound posture of pinning the arms to the side of the body and leaning far forward over the skis (see Fig. 1.3).

In 1985, Sweden's Jan Boklöv introduced the V style (or flying V); and he began to soar further than anyone; even further than the previously unbeatable flying Finn, Matti Nykänen, who used the traditional parallel style. However, Boklöv was unable to gain any victories because his scores were continually penalised for poor flight and landing technique. But in 1989, Boklöv finally secured the Federation of International Skiing's World Cup title, and ski jumpers worldwide began adopting Boklöv's flying V technique.

The V-style jumping technique revolutionised ski jumping by manipulating the drag and lift forces in favour of the jumper. Scientific examination found that the V style, with an angle of 15 degrees formed between the two skis, increased the surface area of the skier and their skis to the oncoming airflow, compared to parallel-style postures. This produced both greater lift and drag forces on the skier. However, the oncoming airflow passes over the skier somewhat like it does over the wing of an aeroplane, and as such, the lift force is increased to a greater extent than the drag, resulting in greater flight time. In fact, wind-tunnel testing reports that the V-style technique may provide as much as 28 per cent more lift than the traditional parallel style of jumping.

FIG. 1.3 V STYLE SKI JUMPING

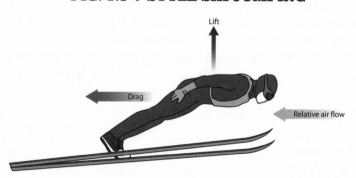

Note: The skis are wide apart near the skier's head and form a point behind the body.

Nailing the run

A self-styled Norwegian fakir added a bizarre sideshow to the World Cup downhill race by tobogganing down the mountainside – on a bed of nails mounted on skis. Naked above the waist apart from a turban on his head, Inge Vidar Svingen travelled about 100 metres down the slope, lying on his back on a bed of 270 nails, each 15 cm long. 'It was cold but I concentrated so much that it didn't hurt,' he said after his run.

BEND IT LIKE BECKHAM

Amongst the world's premier athletes in any given sport, a select few possess the skills, or a skill, that can turn a game. Be it the magic boot of Frenchman Zinedine Zidane, or when England skipper David Beckham or Pavel Nedved of the Czech Republic stand over the ball at a free kick, players and fans alike hold their collective breath. Why? Because these masters can bend a soccer ball with a level of accuracy and speed which invariably leaves even their peers in awe.

At a set piece, like a free kick 30 metres from goal, opposition players will literally form themselves into a human wall to block the ball's direct route to one half of the goal mouth. The goalkeeper will take responsibility for the other half of the net, whilst also contending with a slower strike that may be lifted over the defensive wall.

Despite these obstacles, Zidane, Beckham, and Nedved continually trouble the world's best keepers, and will often billow the back of the net in the doing. This is even more incredible when one considers that the kick-taker holds no real element of surprise, since the keeper is well aware that the ball will eventually head his way. To bend a soccer ball around a wall of players, keep it under the crossbar, and beat an outstretched keeper is to possess a very keen awareness of the physics of ball flight. Whether they know it or not, these footballers have acquired such a knowledge through thousands of hours of practice.

When a soccer ball is struck with spin, two general forces act upon its flight. The *lift force* makes the ball curve, whilst the *drag force* slows its forward progress. However, their distinct contribution is greatly

Eddie the Eagle

In 1988, Michael 'Eddie the Eagle' Edwards, an English plasterer, competed at the Calgary Olympics, scoring less than half the points of any other jumper in the competition – but garnering cult status.

affected by the air flowing about the ball at any given time. When travelling slowly, air flows smoothly at the ball's surface (called the *laminar boundary layer*) but it separates from the ball as it passes by, creating turbulence behind the ball (see Figure 1.4, left). This turbulent wake creates a drag force that slows the ball; the bigger the wake, the greater the drag.

However, at higher ball velocities, the laminar airflow rushing past the ball can become turbulent (see Figure 1.4, right). This now-turbulent boundary layer actually decreases the degree to which air separates away from the ball, thereby minimising the turbulent wake behind the ball; the result being a reduction in the drag experienced by the ball. What this means for a goalkeeper is that a well-struck free kick not only travels at high speed, but it does not slow down at the same rate as one would expect.

But there is still more physics to contend with. At a given spin rate, increasing a ball's velocity reduces the lift effect. Therefore, a fast-moving ball will not curl as much. At first thought, this may appear beneficial for the keeper. However, as the ball slows along its goalward path, its sideways deviation will suddenly become more prominent.

FIG. 1.4 AIRFLOW AROUND BALL

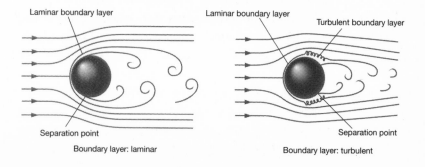

Laminar boundary layer

Separation point

Boundary layer: laminar

Laminar boundary layer

Turbulent boundary layer

Separation point

Boundary layer: turbulent

**Penalty
patience**

When taking a 30-metre free kick, Beckham and co. likely strike the 410–450-gram soccer ball at around 25–30 metres per second; the ball would also be spinning at the relatively high rate of eight to ten revolutions per second. With this motion, the airflow about the ball will be turbulent, providing relatively little drag – thereby better maintaining ball speed. But at some location during its one-second journey, ball speed slows enough for the passing air to revert to laminar flow, abruptly raising drag. To bend it like Beckham, this point should coincide with the opposition's defensive wall, because with drag force increasing and ball speed braking, the lift force can now play its part. As such, the ball will actually begin to curl around the wall of players. If struck just right, the ball could move by as much as 4 metres left or right, making any goalkeeper a mere spectator.

DROP-PUNTING THE PLACE KICK

While the drop punt is the predominant kick used in Australian Rules football these days, (with the rare exception of the occasional torpedo punt – aka the spiral punt), this was not always the case; nineteenth and twentieth-century Australian Rules was defined by the prevalence of place kicks, flat punts, drop kicks and stab passes, with each kick having its own pros and cons.

While the flat punt was deemed safe and reliable, it was difficult to mark due to its spin, and was easily affected by the wind. Not surprisingly, the manufacture of Australian Rules footballs had a major influence on kicking technique. The drop kick and stab pass required precise timing between boot and ball, just as the ball landed on the turf. Tom Sherrin, a student of the game, designed his footballs to be blunter at the ends than the rugby balls imported from England; it was reasoned that the blunt end allowed the ball to 'sit up' for a fraction of a second at the critical moment of foot–ball contact. In contrast, a rugby ball, because of its shape, could not be sent on the low skimming-and-spinning trajectory achieved with the stab pass. Although the stab kick was a low and accurate kick, the timing demands and the high levels of muscular control required made it a difficult proposition. Similarly, while the drop kick could be long and penetrating, again it required precise timing, and couldn't be trusted in wet conditions.

Although even back in 1912 the drop kick was already being tagged as something of a lost art, it was not until Ron Barassi famously outlawed the kick in the late 1960s/early 1970s, when coaching the Carlton Blues, that it finally disappeared from the game. Barassi felt that the drop kick was not a 'high percentage' kick, as it had little margin for error. Instead, he emphasised the drop punt, which allowed greater precision, thereby increasing his team's chance of maintaining possession. The drop punt has maintained its status in Australian Rules as the most prevalent kick in the modern era, not only for its accuracy, but also because it can be kicked long distances and it's the easiest kick to mark.

The torpedo punt, renowned for the aesthetic quality of its curving and lengthy flight path, has remained in the game for those rare occasions where perhaps a forward player has a set-shot for goal from outside 60 metres after the siren has blown, for valuable distance when the ball is severely waterlogged, or when a disobedient back man simply neglects his coach's orders.

Where did the footy come from?

Hatsell King sold locally made footballs from the Melbourne suburb of Carlton from 1879. A few years later Tom Sherrin commenced production in the rival suburb of Collingwood and his 'Match II' footballs were soon being used throughout Australia.

How to kick a big roost

Researchers at the Australian Institute of Sport have attempted to answer an important football question: what factors allow a player to kick a ball long distances? To do so, footballers from the Australian Teal Cup team (the junior national squad) were required to drop-punt for maximum distance while aiming for goalposts. Based on their kicking distances, the players were then divided into two groups: a long-kicking group that averaged 48 metres per kick, and a short-kicking grouped that averaged 43 metres. Subsequently, the biomechanical qualities of each group were examined by dividing the kicking action into four distinct phases and looking for differences between the long- and short-kickers.

The first phase considered the grip on the ball and run-up approach. Results demonstrated that greater consistency and distance were achieved by players who gripped the ball near the upper portion of its lacing; the further the grip pressure was away from the centre of the ball, the greater the chance of unwanted rotation being imparted on the ball. The length of the run-up did not influence the length of the kick, although the angle of approach did. Specifically, greater distance was achieved by employing a slightly curved run-up. This allowed for an increased contribution from the hips, thereby allowing for a greater range of motion for the kicking leg to move through, which in turn generated greater velocity.

The second phase of the kick related to ball release and the back swing of the leg. The more efficient kickers were found to release the ball close to the bellybutton and in line with the kicking leg. The back swing of the leg also differed between the two kicking groups, with the long-kicking group demonstrating a larger range of leg movement.

The forward swing of the kicking leg also highlighted key differences between the kicking groups. Specifically, the long-kickers flexed their kicking knees more and possessed greater leg velocity and foot momentum at impact than the short-kicking group. Interestingly, actual foot speed measured in isolation wasn't a determining factor in the distance kicked, although, obviously, this is an important factor when linked to how the ball is contacted.

The final phase of the kicking action that was analysed was the follow-through; of particular importance was that the long-kicking group's legs did not cross the body but stayed in line with the target until hip rotation moved the leg out of alignment.

Winged defender

A bird decided the outcome of a football match between Botafogo and Gremio when it deflected a goal that would have been the winner. The bird flew in front of the goal and prevented Botafogo striker Fabio's ball from entering the Gremio net, three minutes from time.

Famous roosts in Australian football history			
Distance (Metres)	Player (Club)	Year	Description
105.5	Fred Fanning (Melbourne)	1939	Massive drop kick in reserves grand final v Richmond
98.5	Albert Thurgood (Essendon)	1899	Place kick measured by officials and journalists at training
85	Dave McNamara (St Kilda)	1923	For a point against Collingwood
85	Jeff Fehring (St Kilda)	1981	Torpedo goal from behind the centre at Moorabbin
82	Ben Graham (Geelong)	1999	Torpedo kick in from full back v Port Adelaide
80	Ben Graham (Geelong)	1995	Kick in to centre wing at Whitten Oval
76.5	Fred Hughson (Fitzroy)	1943	Drop kick outguns a US serviceman's gridiron throw in an organised competition
70+	Malcolm Blight (North Melbourne)	1976	Kicks the winning goal at Carlton with a torpedo after the siren
32 High	Bill Brownless (Geelong)	Early 1990s	Becomes the second man to clear the silo at Mirrool, NSW
65 foot	Ernie Walton (Carlton)	1903	Wins a long-kicking competition at Burrumbeet with a drop kick

Source: Adapted from C. Happell (1999) *The Age* newspaper.

Jonny Wilkinson knows his place

While the place kick may have disappeared from Australian Rules football, it is ever-present in rugby union; its influence on a game's result graphically illustrated by the exquisite kicking skills of Jonny Wilkinson in the 2003 Rugby World Cup. Pundits have speculated about what makes such players – particularly Wilkinson, and to a lesser extent Australia's Elton Flatley and Matt Giteau – such consistent place (or penalty) kick performers. One popular theory is that the pre-kick routines of the best kickers are what separate them from the rest.

However, recent analyses of goal-kicking performances at the 1999 World Cup provide some interesting science to refute the goal-kicking theories portrayed by the media. Video footage of 572 place kicks, attempted by 39 players across 41 matches, was analysed to determine the impact of the consistency of pre-performance routines on goal-kicking success.

Two specific elements of a kicker's pre-performance routine were investigated. Firstly, *physical preparation time*, which referred to the time from when the kicker takes his hands away from the ball after placing it on the tee to the end of his walk back; for example, four steps back and two steps to side. The second measure of interest was referred to as *concentration time*, and commenced at the end of the walk back until the initiation of the run-up – essentially, it's the time that the kicker spends standing still after stepping back from the ball. This is the phase where Jonny Wilkinson completes his now-famous imagery routine (see page 19).

Jonny's secrets revealed

After analysing videos of England's star kicker Jonny Wilkinson, scientists at University College Worcester believe they have unlocked the key to his rugby kicking success. It is:

$$KP = CSP - EnC(s + w + r + y)^n + PsS\,(cr + sc + mt + x)^n + PhS\,(c \times t \times w)$$

KP = kicking prowess; CSP = closed skill performance; EnC = environmental conditions; PsS = psychological state; PhS = physical status.

CSP involves factors such as angle of approach to the ball, run-up speed, foot and ball placement, and kicking leg velocity. EnC, PsS and PhS include the factors of playing surface, wind, rain, anxiety, crowd, fatigue and workload.

Results revealed that as the difficulty of the kick increased via a combination of an increase in distance and angle from the posts, the kicker's concentration time also significantly increased. In contrast, physical preparation time was only slightly affected. Specifically, kicks that resulted in a conversion rate of only 69 per cent elicited concentration times of 11 seconds, whereas the easiest kicks (success rating of 98 per cent) required only 7 seconds of concentration. The physical preparation time of these kicks took approximately 11 seconds and 9.5 seconds, respectively.

Further analyses examined the situational pressure on the kickers and whether this was reflected in the kickers' pre-performance routines. Only kicks completed in the second half were analysed, and high-pressure kicks were considered those where the score was separated by three points or less (that is, an opportunity to draw level with the opposition or clear out by six points). A slight increase in concentration time was found in the high-pressure situations – similar to the results of research that has investigated golf putting.

Interestingly, there were no significant differences between the best- and worst-performing kickers in the tournament. The fact that all those analysed were at an elite level is probably the key reason for this. However, it is important to note that large differences did exist between individual players. For example, concentration times ranged from 3 to 14 seconds. Such times reveal that the International Rugby Board's relatively recent rule requiring penalty kicks to be taken within 1 minute of being awarded seems to be a reasonable request easily met by most players.

Another common perception, promoted when discussing the success of penalty kicks, is that it is more difficult for a kicker to score from the same side of the pitch as their kicking foot (that is, a right-footed kicker finds kicking from the right side of the pitch harder than kicking from the left side). Success rates were found to be 73.8 per cent on the easier side and 72.5 per cent on the supposedly harder side of the field. So much for that theory!

It seems that the timing of a pre-performance routine is not the key factor in determining a kicker's success; rather, it may be what one thinks about or visualises that's more important.

Efficient kicking: it's all in the head

What goes through a player's mind as they prepare to execute a skill that has been practised many times before? When standing with the ball in hand 40 metres out, directly in front of goal, what do AFL footballers like Bomber Matthew Lloyd and Magpie Chris Tarrant think about: perhaps how they should guide the ball onto their boot, or the kick's outcome? Lloyd's 2004 goal-kicking success rate of 73 per cent relative to Tarrant's 54 per cent would suggest there are differences.

Can goal-kicking success rates be related to what players focus their attention on as they execute a kick? A flurry of sports science research over the last decade has tried to address this issue by determining the optimal strategy used by athletes to focus their attention as they practise and perform the skills of their sport.

Essentially, two types of attentional focus have been examined. An internal focus of attention is said to occur if the player's attention is directed to his or her body movements, such as focusing on guiding the ball onto the boot when kicking. Attention directed to the effect of the movement, such as the flight of the football, is termed an external focus.

Old ball please

The world's oldest football has been displayed for the first time in centuries at a Scottish museum in Edinburgh. Made of pig's bladder and wrapped in leather, the small ball probably belonged to Mary, Queen of Scots and dates from 1560-1570.

The typical finding to emerge from these attentional focus comparisons is that the learning and subsequent performance of a skill is superior if the player has adopted an external focus of attention. For example, one such experiment that examined the learning of a chip shot in golf found that players who focused on the movement of the golf club's head during the swing performed more skilfully than those players who focused on their arms during the swing.

The logic behind the use of an external focus of attention relates to the old coaching chestnut 'paralysis by analysis'. Due to the amount of practice an elite athlete has devoted to their skills, they generally can perform the skill automatically, without conscious effort. The introduction of an internal focus of attention strategy, which forces the player to focus directly on the movement, disrupts their normal unconscious skill processing. A similar explanation has been put forward as a reason why some players choke under pressure: conscious thought about a movement turns the muscle memory of an elite performer into that of a novice.

Interestingly, when a player is kicking poorly, coaches generally try to improve performance through technical instruction that is usually internal in focus, despite research evidence indicating otherwise. To convince athletes and their coaches to make a change to an external focus of attention requires testimony from other successful athletes, and the strongest support for such an approach comes from Jonny Wilkinson – England's rugby union goal-kicking machine.

Back in 1998 when Jonny was having problems with his kicking, it was decided to forget about technique (internal focus) and focus on 'Doris'. Basically, every time Jonny prepares to kick, he externally focuses his attention on an imaginary woman called Doris sitting in the stands behind the goalposts. Initially his focus was to hit her, and then as his skill level increased, he narrowed his attentional target to kicking a newspaper out of her hands, and later, a soft-drink can. The results of this technique speak for themselves and might convince other less-consistent performers to switch their focus to the external.

TECHNICAL TALES: DIVING INTO SWIMMING RESEARCH

Back in the seventeenth century, swimmers used the 'bottom first' approach to enter the water. Fast-forward a few centuries and there is now concerted research directed towards optimising swim-start performance. The importance of start technique cannot be underestimated, particularly in short sprint events such as the 50 metres freestyle, as it has been calculated to contribute up to 30 per cent of the total race time. While the goal of any swim start is to get off the block as quickly and as forcefully as possible, the typical techniques employed by swimmers all possess biomechanical compromises

Airborne exercise

Emirates Airlines was the first customer for a new exercise product to prevent the occurrence of deep vein thrombosis on long-haul flights. The Airogym is a small cushion that passengers can rest their feet on, exerting downward pressure through four different exercises. Clinical trials were conducted on the Airogym and it was found to increase blood flow from 25 to 50 per cent.

Dive start comparisons	
Start technique	**Advantages / disadvantages**
Grab Hands grasp front edge of block with feet side by side approx. 15–30 cm apart Knee and hip extensors provide most of the force	Only small movement forward required for body to generate propulsion Valuable for explosive swimmers as they can generate a large amount of force quickly
Track As name suggests, one foot back and one foot forward. The front leg provides the most force and so the dominant leg should be forward. Swimmer initially pulls on the block with arms as well as driving forward with rear foot	May be valuable for those swimmers who have greater strength in a dominant leg
Slingshot Adapted from the track start. Swimmer leans back as much as possible rather than forward, loading the shoulders and front leg like an elastic band	May be valuable for swimmers with large upper body power Longer block time than other starts

Source: Adapted from Lyttle, 'Start right — A biomechanical review of dive start performance'

based on the laws of physics. Put simply, there is a trade-off between the time spent on the block and the amount of force generated. While a swimmer may generate more force, and hence greater take-off velocity by summating force on the block over a longer time period, this may be ineffective relative to an opponent who has opted for a strategy of getting off the block quickly with a little less force. Not surprisingly, swimming scientists are interested in providing swimmers and coaches alike with a definitive starting strategy. At this stage, the answer seems to depend on the physique of the swimmer and the amount of practice time spent perfecting their technique.

SURF'S UP

Although Hawaiians were known to surf well before the nineteenth century, and there is little doubt that Aboriginal people surfed Australian waters before the arrival of Captain Cook, incredibly, the evolution of surfing in Australia started in controversial circumstances.

Tommy Tanna from the Marshall Islands was recorded as the first bodysurfer in Australia, riding the Manly waves and teaching a few Manly locals back in 1890. However, it was not until William Goucher defied the law of the time and entered the surf at Bondi in daylight hours in 1902 that bodysurfing began to develop. Although Goucher was arrested and subsequently charged, he had opened the floodgates.

The logical extension to bodysurfing was of course surfboard-riding. The first appearance of surfing in Australia is linked to the Olympics. The 1912 Olympics 100 metres swimming gold medallist, Duke Paoa Kahanamoku, was invited to Australia in 1915 by the New South Wales Swimming Association to give a swimming exhibition at the Domain Baths in Sydney. While in Australia, Duke fashioned an 8 foot 6 inch *alaia* board out of native Australian sugar pine. On a summer's day at Freshwater Beach in Manly, Duke rode the board and inspired locals like Claude West, Isobel Latham and Snowy McAllister. In fact, Latham was the first Aussie to ride a board with the Duke. Meanwhile, Claude West made a replica of the Duke's board, and Snowy McAllister went on to win the 1928 and 1930 Australian championships, performing a headstand on his longboard to win the 1930 title.

Know your waves

The search for the ultimate wave takes some surfers all over the globe. The search for a remote shoreline with great waves, and hopefully no angry crowds, is an integral part of the total wave-riding experience. Sometimes one could be led to believe that surfers take more pleasure

The father of modern surfing

Duke Paoa Kahanamoku was an all-round waterman. In addition to his surfing prowess, which he used to popularise the sport around the world, he won five swimming medals over three Olympic Games, and was a three-time world record holder in the 100 metres freestyle. He was also credited with developing the flutter kick to replace the scissor kick in freestyle swimming.

trying to find the perfect wave than actually surfing it. A good wave can't be too small – such that it offers little challenge – but it can't be too big either, such that it's just plain frightening. So what constitutes a good wave?

Every board-rider will give a different answer, but most would be happy with a curving wave greater than 2 metres high, with enough drive to carry them along at around 10 metres per second. Such a wave allows surfers enough height and speed to skirt along its crest, drop down its face, or in some cases, get covered in a tube.

Most great surf spots have their waves breaking over reefs or sandbars. As a wave heads towards the shore, its energy is compressed by the rising ocean floor. This makes the wave steeper and the water move in a circular motion. When the speed of the water at the crest surpasses that of the wave, it breaks. As the wave moves towards the beach, the water on the crest begins to break diagonally from the wave front. This is called the peel angle. The smaller the peel angle, the faster the breaking white water travels along the wave. The surfer needs to outrun this white water to keep the ride going.

The height of a breaking wave depends on the depth of the water. The ratio of the water's depth to the wave's height is around 1:3. Therefore, to get that 2-metre wave, the water below needs to be 2.6 metres deep.

A spilling wave (or roller), where the crest simply overturns down the wave face, is ideal for bodysurfing; however, if the crest overturns completely, all at the same time, the crest can turn into a large jet of water – referred to as a dumper – and is not much fun for anyone. But if the jet of water plunges laterally across the wave face, a tube can be created. This allows a board-rider to visit the much-sought-after 'green room' by disappearing for a few seconds under the wave's curling lip. For these waves to form, the slope of the sea-floor behind the reef needs to be rising between 1 in 20 and 1 in 40.

The preferred surfing conditions are to have waves at a constant

	Development of the surfboard
Year	**Development**
Mid 18th	Crudely moulded out of solid wood century Weighed approximately 150 pounds
1920s	Solid redwood plank 10 foot long Acted like a sponge when in water
1930s	'Hot-curl' boards made of composite wood Lighter and up to 16 foot long
1940s	Rudder added to help with stability Resin and fibreglass coating the wood
1950s	Balsa wood Still 10 foot long
1950s/60s	Introduction of polyurethane foam and fibreglass Lightweight boards that were easy to manoeuvre
1960s	Between 1968-1970 the average length of a board went from 10 foot to 6 foot and lost 8 pounds
1970s & 80s	1973 – Jack O'Neill invents the leg-rope 1981 – Introduction of the tri-fin (thruster)
1990s	Longboards back in vogue Rail curve, tail design and bottom contour adapted to suit specific wave conditions Tow in surfing arrives, making big waves more accessible
21st century	Hydrofoil board designed to eliminate surface tension, creating a smooth ride on large, bumpy waves Potential to make 100-foot waves accessible

Pipeline power

If the energy contained in a
10-foot pipeline wave could be channelled into an
electrical generator, the resulting wattage would
light up a small town for a night.

height and rolling in at regular intervals. This regular rhythm is music to the waterlogged ears of all 'skegs'. An offshore wind is also important for forming the perfect wave – allowing it to 'hold up' so the pleasure continues for longer.

The art of bodysurfing

Bodysurfing mathematician Professor Neville de Mestre has provided an excellent summary of the physics of bodysurfing, explaining why some of us seem to catch waves with the ease of a dolphin while others behave more like a floating log.

Approaching waves travel at approximately 3 metres per second (m/s), whereas a good swimmer can sprint for a short time at approximately 2 m/s. Hence, to successfully catch a wave rather than have it pass you by, a bodysurfer must accelerate quickly to the wave's speed.

A wave about to break creates a relatively large force inside itself, but below the crest. Taking advantage of this force to propel oneself through and out in front of the wave is called 'porpoising', as it is the technique used by dolphins and porpoises when playing in waves near shore. While easy to do with your feet on the sand in shallow water waves, more swimming skill and speed is required in deeper water.

When looking at the surf on any summer weekend, it's clear that there are many bodysurfing techniques available. The two most prevalent techniques are the arms back or arms forward approach. The arms back approach requires the bodysurfer to put their arms by their side with their head up, protruding ahead of the wave. But a longer ride can usually be obtained by pointing one's arms out in front in a diving position; the face is placed into the water and distance can be gained by stroking with one arm from time to time. Surf-lifesaving competitors are seen to almost float above the water as they approach the shore by using their hands to 'hydroplane'. Interestingly, while experimentation is encouraged, it seems that attempting to bodysurf sideways or feet first will ultimately result in a short ride at best.

When milking the foam section of a ride, it is useful to kick as the bodysurfer's legs begin to create drag and only a small amount of their body is in the turbulent surf front – where the power is. As a result, it is considered advantageous to have a short body and short legs if you wish to ride a wave for longer distances.

Shark repellent

Ever since Batman sprayed a can of shark repellent onto the nose of a Grey White hanging off his leg, surfers have craved a repellent of similar strength. In 2002, an Australian company, SeaChange Technology, developed the first ever recreational shark repellent. The *Shark Shield* is a small electronic device that fastens to the ankle of a swimmer or surfer and repels sharks by emitting a 5-metre electromagnetic force field. This magnetic field impacts the shark's central nervous system, causing pain and muscle spasms. Early models of the device were used in the Sydney 2000 Olympics.

Fifteen of the best surf flicks

Movie	Year
High on a Cool Wave	1959
Gidget	1959
The Endless Summer	1964
Cat on a Hot Foam Board	1967
Morning of the Earth	1972
Crystal Voyager	1974
Tubular Swells	1976
Big Wednesday	1978
Puberty Blues	1981
Mad Wax	1987
The Green Iguana	1992
Occy the Occumentary	1998
Laird	2001
Billabong Odyssey	2004
Step into Liquid	2004

A THREE-DIMENSIONAL RE-CREATION OF BRADMAN

Professor Adrian Lees, an English sports scientist, developed a three-dimensional computer re-evaluation of the supposedly 'unorthodox' batting technique of Sir Donald Bradman. Many cricket coaches have shunned the Don's batting technique, claiming it to be unorthodox because he used a backlift which sent his bat arcing towards the *point* fielding position rather than straight up, as is espoused in many coaching manuals.

Professor Lees required two batsmen to play in either a conventional or a Bradmanesque manner. Through the use of a high-speed motion analysis system comprising six cameras and 16 electronic sensors attached to the players (see Figure 1.4), three-dimensional computer images of the strokes played in both styles were produced. The motion analysis system captured 240 samples per second (as opposed to 25 samples per second available via a standard video camera), allowing the three-dimensional figures to be analysed with great precision.

The results revealed that, while a batsman using either technique would actually play the ball with a straight bat, the Bradman technique had two advantages. Firstly, it allowed the player to delay the moment of shot selection, and secondly, the forward motion of the Bradman technique automatically put him on his toes. These advantages potentially would have afforded Bradman some extra milliseconds of decision-making time and enhanced balance.

Barbie can't bodysurf

Experiments using Barbie dolls to create small-scale bodysurfer models have typically resulted in data of little value, as, surprise surprise, Barbie doesn't behave like a human at all – she's more like a log! Specifically, humans use feedback to regulate their body position to ride a wave; a critical feature not captured in any Barbie replication-type experiments.

UPDATE FROM THE LAB
Back injuries in cricket

There is a common perception amongst the cricket fraternity that fast bowlers are mad – and if one scratches the surface of the physical demands placed on a fast bowler, it becomes difficult to disagree. Approaching the crease at approximately 6 metres per second or approximately 21 km/h, a fast bowler generates an average force of seven times his own body weight every time his front foot contacts the pitch at the point of delivery. Coupled to this is the need to control severe high-speed rotation of the trunk in order to successfully summon enough force to trouble a skilled batsman. Cricket may be considered a non-contact sport, but try telling that to the body of a fast bowler.

In our previous book, *Run Like You Stole Something*, we featured some preliminary research focusing on back injuries in cricket highlighting that, while variety is the spice of life (and certainly diversity in sporting technique is to be welcomed), this rule doesn't apply equally to all sports. In the case of cricket fast bowling, it becomes downright dangerous to have incorrect technique. To possess a 'mixed' bowling action is associated with an increased risk of career-threatening lower-back injury. A 'mixed' action occurs when the bowler adopts a more front-on alignment of the shoulders at back foot impact, but cannot maintain this position just before front-foot, thereby impact rotating the shoulders to a more side-on position. This counter-rotation of the shoulders places large strain on discs in the lower back, more so than bowlers with a less front-on or side-on action.

Prior to modern-day coaching innovation, University of Western Australia researchers examined the injury rates of 82 teenage fast bowlers in the 1986/87 season; 38 per cent were reported to have sustained a serious injury from the stress of bowling. Current Cricket Australia injury surveillance figures on the same demographic reveals that the figure is now around 21 per cent – an improvement predominantly due to Australian coaching innovations and research dedicated to optimising the pace-bowling action to reduce injury rates.

Recent injury surveillance research, based on eight seasons of first-class cricket, suggests that the injury rate in fast bowlers is 18 per cent. It is also evident that lower-back stress fractures are not as common in cricketers at the first-class level relative to their younger counterparts,

Indian philosophy?

'It is a coincidence that two great philosophers should share their birthday today. Like Confucius, Bradman perfected a simple philosophy – namely that the ball is there to be hit and the runs are there to be made.' India's Hindustan Times newspaper compares Sir Donald Bradman to Chinese sage Confucius.

but these injuries are by far the most debilitating, resulting in 120 match days being missed on average. Closer inspection of those star players injured reveals that many of the injuries are more likely caused by workload than bowling action deficiencies. Season 2003–04 saw Australia play 17 tests and 37 one-day matches; this is considerably more than the requirements of a test player some twenty years ago, yet the seasonal incidence of injury remains roughly the same.

Some cricket coaches have suggested the need to adopt a rotational system for our premier fast bowlers to reduce their workloads. Recent evidence on bowling workloads would suggest such a strategy may be prudent. In monitoring the training and match workloads of 70 first-class bowlers over two seasons, it was found that 123–188 deliveries a week was the magic average number of deliveries required to minimise the likelihood of injury; players who bowl more than this amount have a 1.9 times greater injury risk; players who bowl fewer have 1.4 times the chance of injury.

To bowl a cricket ball is a difficult skill to learn – to then bowl with control and pace is an added complication. The need for repetition, to ingrain the correct movement pattern over time, is a necessity. However, unlike an elite netball shooter who puts up hundreds of thousands of shots in a career to gain the necessary repetition, injury prevention issues quite rightly temper the enthusiasm of fast bowling coaches. The competing forces of skill learning and overuse injuries are not easily resolved and are prominent in the minds of Australian coaches and sports scientists alike, as appropriate evidence-based strategies are developed. Perhaps it is time to recognise that pace bowling will always cause attrition due to the extreme forces generated on the human body. Injury rates can be minimised, and have been, yet they are unlikely to be removed.

Mick Jagger during an Ashes series
'Watching the Aussies is like a porn movie; you always know what is going to happen in the end.'

Eight common (yet controversial) rules of backyard cricket

Rule	Explanation
Any wicket	A batsman can be run out at either end of the pitch 1. Utilised when only one batsman is at the crease 2. An umpiring nightmare
Automatic keeper	An edge behind is automatically out 1. Employed when no wicket-keeper is used 2. An 'automatic slips' cordon of designated size can also be added
Bat-for-ball	Whoever makes the dismissal goes into bat 1. For example: if you catch the ball, you bat 2. Uncoordinated players (who can't bowl or catch) may never get to bat
Can't go out first ball	Self-explanatory 1. Makes a hat-trick impossible 2. A rule for wusses
No LBW	Self-explanatory, and necessary (in most cases) because: 1. Without an umpire, everybody has a different opinion 2. With an umpire, they still probably have no idea
One hand, one bounce	If the ball is hit and is caught in one hand by a fielder after bouncing only once, the batsman is out 1. Only suitable when player numbers are small 2. Discourages big hitting because fielders can wait for a high ball to bounce
Six-and-out	If you hit the ball over the fence, you score six runs but you are out 1. Helps to reduce 'lost ball' incidents 2. Imperative if the neighbour's fence is high, the neighbour is a jerk, or their dog is big and angry
Tippity-run	The batsman must run whenever they strike the ball 1. Produces a quick turnover of batsmen 2. Makes it difficult to settle in for a big innings

Note: The implementation or not of any of these rules will vary upon the size and condition of the backyard venue, and the number and skill of the combatants.

A defining feature of many games is the type of projectile used. Of course it takes two to tango, and inextricably linked to the projectile is the method of propelling it. This chapter highlights the diversity that exists in the world of sporting projectiles, and delves into the complexities involved in optimising their performance out on the park.

The Samson theory of professional tennis: Past generations believed that court performance was directly related to the quantity of hair on one's head.

NEW BALLS PLEASE

2

The science of sporting projectiles

RECORD BREAKER
Nadia Comaneci –the 'perfect' human projectile

At the 1976 Montreal Games, Romanian gymnast Nadia Comaneci made Olympic history by being awarded the first perfect score of 10.0 for her uneven bars routine. By the completion of the Montreal competition, Comaneci's skill and bravery across all apparatus resulted in seven scores of 10.0, giving her the All-Around individual championship. When asked after the competition whether she had plans to retire, she replied, 'I'm only 14' (years old).

In 1980, she was runner-up in the All-Around competition, but only after it took 28 minutes for her score on the balance beam – the final apparatus of the competition – to be announced. She needed a score of 9.9 to take gold (and had previously scored a 10.0 on the beam), but an overall score of 9.85 – courtesy of two scores of 9.80 from the Russian and Polish judges – relegated her to the silver medal. In 1989, she defected from Romania.

A SLICE OF GOLF BALL RESEARCH

Physicists with a penchant for flight have long recognised golf as the ideal sport for the playing of mind games. In 1949, a paper entitled 'The Aerodynamics of Golf Balls' appeared in the *Journal of Applied Physics*, spurring scientific pursuit of the optimal golf ball design. But much to the chagrin of golf's law-makers, this scientific dabbling into the physics of golf has itself resulted in battles for the fairway.

The trajectory off the tee involves two implements – the club and the ball. Both objects have been greatly studied, but many experts feel that the ball offers the greatest potential for maximising the length and accuracy of ball flight.

The original fifteenth-century golf ball, known as a *featherie*, involved stuffing boiled goose feathers into a wet leather pouch, then stitching it shut to dry, and dabbing it in white paint. The feathers would then expand, adding to the liveliness of the ball. Like many great inventions, wet weather tested its quality. Unfortunately, the featherie became sodden and heavy, losing its shape after repeated hits with an iron. Crucially, the wet would reduce the ball's carry. Four centuries later, artisans heated gutta-percha gum from the Malaysian tropical tree species *palaquium gutta* into a smooth sphere. Alas, this ball did not offer much in the way of distance or accuracy, dropping to the ground like a dead bird.

But upon observing that the length and predictability of the gutta-percha ball improved with increased wear and tear, an English engineer patented a ball that contained evenly distributed circular depressions on its surface. This design reduced aerodynamic drag and improved the ball's lift. The science of the golf ball was under way, much of it revolving around dimple number and pattern (see Fig. A, illustrated section).

Target golf
In 1457 James IV banned the game of golf in Scotland for he feared his soldiers would not devote enough time to the practice of their archery skills.

Dimples change the face of golf

Most professional golfers today use balls that are 1.68 inches (~ 4.27 centimetres) in diameter and weigh about 4.6 grams. The average size of a dimple is 0.381 centimetres, and a ball with 300 to 500 dimples appears to fly best. The dimples must cover a ball's surface in a fairly even manner or else the ball will swerve unpredictably. The number and symmetry of the dimples is therefore of great importance; if evenly spread about the ball, the result will be 336 dimples.

However, scientists over the years have added hundreds of extra dimples, removed dimples, designed larger but shallower dimples and altered the dimple shape. When the flight of balls with hexagonal dimples was compared to that of the standard circular-dimpled balls, the hex-dimpled balls flew 6 metres further. The dimple arrangement has

Speed golfing
The initial velocity of a driven golf ball is in the vicinity of 75 metres per second; it is also spinning backwards at about 3500 revs per minute (or 60 revs per second).

also been extensively considered: recurring patterns such as icosadeca-hedrons, icosahedrons and cuboctahedrons have improved the golf ball's flight capabilities. To ensure that ball science does not outplay the actual golf courses, the flight distance of a golf ball must not exceed 296.8 yards under the strict *laboratory* testing conditions outlined by the United States Golf Association (USGA) in 1976. The Professional Golf Association (PGA) has also set a minimum ball diameter at 1.68 inches (~ 4.27 centimetres) to keep flight distances under control.

But this has not stopped scientists from challenging golf convention. Some most interesting work was conducted at San Jose University in the 1970s. With limits being set on the flight distance of golf balls, two non-golfing scientists decided to straighten out the hook-and-slice problem. They proposed that a ball with shallower dimples at its poles and deeper dimples around its equatorial circumference would produce a gyroscopic effect, reducing unwanted ball swing by as much as 75 per cent. They came up with the *Polara*, affectionately known as the 'Happy Non-Hooker'.

The Polara did as promised – it self-corrected during a wayward tee-off. So the USGA took the ball to court and, in the process, had to rewrite the rules of ball design to ban the Polara from the professional game. But the Polara had one major let-down; its flight distance was compromised. Having more accuracy but less distance was a trade-off that most golfers weren't happy with, and once again, as its nickname suggested, the 'Happy Non-Hooker' just wouldn't go all the way.

On the PGA Tour, balata (soft-cover) balls are often used because they spin more once they reach the green. Amateur hackers, on the other hand, usually play with Surlyn (hard plastic cover) balls for the extra bounce and roll, for distance. Many of today's balls take advantage of an early three-piece design – a small rubber core wrapped in rubber thread, encased by a urethane cover (see Fig. B, illustrated section). But Titleist released a ball called the *Pro V1* – a ball with a large solid core, covered by two casings. Some players claimed that it

Don't make a splash

To save from extinction the longest drive competitions on cruise ships, the Aquaflyte ball was invented in 1990. The ball – covered in paper pulp, seaweed and a water-soluble gelatin, complete with a sodium bicarbonate core – dissolves in seawater after a few days and is harmless if swallowed.

added 15-plus metres to their driving. Bridgestone also released a two-piece ball – the *Precept MC Lady* – designed to provide women players with extra distance. Many men have also taken to it, but refer to it masculinely as the 'laddie' or the Purdham.

Conventional balls also have a seam where the two halves of the outer casing join; and at this equator, no dimples exist. Under certain conditions, this seam has the potential to produce asymmetric airflow about the ball – not desirable at the professional level of the game. Therefore, golf balls have been produced that have multiple seams in order to increase the symmetry of the ball; some designs have even made use of 10 seams!

But despite all the brain power expended on its specifications, a golf ball still needs a good whack. In fact, average PGA Tour scores have only improved by one stroke over the past 17 years – so for once, it may be a case of brawn over brains.

Golf rules

The number of rules pertaining to the treatment of the golf ball far exceeds those of any other feature of the game.

ANYONE FOR TENNIS?

When one compares tennis in days gone by with the modern game, the most frequent observation is that the speed of the game has increased. Numerous reasons have been cited for this change of pace; in particular, improvements in equipment technology and training approaches have created higher ball velocities and stronger, faster players. One of the most notable and frequently discussed performance changes is that tennis players now consistently serve the ball faster and more accurately than ever before. A quick glimpse at the radar reveals that many of the top male players in the world successfully hit their first serve in excess of 200 km/h.

This great change in the speed of the game has followed the technological advances in racquet construction. Compared to the wooden racquets so ably handled by Björn Borg, today's racquets are stiffer and lighter. They are over 60 per cent bigger, 100 per cent thicker, and 20 per cent lighter, while the 'sweet spot' of today's larger-headed racquets is at least double the size of the old wooden faithful hidden in the back of your cupboard.

Experiments at the University of Pennsylvania showed that a 33 per cent increase in racquet weight produced only a 5 per cent increase in ball speed. However, a 33 per cent increase in racquet head speed got the ball moving 31 per cent faster. Therefore, the lighter frames provide players with a greater ability to generate more speed in their stroke. The greater stiffness of the modern implement also means that less of the ball's energy is absorbed by the racquet during its 5-millisecond vacation on the strings.

These technological improvements in racquet design can be greatly attributed to materials such as graphite fibre and titanium – and many years in the laboratory. The International Tennis Federation (ITF), tennis's governing body, does have limitations on racquet design, but the scientists keep coming up with new ways to make racquets move the ball still faster. So what is the answer?

The bear essentials

The first world ice golf championships were held in Greenland. Competitors used bright-coloured balls, the greens were sprayed with red dye, and each player was advised to bring along a strong eight-iron just in case they came across any polar bears.

Technology has changed stroke mechanics

Tennis heros of the late 1970s and early 1980s such as Ken Rosewall and Chris Evert-Lloyd had classic ground strokes characterised by the player standing side-on to the approaching ball and then smoothly accelerating the racquet through the ball, transferring their body weight with a step; the result was a graceful, flowing motion causing the ball to leave the racquet with slight top spin or a flat trajectory. Modern ground strokes are hit from an open stance (or front-on) to the ball with a western grip (the palm of the hand is on the underside of the grip). Players wind themselves up and then uncoil like spring, using the large muscles of the trunk to increase force as they intercept the ball. The amount of uncoiling, or rotation, results in a powerful stroke hit with lots of top spin, and often the player leaves the ground in the process. The combination of a larger sweet spot and lighter-weight racquet has allowed even novices to swing with greater abandon and success.

World record

Andy Roddick currently holds the world speed record
for a tennis ball – 246.2 km/h – making him the fastest
server in world tennis.

Is bigger better?

In an attempt to halt this speed, the ITF has proposed
not to change the racquet, but the balls. Currently, balls
are strictly regulated in size, weight and rebound. The
ITF allows a 5 per cent variation in diameter and a 3 per
cent variation in weight. When dropped from 254 centimetres (8 feet 4 inches), the ball must bounce back to
a height between 135 and 147 centimetres (4 feet 5
inches and 4 feet 9 inches).

Over the last couple of years, the ITF has implemented rule changes pertaining to the types of balls that
can be used in tournament play. These changes are
aimed at adjusting the speed of the game, slowing play
to make it more attractive to learners whilst also providing flexibility to manage changes to the professional
game if necessary.

Jason who?

While everyone
knows Tiger Woods,
not many know
Jason Zuback. He is
golf's long-driving
legend – able to hit
drives in excess of
340 metres. Zuback
has become a cult
hero in recent years:
he can hit a ball at
336 km/h and wows
fans by slamming
golf balls through
telephone books.

As a consequence, there are now three official ball
types (Types 1, 2 and 3) that can be used at all levels of
tennis. The type that is most likely to have a profound impact on the
future of the game is the Type 3 or 'oversize' tennis ball. Designed for
play on fast-pace courts, the Type 3 ball is approximately 6 per cent
larger in diameter than a standard ball (now called a Type 2 ball) but
possesses the same mass.

Diligently, the ITF has completed a number of research studies investigating the impact that Type 3 balls would have on both tennis performance and the muscles of those hitting them. Not surprisingly, the
larger ball had a 12 per cent increase in drag relative to the standard
ball, thereby slowing the ball more quickly during its flight, and giving
the receiving player more time in which to prepare and execute a stroke.
Logically, while initial ball velocity off the racquet was not different
from that of the standard ball, by the time the ball had crossed the net,

differences in velocity were evident. In real terms, when facing a serve of 190 km/h, the slowing oversize ball provided the receiver an extra three one-hundredths of a second in which to react, or about 10 per cent more time.

Giving great optimism to tennis hackers everywhere was the improved accuracy that came with using the oversize ball. UK findings based on a continuous hitting test demonstrated that players had twice the accuracy with the oversize ball relative to the standard ball. Rally lengths were found to increase by approximately 10 per cent and point outcomes were more likely to be the result of a winner rather than an error. Likewise, American researchers found that service accuracy improved by 19 per cent when the larger ball was used.

An issue easily forgotten by those enjoying their new-found hitting accuracy was that of whether the larger ball would cause an increase in overuse injuries, as players used greater effort to hit it. While preliminary evidence provided some cause for alarm, more recent, better-controlled experimental work has revealed that the muscle-force activation patterns of players when serving was consistent between ball types. The perception that greater effort may be required when hitting the oversize ball was unfounded. Overuse injury problems are no more likely to occur than with the standard ball.

While the 'power machines' playing at the elite level may lament the introduction of the oversize ball, hackers around the globe will be finding tennis just that little bit easier. And from a spectator's perspective, the larger ball also makes watching tennis that little bit easier. Whilst difficult to forecast the long-term impact that such a ball may have on the game, obviously anything that attracts more people to the sport has to be considered positive.

Did you know?

In the US, you get three tennis balls in a canister whilst in Europe you will usually get four balls; in Japan, you only get two.

Evolution of the tennis racquet

Year	Development
11–12th century	French monks played by hand
14th century	Italians started using a wooden-framed racquet with strings made of gut
1500	Racquets in widespread use Long handle and a small, teardrop-shaped head
1874	Major Walter C. Wingfield patents the equipment and rules of outdoor lawn tennis
1900s	Wooden racquets evolve slowly Quite heavy – 13-14 ounces (368 grams) Small heads – approx. 65 square inches
1967	Wilson sporting goods introduce a metal racquet (T2000) Stronger and lighter than wood Jimmy Connors its most famous user
1976	Howard Head introduces the first oversized racquet – Prince Classic Aluminium frame with a string area 50 per cent larger than standard wood racquets Weed USA tries to market a similar racquet in 1975 with little success
1980	'Graphite' racquets – a mixture of carbon fibre and plastic resin – become the hallmark of quality The Dunlop Max 200G, used by McEnroe and Graf, weighed 12 ounces (340 grams)
1987	Wilson develop the 'Widebody' racquet to increase racquet stiffness without using stiffer materials Frames are 39 mm wide, more than twice the width of a wooden racquet
2000	Average racquets now weigh approximately 10.5 ounces (297 grams) with some as light as 7.5 ounces (210 grams) New materials mixed with graphite include: ceramics, fibreglass, boron, titanium, Kevlar and Twaron
21st century	Head has developed a racquet that uses piezoelectric technology to convert vibrations into electrical energy that subsequently dampens the vibration

Fresh air shot

A Toronto-based inventor, Oliver Tiura, has designed a tennis racquet with a ventilated handle. The racquet has a hole near the base of the head so that on every stroke, air funnels through the hollow handle. The air then comes out through holes in the handle and into the palm of the player, helping to rid the area of sweat and improving the player's grip on the racquet.

Get off the grass

A huge factor contributing to ball speed is court surface; the difference in Grand Slam court surfaces is as clear as red and green. Each of the four Grand Slam events is contested on a different surface: rebound ace at the Australian Open, clay at the French Open, grass at Wimbledon and hard court at the US Open. Not only does the surface affect ball speed, but also the fortunes of some of the game's stars. This is most evident at the French Open which is decided on Roland Garros's dusty clay courts.

This clay conundrum has motivated sport scientists to investigate why court surfaces can turn the unbeatable into hacks. Typically, the approach employed to analyse the impact of court surface on elite tennis performance has been by notational analysis. Most recently, an analysis of some 175 Grand Slam matches between 1997–1999 was undertaken to determine the frequency of a wide range of variables thought likely to influence the result of a match. This resulted in 313 hours of broadcast footage – equating to 31,558 points – being analysed. The key aim for the researchers was to identify, in each of the four Grand Slams, the distinguishing subtleties and nuances in the way a point was played.

As any tennis connoisseur would anticipate, the French Open produced significantly longer rallies than any of the other Slams. On average, each point lasted for 9 seconds in women's matches and 7.5 seconds in the men's competition. In comparison, rallies on the slick grass of Wimbledon lasted for 6 and 4 seconds, respectively, for women and men. Players also produced a significantly lower shot rate in Paris relative to the other tournaments.

The above evidence indicates that the clay game possesses a decidedly different temporal nature – but what properties of clay contribute to this change? The ball is known to collide with the clay surface with a higher coefficient of friction, effectively slowing down the ball's speed. Clay also possesses a higher coefficient of restitution than the other Slam surfaces, resulting in a higher ball-bounce. These two factors combine to afford players more time to hit a return stroke.

Despite the ball-to-court collision lasting only 250 milliseconds, its influence on playing time is significant. The steepness of the trajectory of 'ball flight in' relative to 'ball flight out' determines surface speed; the greater the difference between these trajectories, the slower the surface. For a ball struck with top spin of 900 revolutions per minute (slightly less than an average female ground stroke), the slow courts of Roland Garros produce a bounce some six degrees steeper than Wimbledon's grass. Coupled with this is the ball's velocity. In Paris, a ball travelling at 30 km/h immediately prior to biting the dust will reach a player standing 2.5 metres away some 3 km/h slower and 320 milliseconds later than its Wimbledon equivalent. The combination of friction with the coefficient of restitution determines why a ball fights against clay or glides over grass.

The effect of this increased time is most evident in the battle of serve-and-return. Slower ball speeds caused by the clay surface negate the impact of serve dominance; 'aces' and outright service winners are fewer in Paris relative to the other tournaments.

Not surprisingly, the time taken *between* points is longer at the French Open than any other Grand Slam; this can be attributed to players needing more time to suck in the O_2 at the end of each point. The flip side of longer rallies is that more shots are required before a winner or error is produced. Therefore, winning on clay becomes a game of attrition; as match durations also increase, players must resist the effects of fatigue for longer. As such, stroke velocity decreases, while error rates increase.

To make it to the last weekend at Roland Garros is like making it to the finish of that other famous French sporting event – the Tour de France; significant amounts of staying power are required – more than any other Grand Slam.

Feat of clay

Pete Sampras holds the record for most Grand Slam singles tennis titles won by a man, with 14 wins. While he won the Australian Open, US Open and Wimbledon he never captured the French Open title played on clay. In fact, in his last five French Open appearances Sampras exited Roland Garros in either the first or second round.

Tennis origins

Royal tennis originated during the Middle Ages and is played on an indoor court using balls made from sheepskin filled with sawdust, sand or wool. These balls didn't bounce on grass courts, so it wasn't until the nineteenth century when rubber trees were commercially grown that the first lawn tennis balls were made and lawn tennis as we know it today caught on. Initially, a two-piece, hollow rubber ball was used, but it was found to be too slippery in wet conditions – so a flannel covering was invented. Today's balls are covered with a mixture of wool and man-made fibres.

There's money in tennis

A British quiz show contestant won $319,000 despite getting a question wrong. He said 24 is the minimum number of strokes needed for a tennis player to win a set. The producers later said the answer is 12 if the opponent double-faults every serve.

Calling the lines

Cyclops made its Grand Slam debut at the 1981 US Open. It was first used in Australia at the 1988 Open – the first year the Open was held at Melbourne's Flinders Park (now known as Melbourne Park). Cyclops transmits five infra-red beams across the court from a position on the service line. The system is positioned in such a way that one infra-red beam runs along the good side of the service box line, and the other four run on the fault side, up to 45 centimetres from the line. When a ball hits on the line (or just inside the line), it momentarily breaks the first beam and turns off the others. If the serve is long, it breaks one of the four other beams. Cyclops's developer claims calls are more than 99 per cent accurate, barring extreme temperature changes that can affect the court surface.

Meanwhile, a new line-call system – a sensor embedded in the line that triggers when the ball hits the chalk – is supposed to increase the accuracy of the other line calls in tennis by 100 per cent. Linespeople are provided with earphones and are alerted by a signal if the ball is in. The system is supposed to be so accurate that it can even tell the difference between when a ball hits the line or someone's shoe.

Grass has been slammed

Unlike the four different surfaces played on in modern Grand Slam tennis, 31 years ago three of the four Grand Slam events were actually played on grass. Now the professional circuit spends less than one month of the season playing on grass. This change in court surface is another reason for the prevalence of modern ground strokes that have been optimised for high-bouncing, medium to slow paced court surfaces rather than the fast, low-bouncing grass.

Wimbledon champion Goran Ivanisevic
commenting on the state of US linespeople
**'They need more young people calling the lines in the States –
there are too many older people who can't see.'**

BATTER UP

Baseball is all about matching up against the ghosts of the past. Professional records span as far back as 1876 when the National League was founded in the US (the American League came into being in 1900), which means that batters and pitchers across the centuries past and to come can be compared and judged. But with the distance between the pitcher's mound and the batter's box (or more accurately, the pitcher's plate to home plate) being only 60.5 feet (18.44 metres), and having baseballs of only 2.90 inches (7.3 centimetres) in diameter being delivered at speeds nearing 160 km/h to hitters wielding a rounded bat of no more than 2.75 inches (~ 7 centimetres) in diameter, delicacy exists in the balance of power between pitcher and batter.

The history of baseball charts several small but vital adjustments to the game in order to maintain the unique pitcher–batter equilibrium. Lengthening the throwing distance and lowering the height of the pitching mound have tempered the dominance of the pitcher. At the opposite end of the equation, the resistance by Major League Baseball (MLB) to the introduction of the aluminium bat (despite its enhanced durability) has helped restrict modern-day hitters from crushing pitching reputations as well as every hitting record in existence. However, the staunch position by MLB to stick with tradition and demand the use of the wooden bat may do much more than just keep opponents on an even keel – wooden bats may indeed save lives.

Ball bender

In 1959, wind-tunnel experiments by physicist Lyman Briggs showed that a baseball could curve up to 17.5 inches (~ 44 centimetres) during its short journey from the pitcher's hand to home plate. He demonstrated that spin, and not speed, was most important when throwing a ball for maximum curve. The 17.5-inch deviation was achieved with the ball spinning at 1800 rpm at a speed of about 108 km/h; this is achievable for a professional pitcher.

Basketballer Charles Barkley
'Two people have ruined history – Spud Webb and Tiger Woods. Now every munchkin thinks he can play basketball.
And everyone thinks they can play golf.'

Wood versus aluminium

When the game of baseball started to take shape in the mid-nineteenth century, the BYOB rule applied – Bring Your Own Bat. Players soon realised that they could hit the ball further with a round bat and this shape was quickly adopted by most players. In 1859, baseball's then governing body limited the width of the bat to 2.5 inches (6.25 centimetres) and players responded by seeking the services of woodworkers to shape their bats for optimal length and weight distribution. In 1895, the width restriction was increased to 2.75 inches (6.9 centimetres) whilst the length limit remained at 42 inches (105 centimetres), as it still does today.

Aluminium bats arrived on the landscape around 1970 and were approved for use at virtually all levels of baseball except Major League Baseball where the rules state that the bat must be made from one solid piece of wood. However, there's been no shortage of attempts to illegally manipulate the implement. Weight has been added by hammering nails or phonograph needles into the barrel. To lighten the stick, players have drilled holes to insert cork or super balls. But unfortunately, wood breaks. This has resulted in some embarrassed faces in the batting box when the shattering of a bat sends cork flying or super balls chaotically bouncing about the diamond.

Firstly, does aluminium actually perform better than wood? Early research by engineers at Arizona State University, using a radar gun, found that a ball coming off the sweet spot of a metal bat travelled 6.5 kilometres per hour (km/h) faster than off wood. This means that the defence has less time to react to a batted ball, giving the hitter a greater chance of reaching first base on a hit. Furthermore, this improvement in ball velocity off an aluminium bat translated to a flight distance some 10 per cent greater than that achieved off its wooden equivalent. Again, not only does this make the outfielders' job more difficult but it also leads to more home runs.

However, more recent work from the University of Western Australia (UWA), using high-speed cameras, reports that this difference in ball speed off an aluminium bat compared to a wooden bat is much greater than previously reported. In fact, the UWA findings showed that a metal bat can swat the baseball some 35 km/h faster! This not only increases a batter's chances of beating the fielders, and the home run fence, but may also present more dire consequences for the pitcher than just damaging his pitching averages. But more on that later.

But why does aluminium produce these significant improvements in ball rebound? In part, aluminium has greater rigidity and strength than wood. More importantly, aluminium bats can be constructed lighter. This means that higher bat speeds can be generated for the same length of bat, and bat speed is a critical factor in hitting range; it has been estimated that increasing bat speeds by only 1 metre per second will increase the optimal range of a hit by nearly 5 metres.

Foulproof protection

In the 1920s, a travelling salesman called Foulproof Taylor sold 'protectors' (also known as a 'box' or 'cup') to boxers and spectators at carnivals. Foulproof would invite spectators to punch him below the belt to show the effectiveness of his merchandise. If the crowd was not responding, he'd even allow them to whack him between the legs with a baseball bat.

Lively balls

Over the last few years, many longstanding home run records have fallen. As such, questions have been raised about the liveliness of the balls being used in Major League Baseball. Analysing baseballs from 1963 through to 2000, forensic scientists at the University of Rhode Island suggest that modern balls are flying 10 per cent further than past generations. The composition of the 1989, 1995 and 2000 balls differed from earlier balls, having a greater concentration of rubber in their cores, as well as a synthetic material in their wool windings. When dropped from a height of 462 centimetres (15 feet 2 inches), the 1995 and 2000 versions bounced to a height of 208 centimetres (6 feet 10 inches) whilst the older balls only reached 157 centimetres (5 feet 2 inches).

Right number, wrong answer

In 1997, a Florida Marlins bat-boy answered a phone call in the clubhouse. The caller told the boy, 'This is Bill Clinton', to which the boy replied, 'Yeah, and I'm Elvis' and hung up. Two security guards then came running at him saying, 'Hey, get off that phone. The president is going to call any minute.'

Bat weight also affects the speed at which a ball cannons after contact. Once again, the greater the bat weight, the greater the momentum. But if a hitter swings a bat that is too heavy, their accuracy in bat–ball contact will be jeopardised. Researchers at the University of Arizona examined this issue of ideal bat weight and found that 75 per cent of professional ball players were already swinging a bat of the weight most appropriate for themselves. Here, aluminium again has advantages over wood because metal allows more flexibility during bat construction when searching for the optimal combination of bat weight and swing speed.

Interestingly, the metal bat has gone a long way to restoring the lost equilibrium between batter and pitcher in softball. With the advent of the windmill-style pitching delivery, many softball pitchers now fling the ball at similar speeds to that of baseball chuckers. Unfortunately for softball batters, the distance from the pitcher's mound to home plate is only 46 feet (14 metres) – don't blink or you'll miss it. But since the introduction of aluminium to the hitter's arsenal, softball batting averages have risen dramatically. With that touch more bat speed that aluminium can provide, the hitters can get the stick over the plate a little quicker, and at least have a chance of getting bat on ball.

How to hit a home run

Researchers from the University of California and the University of Cambridge have calculated the optimal conditions for hitting a baseball the furthest possible distance, using typical bat and ball speed parameters observed in Major League Baseball.

1. Most importantly, the faster you swing the bat, the further a baseball will travel: the ball travels almost an extra 5 metres for every 1 m/s increase in bat speed.

2. For a given pitch (e.g. *fastball, curveball, knuckleball*), the faster the delivery, the further the distance the ball will rebound off the bat.

3. For a typical fastball pitch, the batter's swing should 'undercut' the ball below its centrepoint by 2.65 centimetres, with an upswing angle (from the horizontal) of 9 degrees. Undercutting the ball at impact also enhances the backspin carried by the baseball in flight.

4. Contrary to popular belief, an optimally hit curveball can be hit further than an optimally hit fastball – this is due to differences in the amount of backspin carried by the batted ball. Once hit, a fastball has approximately 30 per cent less backspin than a curveball: as such, a curveball will travel an extra 4 metres. (Note: Backspin increases the lift effect experienced by the ball, helping keep it airborne for longer. When hit, the spin of a fastball must be reversed to produce backspin in flight; in contrast, the top spin of a curveball actually augments the resultant backspin of the struck baseball.)

Source: Sawicki, Hubbard and Stronge, 2003

A deadly game

More than home runs and strike-outs are at stake when swinging an aluminium bat. When you consider that a baseball is deformed to half of its original diameter when being hit and that it only remains in contact with the bat for 2 milliseconds, these statistics clearly highlight the high-speed nature of the event. Subsequently, the major cause of death in baseball is when a pitcher gets hit by a ball smashed back in his direction. At Little League level, 75 per cent of all injuries are the result of being struck by a batted ball, and in the US alone, 88 Little Leaguers between 1973 and 1995 died from head injuries on the diamond, most from being struck by a well-hit ball.

Despite the pitching distance being set at 18.44 metres, by the time the pitcher has stepped forward from the pitcher's plate and extended his entire body toward home plate in order to transfer as much speed as possible to the ball by the time he releases it, the pitcher is more likely to be about 16 metres from the bat. This is where the speed at which a ball rebounds from the bat, called its *exit speed*, becomes vital.

From a distance of 16 metres, the scientists at UWA calculated, a pitcher needs at least 400 milliseconds to evade a ball batted straight back in his direction. This is approximately the time taken for a ball to ricochet back to where the pitcher is standing if struck with an exit speed of 150 km/h. Using high-speed cameras to film elite baseballers swinging wood and aluminium bats of equivalent dimensions, the research team found that wooden bats could produce exit speeds of around 150 km/h. However, the aluminium bats produced ball velocities in *excess* of 160 km/h. Results from the UWA study indicate that the exit speeds of a well-hit ball from a wooden bat provide just enough time for a pitcher to take some evasive action. However, a ball off the sweet spot of an aluminium bat can exceed, perhaps by 100 milliseconds, that 400 milliseconds threshold needed for a pitcher to react.

Importantly, this work also highlighted that the weight distribution in a bat, and not the mass itself, is a determining factor in the speed at which a bat can be swung and, therefore, the exit speed of a batted ball. The differing density of aluminium compared to wood allows a metal bat to be constructed with more weight in the handle compared to a wooden bat with its relatively heavy barrel. More weight distributed in the bat handle confers a smaller moment of inertia when generating a swing. As such, aluminium bats can be accelerated faster, resulting in a greater bat head speed at ball contact – and a greater exit speed for the ball.

Illegal pitch
Michael Jackson impersonator, Frederick Oliverier, persuaded the New York Yankees to let him throw the first pitch. Police later arrested him when they noticed him sitting in the home team's dugout. He faces charges of criminal trespass and false impersonation.

Of cork and nails and super balls

Considered the equivalent of cricket ball tampering, corking a baseball bat is one of the game's biggest sins. In 1974, legendary Yankees player Craig Nettles broke a bat during a game, sending a flurry of super balls bounding about the infield. Then in 2003, Chicago Cubs super-slugger Sammy Sosa became the fifth Major League player since 1975 to be outed for using a corked bat. In a game at Chicago's famous Wrigley Field against the Tampa Bay Devil Rays, Sosa was caught with his pants down when the bat he was using broke to reveal shards of cork. Of course, he was ejected from the batting box, suspended for a few games, and embarrassed to be exposed as a cheat. But why all the fuss? Does corking a bat really provide an advantage to the hitter?

The MLB rulebook states that a bat must be round and made of *solid* wood, can be any weight but no wider than 2.75 inches (7 cm). The rules have remained the same for an eternity, and like most other sports, players have continually pushed these rules in search of a performance advantage. Players 'cork' a bat by drilling a one-inch (2.5-centimetre) diameter hole into the barrel about 6 to 10 inches (15 to 25 cm) deep, filling the space with cork. They then seal the bat with sawdust and glue. As mentioned earlier, this form of illegal manipulation makes the bat lighter. Sosa typically uses a 33-ounce (935-gram) bat, but its weight when corked would alter by 1 to 1.5 ounces (~28 to 42 grams. This supposedly gives the player increases in bat speed, and hence greater exit speed for the ball and more legs with the hit.

But if Sosa had read *The Physics of Baseball* by Robert Adair, he may have saved himself some embarrassment. In this biomechanics bible of baseball, Adair demonstrates that cork weakens the bat, as Sosa eventually discovered. The energy transferred from the bat to the ball at impact is reduced by about 2 per

The shaking heart

Of 128 reported cases of commotio cordis (shaking heart), 67 incidents have resulted from baseball and softball players being struck in the chest by a baseball. This rare form of cardiac arrest appears only to occur if an individual is struck in the chest at a precise moment in an exact location with an explicit force or speed. In fact, to fall victim to this condition, the impact to the chest must occur within a specific 15-millisecond window during a heartbeat.

cent when using a corked bat. In performance terms, this equates to the ball losing approximately one metre of distance in a 120-metre drive, despite the extra bat speed.

Sosa, a potential 'Hall of Famer', ended the 2005 season with 588 home runs, most likely in the absence of cork. X-rays of 76 of his bats impounded from the locker room, and a further five resting in the Hall of Fame, have shown no traces of cork. Perhaps he should have followed the old adage – if it ain't broke, don't fix it.

Death by sporting implement (of the 'living' or 'undead') in the movies	
Shaun of the Dead	Cricket bat (great for whacking Pommy zombies)
Caddyshack	Golf club (as a lightning conductor)
The Untouchables	Baseball bat (don't backchat De Niro)
Rollerball	Rollerball (those balls are damned heavy)
Down By Law	Billiard ball (it was self-defence)
Shaolin Soccer	Soccer ball (who would have guessed?)
Dawn of the Dead	Croquet mallet (there's more than one way to stop a zombie)
Fatal Games	Javelin (it was inevitable)
Mystery Men	Bowling ball (by someone called 'The Bowler' funnily enough)
Lethal Weapon 2	Surfboard (Mel is an Aussie, after all)
Wishcraft	Bowling ball (it appears to be very useful for killing)
Gladiator	Trident, sword and tiger (well, they were sporting implements back then … kinda)
Running Man	Ice hockey stick (the character 'Sub-Zero' carried a very sharp one)
'Salad Days' directed by Sam Peckinpah (A *MontyPython's Flying Circus* sketch)	Tennis racquet and ball (it's a TV show but it's rare to witness such violence associated with tennis)
Shaun of the Dead	Totem tennis pole (zombies just keep coming)

WHAT MAKES FRISBEES FLY?

There is no doubt that the first inkling of throwing a *Frisbee* came from the primitive days when hunters needed a projectile – be it a stick or rock – to stop fast-moving animals. The Aboriginal people then steered us closer to the modern-day Frisbee with their expert usage of the boomerang. Deliberately carved in the shape of a curved air foil, these wooden sticks were not only designed to knock out any small game in range, but also to return to the thrower. Despite these early indications of man's ability to design a hand-launched flying object, it was not until the late nineteenth century, when new, lightweight materials were produced, that the concept of Frisbee began to take off.

In the mid-1870s, William Russell Frisbie opened his own bakery called *The Frisbie Pie Company*. The family-run business decided that pies would be packaged in metal pie tins approximately 10 inches (25 centimetres) in circumference. On the bottom of these tins were stamped the words *Frisbie Pies*. Once the pie was eaten, college students from Yale created a mini-craze by engaging in pie tin tossing.

Thirty years later, Fred Morrison and Warren Francioni decided to extend the flight of the early pie tins. Originally they welded rims onto the pie tins, but as could be expected, the weight, amongst other factors, rendered the concept useless. That was until Morrison was able to utilise plastic. His original disc was called *Morrison's Flyin' Saucer* and was made from a plastic compound called butyl stearate. But this

X-ray specs

Researchers at the National Institute of Standards and Technology in the US aimed to determine the optimal 'non-destructive' method for ascertaining whether a wood baseball bat was corked or not. Using a variety of devices including ultrasound, X-ray and CAT scanners, the scientists concluded that medical X-ray devices were best. Besides its definitive results, X-ray technology was also the quickest and most practical approach, particularly because most baseball grounds had X-ray machines on hand to diagnose player injuries and they were also handy for assessing suspect bats.

Swish science

The minimum entry angle for a swish in basketball is reported to be just under 33 degrees; this presents a rim size of 9.71 inches (24.3 centimetres), the same size as the basketball's diameter.

Boomerang discovery

Archaeologists have found what they describe as 'sport boomerangs' dating back to 12,000 BC in locations as diverse as Australia, Egypt, North America and Europe.

model didn't last long, as the formulation was too brittle. In 1951, Morrison re-designed the Flyin' Saucer, renaming it *Pluto Platter*. He went on to sell this model for a few years before turning over his idea to another company: *Wham-O*.

Shortly afterward, one of the co-owners of Wham-O, on a promotional trip, came across students who were familiar with the idea of disc flying, except they used the name *Frisbie*. Realising a good opportunity, Wham-O subsequently commenced production in 1957 of the first plastic disc trademarked *Frisbee* (not 'Frisbie').

Frisbee physics

The design of the Frisbee has not changed a great deal over the years, for a very good reason. Its pie-tin characteristics – being circular, fairly flat, with sloped or rounded edges – are critical to its ability to fly. In particular, the rounded edges of the Frisbee behave like the front edge of an aircraft wing. As air passes over the curved upper surface of the Frisbee it speeds up, creating a low-pressure region on top of the Frisbee. Below the Frisbee, air passes more slowly, creating a high-pressure region. The difference in relative pressure gives the Frisbee lift; this is called the 'Bernoulli effect'. In addition to being designed to generate lift, the requirement to throw the Frisbee with spin is also critical, as without a good tweak it wobbles and falls quickly. Although the shape of the Frisbee may generate lift, the Frisbee is unstable and cannot stay upright, and eventually stalls without spin.

Amazingly, scientific research on Frisbee flight has taken off in recent times. Early work used wind tunnels to measure the aerodynamic lift and drag forces on the Frisbee as a function of the throwing angle. More recently, scientists have shifted their attention to quantifying pitching and rolling moments of the Frisbee in flight, and to the biomechanics of the Frisbee throwing

Aerobie

In 1978, an aerodynamicist called Alan Adler, not content with the stable but relatively short flight time of a Frisbee, developed a flying ring called the Skyro. With a low-drag shape relative to the Frisbee, the Skyro could be projected massive distances. However, the catch was that it would only do so at one specific speed, meaning that it was unstable to the majority of average throwers. Based on a computer simulation of ring flight, Adler then developed a ring that produced perfect balance at all speeds. After a number of prototypes, the Aerobie was born in December 1984. On 30 January 1985, Scott Zimmerman threw an Aerobie 1,125 feet (343 metres), setting a Guinness World Record for the longest throw of any heavier-than-air object.

action. Specific techniques, such as the backhand throw, have been analysed through the use of high-speed video cameras that allow the joint angles of a thrower to be captured. Additionally, flight data can be collected via a three-dimensional motion analysis system, like those used to quantify the bowling mechanics in cricket (see page 55). Opto-reflective markers are placed on the Frisbee so that it can be tracked with great precision over an 18-metre flight. The end goal of such research is to model the flight of the Frisbee and simulate the resulting trajectory for any set of initial release conditions; such investigations are aimed at optimising the ability to throw the Frisbee.

Did you know?

It is claimed that, in the US, more Frisbees are sold each year than baseballs, basketballs and footballs combined.

Flying by the crotch of your pants

An angler, who had failed for 11 years to catch salmon in a Scottish river, finally succeeded when he used a fly featuring a tuft of his wife's pubic hairs – his theory: that pheromones might attract the fish. 'Sure enough, on my eleventh cast, I hooked a beautiful four-pound fish,' he said. 'My problem is not so much that I have run out of raw materials for my fly-tying, but what to call this superb new fly.'

The Bernoulli effect

The Bernoulli effect is an explanation of how the wings of aircraft help generate lift for the aeroplane. Pressure is lower in a moving fluid than in a stationary fluid. By installing an air foil shape (curved on the top and flat on the bottom) in a stream of moving air, one creates an area of fast-moving air (on top) and an area of slow-moving air (on the bottom). This creates a difference in pressure above and below the air foil, which in turn generates lift.

TECHNICAL TALES: THE JAVELIN

The modern javelin weighs 800 grams and is made of steel. However, it was not until the 1956 Olympics that steel became the material of choice. Back then, most throwers still used wooden javelins, but this all changed when Norwegian Egil Danielsen smashed the world record at the Games with a borrowed steel javelin.

Javelin takes place on a runway between 30 and 36.5 metres in length, making it the only throwing event that does not take place in a ring. However, one of the earlier throwing techniques used a *rotational* style – somewhat akin to the discus technique – but due to fears for spectator safety, this practice was banned.

Spectator safety became a real concern again in 1984 when the great javelin barrier was broken – a distance of 100 metres. On 20 July 1984, Uwe Hohn of East Germany released a massive throw of 104.80 metres; a throw so big that it instigated an entire alteration to javelin construction.

In 1986, the International Amateur Athletic Federation (IAAF) introduced its *new javelin*, where the centre of gravity of the implement was shifted and the tail made narrower; this greatly reduced the distances that javelins were flying. Hohn's record of 104.80 metres was relegated to the history books and the new world record was set at 85.74 metres. However, over the last two decades with the new javelin, throws are again approaching 100 metres.

MOVEMENT ANALYSIS: A PROGRESSION OF PRECISION

Movement analysis was pioneered back in the late 1800s by Etienne-Jules Marey and Eadweard Muybridge, who used still-image photography to make the seemingly invisible movement of humans and animals into a visible permanent record.

Marey examined the external conditions that influenced actions such as walking, running, and jumping, and the energy expended at each instant. His research produced *Du Mouvement Dans Les Funlctiorls Da La Vie* in 1892 and *Le Mouvement* in 1894. Muybridge produced his book *The Horse in Motion* in 1882 and an 11-volume monolith titled *Animal Locomotion* in 1887. Both scientists' use of still pictures in a time-series allowed high-speed, complicated movement patterns to be understood as never before.

Scientists have continued to take great interest in quantifying the mechanics of motion. Fast-forward 100 years and this interest is never more apparent than in the analysis of cricket bowling techniques. Sport biomechanists, or those sports scientists who measure the effects that force has on the body, have applied a variety of techniques in an attempt to understand the physics of bowling. Their aims have been twofold: firstly, to maximise bowling performance while attempting to minimise injury rates; secondly, and more recently, to determine how the myriad of actions seen in international cricket fit within the laws of the game.

Sport biomechanics captured the public's attention in the 1970s when the legendary fast bowler, Dennis Lillee, needed his technique rebuilt to remove the occurrence of career-threatening stress fractures of the back. As Lillee bowled, high-speed cinematography allowed biomechanists to capture his action at 200 frames of film per second. Recording his technique with such precision allowed the scientists to analyse and correct his technique in minute detail.

Since the successful rebuilding of Lillee, there has remained a

Double-barrelled javelin
Early in the twentieth century, the javelin competition also had a two-handed event, where throwers threw twice, first with the right hand and then with the left – their overall distance being the sum of the two throws.

concerted research focus towards the improved understanding of fast bowling technique. The increase in understanding of the bowling action has, in part, been due to the measurement methods now available. Following the cinematographic techniques came the evolution of VHS video and then digital video, both with the capability of videoing at high speed – a must for the precise recording of blink-of-the-eye movements such as bowling.

Today's most accurate laboratory testing approach allows three-dimensional stick-figure images of a bowler's action to be produced by high-speed infra-red motion analysis systems. Opto-reflective markers placed on key body segments of the bowler, such as at the elbow, wrist and shoulder, are detected by anything from six to 24 infra-red cameras so the joint centres can subsequently be modelled.

Mathematical (kinematic) models are then applied to the bowler's motion to determine key values, such as the degree of trunk–shoulder rotation. This evidence base has developed to the point where scientists can now accurately predict the injury risk of a particular bowling action. Values higher than 30 degrees of counter-rotation are considered a red flag for an increased risk of stress fractures of the back.

UPDATE FROM THE LAB:
HOW MOVEMENT ANALYSIS
TECHNOLOGY CHANGED THE
'CHUCKING' RULE

An obvious application of motion analysis technology has been in relation to cricket's *chucking* rule. Over the past few years, many of the game's elite have been questioned over the legality of their bowling actions – pacemen like Australia's Brett Lee and Pakistan's Shoaib Akhtar have both been investigated. In *Run Like You Stole Something*, we discussed some preliminary research that analysed the action of Sri Lankan spinner Muttiah Muralitharan. In recent times, motion analysis technology has become influential in determining the legality of a bowler's action, and has caused a reinterpretation of the game's rules.

A quick check of the history books reveals that the chucking controversy has never been far from the headlines (see the table on page 59).

Australian Ernie Jones was the first to be called for an illegal delivery in Test cricket during the 1897–98 season against England. Since then, eight more players have been 'no-balled' for the motion of 'straightening the elbow' that defines chucking.

In eighteenth-century cricket, the delivery of the ball was literally that of 'bowling' – an underarm action akin to lawn bowling. Batsmen were able to simply stand still and swing their long club-like bat at the rolling ball. But around 1744, bowlers began lobbing the ball. This now forced batsmen to use their feet to deal with variations in line and length of the delivery. This changed the game of cricket immeasurably, but more changes to the bowling technique were to follow.

A grand rumour tells that the shift from underarm to overarm bowling was pioneered by a woman. Christina Willes was the sister of Kent player John Willes, and she would help her brother practise his batting skills by bowling to him. But sporting attire in nineteenth-century England, especially for a woman, was not always practical for the needs of a sport. Consequently, Christina Willes would be forced to send down her lobbed deliveries whilst trying to contend with a long, billowing skirt. The fullness of such skirts made it virtually impossible to deliver the ball in a purely underarm fashion, so to overcome this problem, Christina was forced to use a round-arm action. This type of action greatly troubled her brother's stroke play in the backyard, and subsequently, on 15 July 1822, at the Lord's ground, John Willes adopted his sister's unorthodox technique and opened the bowling for Kent against the MCC. He was no-balled for throwing.

However, the notion that Christina Willes invented the precursor action to modern-day bowling may be more myth than fact. It has been reported that Thomas Walker of Hambledon experimented with the round-arm delivery in the 1780s, and by 1816, a law had been introduced that outlawed the round-arm technique, noting that the ball must 'be delivered underhand, with the hand below the elbow'.

Wily weights

World shot put champion Alexandr Bagach won the European gold medal only to hear that he had been accused of hiding weights in his socks, helping his rotation in the circle. After much deliberation, officials decided that weighted attachments to the ankle did not break any rules and that Bagach could keep his gold medal.

By 1827, five years after the 'John Willes no-ball incident', the round-arm method had grown in popularity – so the MCC conducted three experimental matches to assess the impact this mode of delivery would have on scoring rates. The round-arm action was subsequently legalised the following year; bowlers were now permitted to raise their hand to the level of the elbow. By 1835, further revisions to the game's laws gave bowlers the right to raise their hand to the level of the shoulder during delivery.

True overarm bowling was not far away, and at The Oval in 1862, Edgar Willsher of Kent was the first player to be no-balled for using an overarm action. He and his team left the field that day in protest and the match was suspended until a replacement umpire (who would not call Willsher for an illegal delivery) was found. But 1864 saw overarm bowling written into the rulebook. However, it took some decades before all bowlers adopted the modern-day technique.

DEFINITION
Law 24 (No ball)
2. Fair delivery – the arm

For a delivery to be fair in respect of the arm the ball must not be thrown.
A ball is delivered fairly in respect of the arm if, once the bowler's arm has reached the level of the shoulder in the delivery swing, the elbow joint is not straightened partially or completely from that point until the ball has left the hand. This definition shall not debar a bowler from flexing or rotating the wrist in the delivery swing.

Muralitharan's movement

The most recent case of suspected chucking has involved Sri Lanka's Muttiah Muralitharan. He subsequently visited the University of Western Australia's biomechanics laboratory on a number of occasions: firstly to have his entire action examined; and most recently, in 2004, to examine his *doosra* delivery. On both occasions, the precision of the motion analysis laboratory has verified the legality of Muralitharan's action. Interestingly, Muralitharan's 'numbers' reveal that the speed at which he circumducts his upper arm from horizontal to the point of ball release (.072 seconds) is equal to or quicker than some fast bowlers. Of course, public opinion disputes these findings, but such opinions are based on the unaligned human eye sitting high in the stands, or on viewing less-than-precise television camera images that are unable to re-create the accuracy of three-dimensional analysis.

DEFINITION
Doosra
Urdu word meaning 'the other'

Players called for chucking in Test cricket	
Player	**Match details**
Ernie Jones	Australia v England at MCG 1897-98
Tony Lock	England v West Indies at Kingston 1953-54
Geoff Griffin	South Africa v England at Lord's 1960
Haseeb Ahsan	Pakistan v India at Bombay 1960-61
Ian Meckiff	Australia v England at Brisbane 1963-64
Abid Ali	India v New Zealand at Christchurch 1967-68
David Gower	England v New Zealand at Nottingham 1986 (Gower threw intentionally)
Henry Olonga	Zimbabwe v Pakistan at Harare 1995-96
Muttiah Muralitharan	Sri Lanka v Australia at MCG 1995-96
Muttiah Muralitharan	Sri Lanka v England at Adelaide 1998-99
Shabbir Ahmed*	Pakistan v West Indies at Barbados 2005
Shoaib Malik*	Pakistan v England in Pakistan 2005
Johan Botha*	South Africa v Australia at SCG 2006
* Cited under the ICC's new reporting methods for chucking.	

Technology is now allowing scientists to analyse action in situ with appropriately aligned high-speed cameras. While it has been suggested that there is a 4-degree error margin in the field relative to a 1-degree margin in the lab, the field-based results are still compelling. Recent results from the placement of two high-speed digital cameras at Test venues have shown that 34 deliveries bowled by 21 different fast

Rock-Paper-Scissors –
The throwing sport at the cutting edge

DEFINITION

Rock-Paper-Scissors (RPS) is a decision-making game of wits, speed, dexterity and strategy, between players who are unable to reach a decision using other means. The result of a game is considered a binding agreement between the players. RPS is a game played by honourable people, and therefore, every effort should be made to commit to the outcome. The game is played by substituting the elements of Rock, Paper and Scissors with standard hand signals.

Throws

Rock: is represented by a closed fist with the thumb resting at least at the same height as the topmost finger of the hand. The thumb must not be concealed by the fingers.

Scissors: is delivered in the same manner as rock with the exception that the index and middle fingers are fully extended toward the opposing player. It is considered good form to angle the topmost finger upwards and the lower finger downwards in order to create a roughly 30-45 degree angle between the two digits and thus mimic a pair of scissors.

Paper: all fingers including the thumb are fully extended and horizontal, with the points of the fingers facing the opposing player. Use of the 'vertical paper' (sometimes referred to as 'the handshake') is considered exceptionally bad form.

The World RPS Player's Responsibility Code

1. Safety First! Always ensure that all players have removed sharp jewellery and watches.
2. Ensure agreement, before the first round, on priming conventions (the World RPS Society recommend the standard three-prime shoot).
3. Always establish what is to be decided or whether the match is to be played for honour.
4. Pre-determine the number of rounds required to win the match (remember, odd numbers only).
5. Encourage novice development by explaining blunders in judgment with a mind towards being helpful. Don't berate.
6. Think twice before using RPS for life-threatening decisions.
7. Always respect foreign cultures. When abroad, consider yourself an ambassador of the World RPS Society.

Source: World RPS Society, 2002, Game Basics. <http://www.worldrps.com/index.html>

bowlers demonstrated some degree of elbow straightening. Similar in situ approaches were also used at the ICC Champions Trophy tournament in England in 2004 and perhaps more importantly, expert two-dimensional analyses were conducted at the 2004 Youth World Cup in an attempt at early identification of any technical problems within the next generation of bowlers.

It is such numbers, generated from in-depth motion analysis, that led the International Cricket Council (ICC) to convene an expert panel to discuss the results and recommend changes to the interpretation of the chucking law. The overwhelming consensus of this ICC-convened committee was that the current tolerance levels for interpreting whether a player had chucked or not were no longer tenable. As a result, it was proposed that the degree of elbow-straightening at the point of ball delivery be relaxed from 5 degrees for spinners, 7.5 degrees for medium pacers, and 10 degrees for pace bowlers, to a blanket arm-extension limit of 15 degrees. Without such a change, 80 to 90 per cent of the world's bowlers, both past and present, would be in breach of the law.

The changing face of sporting equipment signifies the evolution that materials, testing and technology has undergone over the years, resulting in the tumbling of world records on a regular basis.

This chapter is devoted to the science behind some of the great equipment transformations that have revolutionised their respective sports.

The Ken Done conjecture:
Despite enormous innovations in bike equipment and design, no amount of science has been able to make cycling clothes look anything but ridiculous.

EQUIPPED FOR SUCCESS

③

Technical revolutions in sporting equipment

RECORD BREAKER
Sergey Bubka – twenty feet and beyond

On 13 July 1985, Ukrainian pole vaulter Sergey Bubka became the first man to clear 6 metres (19 feet 8.25 inches), but greater heights were to be scaled. Six years later, on 5 August 1991, he finally sailed over the ultimate height – a vault of 20 feet . He is still the only man in the sport's history to ever achieve 20 feet. His vault of 6.14 metres (20 feet 1.75 inches) in 1994 still stands as the outdoor world record; in fact, Bubka holds the first 11heights on the all-time outdoor pole vault list. Indoors, he has gone even higher – 6.15 metres.

A combination of unique factors has been put forward to explain Bubka's unprecedented success. Firstly, he employed a higher handgrip on the pole than his competitors, meaning that at the zenith of his vault, he was able to raise his centre of mass higher. He also had great speed and strength. Utilising a 46-metre approach run, Bubka generated great speed by the time he planted the pole. And his strength allowed him to use poles that were longer and stiffer than were normally used by his competitors; this provided him a better catapulting action.

Since 1983, when he burst onto the international scene as a 19-year-old to score an upset victory at the inaugural World Championships of Athletics, he has set 17 outdoor world records, 18 indoor world records, winning six world championships and capturing the 1988 Olympic gold medal. He is still the only athlete in any event to win six world championships.

THE WINGED KEEL

'Who is first?' asked Queen Victoria. She was informed that the *America* had won.

'Who was second?' she then inquired, to which came the reply, 'Your Majesty, there is no second.'

In 1848, Queen Victoria sanctioned the making of a 'One Hundred Guinea Cup' of solid silver for a yacht race, open to all comers, around the Isle of Wight over a distance of 53 miles. Three years later, Commodore J.C. Stevens of the New York Yacht Club formed a syndicate and designed a yacht that was to be presented in London at the

Great Exhibition of 1851 as an example of American shipbuilding prowess. Whilst there, he entered his wooden schooner, named *America*, in the 'One Hundred Guinea Cup', won it and took it home.

The Cup immediately became known as the America's Cup, named after the winning boat, and was soon entrusted to Commodore Stevens, who established it as a permanent challenge cup for international yachting syndicates, placing it into the trust of the New York Yacht Club. The Cup would remain in American hands for the next 132 years.

Since the establishment of the America's Cup in 1851, the Cup has been challenged over 30 times. The second contest did not take place until 1870, the long pause due primarily to the outbreak of the American Civil War. In this match, Britain's *Cambria* was defeated by the American yacht *Magic*. The two world wars and their subsequent years of recovery also substantially halted racing and, in fact, between the 1902 and the 1958 challenges, the race only took place four times.

The original conditions set out by Commodore Stevens stated that America's Cup races had to be sailed over the course set out for the annual regatta of the Cup-holding club. In 1881, new rules stated that challenging vessels had to be constructed in the country which they were representing, and these yachts were then required to sail 'on their own bottoms' to the port at which the Cup was being contested. What this meant was that a challenger, say from Britain or Ireland for example, would have to cross 3000 miles of ocean prior to competition. This regulation placed severe limitations on the construction of a challenging boat, as it would have to first survive a long ocean passage before it began racing. The American yachts, on the other hand, could be built specifically for one season of racing for a Cup defence. This advantage to the defending American syndicates was somewhat alleviated when boat construction shifted to more durable structures.

In 1957, the New York Supreme Court approved amendments to the rules and construction guidelines so that the '12-metre yacht' could challenge for the Cup. These boats were significantly smaller than previous designs, and because of this, the demand that challenging syndicates had to first sail to the race location from their country of origin was dropped. Britain's *Sceptre* subsequently challenged in 1958 but the rule changes made little difference – *Columbia* retained the Cup for the US.

A rapid evolution in boat design ensued over the following decades

The gamest loser in the world of sport

Irish tea baron Sir Thomas Lipton challenged for the America's Cup five times between 1899 and 1930. Representing the Royal Ulster Yacht Club, every one of his five boats was named Shamrock. After his 1930 challenge failed yet again, he was presented with a gold cup to honour his efforts. He died in 1931, at age 83, as he prepared for his sixth challenge.

with materials moving from wood to aluminium to fibreglass. In 1980, the British boat *Lionheart* arrived with a 'bendy' mast – the mast's upper section was composed of glass fibre and foam so that it could bend. This feature provided the British with the advantage of a greater sail area in certain wind conditions, and had both the Americans and French protesting its legality. In 1987, New Zealand's challenger was the first 12-metre yacht to sport a fibreglass hull. But in 1983, *Australia II* challenged for the Cup with an innovation that, once revealed, immediately became one of world sport's most recognisable designs – the *winged keel*.

AUSTRALIA II AND ITS SECRET WEAPON

The winged keel was the brainchild of Australian designer Ben Lexcen, but as many other syndicates discovered, the simple act of slapping a wing to either side of their keel would not automatically make a 12-metre class yacht perform better. The brilliance of Lexcen was in his ability to achieve the ideal design, not only in the dimensions of the keel itself, but with regards to the mass, length, width, shape, angle and positioning of every component of *Australia II*'s eventual configuration. This involved a long process of thorough and secretive experimentation, being assisted in the field of computational fluid dynamics by the National Aerospace Laboratory in Amsterdam, and conducting tank-testing at the Netherlands Ship Model Basin.

Firstly, the wings of the famous keel were around 2.5 metres long and protruded about 60 centimetres from the bottom of the keel at a downwards angle of near 20 degrees. The wings were responsible for improving the performance of *Australia II* in several ways, but their role in decreasing the drag experienced by the yacht was notable. Normally, the water running off a keel produces a whirl of water (known as a 'vortex') at its rear. This vortex produces a drag effect on the boat, slowing its progress. However, the 'winged keel' of *Australia II* acted to redirect this waterflow along the wings such that *two* vortices were now created, one at the tip of each wing. Ingeniously, when these two vortices met behind the keel, they cancelled each other out, effectively reducing the overall drag.

FIG. 3.1 WINGED AND OTHER KEELS

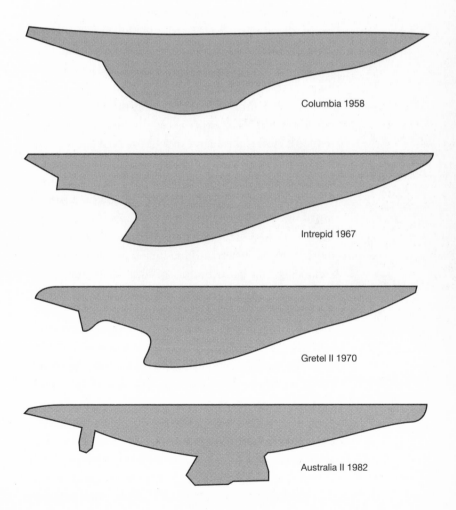

Columbia 1958

Intrepid 1967

Gretel II 1970

Australia II 1982

The boxing kangaroo

The victory of Australia II carries with it many unforgettable images. One such image is that of the boxing kangaroo – a green flag depicting a yellow kangaroo wearing bright red boxing gloves – but this symbol held iconic importance long before 1983. During World War II, the boxing kangaroo was a popular emblem on the Kittyhawk fighter planes of the No. 450 Squadron. However, on these planes, the boxing kangaroo usually wore a slouch hat, as opposed to the image on flags waved during the 1983 America's Cup.

The shape of the keel also contributed great advantages to her performance on the water. The keel was made of lead and sported an inverse taper, sometimes referred to as an 'upside-down' keel. That is, when viewing the keel from the side, the length of its bottom edge was longer than the upper portion attaching to the hull (see Figure 3.1). Furthermore, when looking at the keel from front-on, it did not have the usual V-shape taper from top to bottom, but in fact tapered outwards so that it was thicker at its base than near the hull. Along with the wings themselves, these attributes all contributed to moving more ballast towards the base of the keel, thereby lowering the yacht's centre of gravity almost a metre deeper than other 12-metre yachts.

With its centre of gravity sitting further below the waterline, the *heel* experienced by *Australia II* was reduced. Heel is the degree to which a boat leans to one side as it sails, especially when heading into the wind. Importantly, a reduction in heel is known to improve a vessel's stability and performance. The correct position-ing of the wings on *Australia II*'s keel also helped lessen the yacht's heel. This meant that *Australia II* remained more upright when sailing into the wind, thereby enhancing the contribution of her sails and subse-quently providing more boat speed when sailing into the wind.

Also, because a boat must sail slightly sideways into a headwind in order to maintain forward momentum, the reduced heel allowed *Australia II* to sail more directly into the wind. She was therefore able to cover upwind distances with less sideways deviation than her competitors. This was tactically brilliant because 55 per cent of the total distance of the America's Cup course in 1983 was sailed into the wind – that is, what *Australia II* lost downwind was picked up with interest upwind.

Finally, with Lexcen's keel carrying more weight below the waterline, he was able to reduce the weight of

Australia II's hull (whilst staying within 12-metre yacht specifications). Consequently, the lighter hull resulted in less hull area sitting in the water – a term called *wetted surface*. This smaller wetted surface of *Australia II* not only translated to a reduction in water resistance (drag) but also made her more manoeuvrable, with greater acceleration.

Despite many attempts to expose the winged keel of *Australia II*, including the arrest of a yachtsman from the Canadian challenger caught diving around *Australia II* with an underwater camera, her design was kept a closely guarded secret until 26 September 26 1983. That was the day when *Australia II* passed the American defender *Liberty* during the final race of the event, becoming the first yacht to win a challenge for the America's Cup, and carry the trophy off US soil – 132 years after Commodore Stevens carried Queen Victoria's 'One Hundred Guinea Cup' back to the New York Yacht Club.

The 12-metre yacht

The 12-metre yachts that sailed in America's Cup contests were not 12 metres long – in fact, they were usually around 19 to 29 metres in length. The 12-metre rating is actually derived from the formula below:

$$\frac{L + 2d - F + S}{2.37}$$

where:

L = length in metres

d = girth difference

F = freeboard (the distance between the deck and the waterline)

S = sail area in square metres

Drunken sailor

Russian skipper Viktor Yazykov, whilst sailing the 12-metre yacht Wind of Change-Russia in the 1998-99 Around Alone race, had to deal with an elbow infection that threatened to become gangrenous. Yazykov operated on himself and drained the abscess, losing a lot of blood and passing out – but that may have been the result of the half-bottle of wine he drank to get the job done. After recovering his strength a day later, Viktor discovered that he had made his best progress with the boat on autopilot, covering 239 nautical miles.

America's Cup winners

Year	Defender	Challenger
1851	Aurora, England	**America, USA**
1870	*Magic*, USA	Cambria, England
1871	*Columbia*, USA	Livonia, England
1876	*Madeline*, USA	Countess of Dufferin, Canada
1881	*Mischief*, USA	Atalanta, Canada
1885	*Puritan*, USA	Genesta, GBR
1886	*Mayflower*, USA	Galatea, GBR
1887	*Volunteer*, USA	Thistle, Scotland
1893	*Vigilant*, USA	Valkyrie II, GBR
1895	*Defender*, USA	Valkyrie III, GBR
1899	*Columbia*, USA	Shamrock, Ireland
1901	*Columbia*, USA	Shamrock II, Ireland
1903	*Reliance*, USA	Shamrock III, Ireland
1920	*Resolute*, USA	*Shamrock IV*, Ireland
1930	*Enterprise*, USA	*Shamrock V*, Ireland
1934	*Rainbow*, USA	*Endeavour*, GBR
1937	*Ranger*, USA	*Endeavour II*, GBR
1958	*Columbia*, USA	*Sceptre*, GBR
1962	*Weatherly*, USA	*Gretel*, Australia
1964	*Constellation*, USA	*Sovereign*, GBR
1967	*Intrepid*, USA	*Dame Pattie*, Australia
1970	*Intrepid*, USA	*Gretel II*, Australia
1974	*Courageous*, USA	*Southern Cross*, Australia
1977	*Courageous*, USA	*Australia*, Australia

1980	*Freedom*, **USA**	*Australia*, Australia
1983	Liberty, USA	*Australia II*, **Australia**
1987	*Kookaburra III*, Australia	*Stars & Stripes*, **USA**
1988	*Stars & Stripes*, **USA**	*New Zealand*, NZ
1992	*America 3*, **USA**	*Il Moro di Venezia*, Italy
1995	*Young America*, USA	*Team NZ*, **New Zealand**
2000	*Team NZ*, **New Zealand**	*Luna Rossa*, Italy
2003	*Team NZ*, New Zealand	*Alinghi*, **Switzerland**
Note: Winners are shown in **bold**.		

CLAPSKATES SLASH SPEED-SKATING RECORDS

Existing for centuries, speed skating was initially used as a mode of transportation for people commuting on the frozen canals of Holland. In the competitive arena, elite speed skaters gracefully glide over the ice much in the manner of their ancestors. Yet underlying this ease of movement is finely tuned coordination and balance whilst moving at high velocities.

Traditional skating technique used a gliding action, where the skater is required to push off while the skate continues to glide in a forward/slightly sideways direction. Although investigated by Da Vinci in the early fifteenth century, little change had been made to speed skating technique until the glide technique was challenged in the mid-1980s by Dr Gerrit Jan van Ingen Schenau, a Dutch scientist interested in optimising skating technique.

Ingen Schenau found that the glide action limited the contribution of the powerful knee extensor (or quadriceps) muscles in the front of the thigh. The skater's technical priority to reduce ankle extension caused the skate to lose contact with the ice before full knee extension was reached; this was a deliberate strategy by the skater because if they continued to extend the ankle during the push-off phase, they would increase friction, and potentially drive the tip of the skate into the ice,

Dirty (ice) dancing

The International Skating Union (ISU) has decided to penalise particular moves following complaints that certain lifts were 'undignified'. 'There is a serious concern about the display to the public of undignified poses or positions,' the ISU said. Such moves as the upside-down splits and backward spread-eagles would receive a 0.1 reduction from the judges.

losing balance. In other words, the design of speed skates meant that skaters had to forfeit available leg power in order to minimise increased friction with the ice.

The skaters' adaptation to such a technique was further reinforced in strength-testing results which compared elite speed skaters to a control group. The testing revealed that the elite skaters were able to produce much greater muscle force than the controls in all angles or phases of knee extension except near full extension, where they were not different. Put simply, the elite skaters were not familiar with applying force at a full range of leg extension.

Slap or clap?

Their Dutch inventors call them 'klapshaats'. However, in English, they were initially referred to as slapskates. But since the 1998 Nagano Olympics, they are commonly referred to as clapskates.

After a number of years of biomechanical analyses on activities such as jumping, sprinting and running, where leg extension is unconstrained, Ingen Schenau and colleagues at Free University Amsterdam developed a new type of skate. The new skate permitted the shoe to rotate around a hinge that connected the shoe to the skate blade. To ensure commonality with running and jumping movements, the hinge was placed down near the toes. Such a design theoretically allowed a skater to use more complete knee extension while maintaining a horizontal blade in contact with the ice. Since the new skate was intended to allow the skater to 'slap on' extra ankle extension at the end of the push-off, it was christened the *slapskate* (see Fig. F, illustrated section).

POPULARITY HINGES ON THE TIMES

As with any technical revolution, it took some time before the elite skaters would risk the clapskate in competition. Several versions of the skates were trialled by various athletes between their first release in 1985 and 1991. But it was not until 1994/1995 that the remarkable improvement in performance of a junior Dutch squad was noticed by the skating fraternity, leading to senior elite athletes committing to the new skate.

Theoretical assumptions of the performance-enhancing abilities of the clapskate suggested that by switching to a clapskate, a skater could reach a level of ankle extension comparable to what is observed in jumping and running. Such a technique would allow the application of more muscle force to every stride taken. Based on this idea, a time benefit of approximately 1 to 1.5 seconds per lap was predicted.

Adding further weight to the theory came the practical evidence. First, the speed of the pioneering junior squad back in 1994/1995 was, on average, 0.6 seconds per lap faster at the 500-metre mark and 1.2 seconds per lap faster at 3000 metres. More recently, comparisons made between world record times for Olympic distances at the end of the 1997 season (where traditional skates were exclusively used) and after the 1998 Olympics in Nagano (where most competitors had switched to clapskates) showed that all ten men's and women's senior world records were broken or tied using the clapskate. Furthermore, average lap times decreased by 0.59 seconds for men and 0.52 seconds for women; this translated to average improvements in world record times by 1.9 per cent for men and 1.8 per cent for women.

Did You Know?

The idea of a hinged skate was first patented
nearly 80 years ago.

POLE VAULTING – FROM HARD POLES TO SOFT LANDINGS

Pole vaulting has continually evolved since its initial mention in a 1774 German book on physical culture. In regard to the modern sport as we know it, two areas of technological advance have driven records higher and higher.

Firstly (and obviously), alterations to the pole's construction and, in particular, the material used, have provided vaulters with enhanced performance. Poles have moved from wood to bamboo to steel to aluminium to fibreglass. Because of this continual progress, no other track and field event has produced more world record holders.

Competitors can use poles of any length and any material. The earliest poles were made of ash, hickory or spruce, and had an iron spike at the tip. Bamboo gained acceptance between 1900 and 1915. The 1930s saw the introduction of the aluminium pole, but it lacked the flexibility of bamboo, whilst more flexible steel poles came into use around the late 1940s but they broke easily. Then in the early 1950s, fibreglass poles filtered into the sport, with decathlete Bob Mathias first using one at the 1952 Olympics. It was not until the 1956 Melbourne Games that a pole vaulter used fibreglass in Olympic competition – Georgios Roubanis of Greece. By the 1960s, these poles had revolutionised vaulting technique.

The flexion afforded by fibreglass helped reduce the jarring experienced by the hands when planting the pole; it improved the transition from horizontal to vertical motion; it allowed vaulters to grip the pole closer to its top (allowing for a higher body position at the top of the vault); and its extension helped catapult the vaulter during their push-off at release.

In 1972, a new model of pole appeared called the *Cata-Pole*. However, a dispute over the pole and its material (believed to be carbon fibre) erupted at the Munich Olympics, despite IAAF rules stating that a pole can be constructed of any material or combination. Officials took the strange step of banning its use immediately before competition and many of the favoured

Tough Brits

At the 1908 London Olympics, the joint pole vaulting winners both cleared 12 feet 2 inches (3.7 metres) despite the fact that the British organisers did not provide a sandpit for landing, or even bales of hay.

vaulters were disadvantaged because they had planned to vault with Cata-Poles at the Games. In consequence, the 1968 gold medallist and 1972 favourite Bob Seagren of the US could only manage the silver medal, ending the US domination of the sport. Prior to that, the US had won every gold medal in pole vaulting since the inaugural modern Olympic Games in 1896 (the longest national winning streak in Olympic history).

Buster move

The 1924 Olympic gold medallist Lee Barnes was a stunt-double for Buster Keaton in the film College, where Barnes had to pole vault through a second-storey window.

The second of pole vaulting's great equipment advances is that of the landing pits. Prior to the 1950s, vaulters were forced to land on sand or sawdust. One athlete, writing in his textbook on track and field, described European vaulting pits as 'soft to land on as a cement sidewalk'. By the time foam was introduced, elite vaulters were already clearing heights in the vicinity of 15 feet (4.57 metres), and it is incredible that more injuries did not occur when falling from these heights onto levelled sand or sawdust. In fact, in 1963, American John Pennel became the first vaulter to clear 17 feet (5.18 metres), and this involved landing in a sawdust pit! These days, foam rubber landing bags provide athletes with the safety of a soft landing when attempting heights nearing and exceeding 20 feet (6.09 metres).

GETTING WET WITH SWIMSUITS
The bodysuit cometh

Manufacturers including Speedo, Adidas, Mizuno and Tyr have made various claims as to the performance-enhancing effects of wearing a bodysuit. Their rigidity makes a swimmer more like a spear through the water. The compressive power of a suit may reduce muscle and skin vibration and thus lower turbulence and fatigue. This constricting nature may also aid the flow of blood back to the heart.

Furthermore, bodysuit fabric may include microscopic vortex generators, embedded riblets and/or ridges of stitching, all designed to reduce the drag experienced by the swimmer. The coating of the suits (for example, Teflon) may also prevent water retention around the body, further reducing drag. Performance improvements of 3 per cent have been touted by the companies who produce these outfits. Interestingly, the reductions in drag experienced by swimmers who shave off their body hair also result in performance improvements of around 3 per cent. Therefore, some scientists contend that the bodysuits provide little benefit over that of shaving down and slipping on the conventional lycra.

In 2002, a study published from the Netherlands compared Speedo's *Fastskin* suit against a conventional swimsuit to determine if the 7.5 per cent reduction in drag claimed by Speedo was in fact true. The reduction in drag experienced across a variety of freestyle swimming speeds was only in the order of 2 per cent. This reduction in drag did not prove to be significantly different from the values obtained when front-crawling in a standard lycra swimsuit. However, it has been suggested that the bodysuits quickly become saturated and less buoyant upon wearing, and that swimmers who use the suits don a dry suit prior to a race in order to limit this problem. The fact that the Dutch researchers did not re-suit their swimmers in dry suits between trials may explain why they found little advantage in wearing them over traditional lycra.

But in support of this work was an analysis performed on the swimming times produced at the 2000 US Olympic Trials, where all swimmers were issued with bodysuits. This research hypothesised that, if bodysuits did in fact aid the athletes, their winning times would exceed those predicted from the normal progression in swimming performances observed over time. But in only one event was the winning time significantly faster than predicted, that of the women's 100 metres breaststroke.

One issue that is always avoided by the manufacturers is the notion that the bodysuits may provide a buoyancy effect. Swimming's governing body, FINA, rules that no equipment is allowed that may aid the speed, buoyancy or endurance of a swimmer. Aside from the fact that many of the benefits put forward by manufacturers appear to contravene the regulation in terms of improving speed, evidence suggests that bodysuit designs do provide greater buoyancy for the swimmer.

San Diego State University and Indiana University researchers have provided photographic evidence that suggests that the bodysuits trap air in the fabric, thereby improving flotation above that of conventional swimsuits. This work also indicates that the surface tension of a bodysuit causes air bubbles to adhere to it, further increasing buoyancy.

This buoyancy effect may explain why many male swimmers wear the *Jammer* form of swimsuit, where only the lower hips and thighs are covered. Improved lower body flotation would act to combat 'leg sinking' and raise the body to a more horizontal position, thereby reducing the frontal area of the swimmer exposed to the oncoming fluid flow.

With question marks hovering over the effectiveness, and the legality, of the bodysuit, perhaps all swimmers should be forced to compete in lycra costumes as in the good old Olympic days of 1996.

Triathlon togs

With triathlon events now a huge part of our sporting calendar, and with Australia being an island continent, organisers can drive triathletes into the oceans for the swim leg. But the open water is an uncontrolled environment, and water temperatures (particularly down south) can often be a little chilly. With the swim leg preceding the bike and run efforts, triathletes need to ensure that their bodies are primed for the transition from the aquatic to the terrestrial. Unfortunately, there have been reports of some athletes suffering hypothermia in the cool waters.

Several studies have investigated the effects that different types of clothing have on swimming performance and related physiological parameters. Researchers from Deakin University in Melbourne examined three different clothing conditions: (i) a nylon/lycra racing swimsuit; (ii) a tank-top, thigh-length lycra suit; and (iii) a sleeveless, below-calf-length synthetic rubber wetsuit. Thirteen triathletes completed trials in each of the suits under three different water temperatures – cool (17°C), mild (21.3°C) and warm (29.5°C). What they found was that the athletes swam a 1500-metre distance 10 per cent quicker when wearing a wetsuit compared to the other two swimsuits.

Skinny dipping

Promising US swimmer Matt Zelen was stripped of his 100-metre butterfly win for violating a uniform code – swimming the race naked. Forgetting to tie up his bathers, he felt them sliding off after diving into the pool, but decided to kick them off and finish the race. Apparently Zelen was laughing so hard that he forgot to breathe most of the first lap. 'It was hilarious; if it would have been the backstroke, obviously I would have stopped.'

The enhanced buoyancy when wearing a wetsuit is offered as a major reason for the increase in swimming speeds. This flotation effect may decrease the effort required to maintain the legs in a horizontal position. Furthermore, this horizontal position may decrease the drag resulting from lagging legs. A tight wetsuit may also reduce the friction as the water rushes past the body. These claims mirror the arguments central to the Olympic bodysuit controversy. Another study even reports that the effort required to maintain a particular swimming speed is inversely proportional to the area of the body surface covered by the wetsuit.

The Deakin University study also highlighted that wetsuits helped maintain body temperature in all three water temperatures, whilst in the lycra and racing swimsuits some swimmers had significant falls in rectal temperature when swimming in the cool and mild water conditions. This could be an important factor come the bike transition, as the strain placed on a body struggling to maintain an adequate body temperature may detract from the early stages of the cycling leg.

Those demonstrating the greatest falls in body temperatures were the slower and thinner swimmers. Higher body fat levels provide insulation against heat loss, so swimmers with low body fat percentages are at greater risk of hypothermia in mild and cool water temperatures. Thinner competitors should therefore don the wetsuit – not only to maintain body temperature, but it may also provide a relatively greater buoyancy effect when compared to those with more body fat. And the longer you are out in the water, the greater the reductions in body temperature – so novice triathletes should take note and zip up too. But remember to strip off the rubber suit before getting on the bike, because all the talcum powder in the world won't stop the chafing.

PENNY-FARTHINGS TO SUPERBIKES:
BICYCLE (R)EVOLUTION

Cycling is the most energy-efficient mode of transport on the planet. It takes about 100 calories of energy to power a car 85 metres, but on a bike, you could travel almost five kilometres for the same energy expenditure. Riding a horse at 16 km/h will expend over 200 calories per kilometre but the same speed on a bike will cost only 20 calories; even walking is significantly less energy-efficient when compared with cycling.

The bicycle itself has evolved incredibly since its first appearance as a *Swiftwalker* (see page 83) in the early nineteenth century. Cycling's most famous race, the Tour de France, too, has gone through many changes since its initiation in 1903, none more so than in bicycle technology. In the early days of the Tour, bicycles weighed around twenty kilograms; now they weigh less than nine. Devices like clip-on pedals, aerodynamic wheels and triathlon handlebars have greatly improved cycling performances over French roads. In fact, an aerodynamic helmet worn by Greg LeMond is estimated to have provided him with a 10-second time advantage in the final time trial of the 1989 event – an interesting point when, after 88 hours of racing, he won that Tour by only 8 seconds.

But the progress in professional bicycle technology over the past 30 years has been so intricate at the frame design level, and so influential on elite performance, that cycling's governing body, the Union Cycliste Internationale (UCI), has had to take a stand. To retain the purity of the traditional bicycle design and to return to a level playing field that defines true competition between rivals, rules have been imposed on races and record attempts that restrict a 'free-for-all' in the technology stakes. For example, now the UCI has two categories for its 'one-hour record' (that is, the maximum distance that is covered in one hour): (1) the UCI Hour Record, and (2) the Best Hour Performance.

The UCI Hour Record, based on the effort of Eddy Merckx in 1972 when he covered a distance of 49.431 km, requires that any record attempt must use cycling equipment similar to that used by Merckx, thereby outlawing technological innovations of the last 30 years. This record is now held by Chris Boardman at 49.441 km, set in 2000. The Best Hour Performance, on the other hand, allows cyclists to ride any contraption in any position that their heart (or more accurately, their

Frozen moment

Giovanni Pettenella (Italy) and Pierre Trentin (France) hold an Olympic track cycling record – for standing still. They stood static on their bikes for 21 minutes 57 seconds during their match sprint race in 1964, while each waited for the other to lead off.

sport scientist's brain) may desire. Boardman also holds this record – 56.375 km in 1996. This distinction, says the UCI, will 'allow the respect of a long tradition of a classic cycling speciality, without endangering the vital modern aspect of the sport'.

But for most of us, the bicycle as sporting apparatus or a means of transport is largely devoid of Superbike technology due to cost or safety issues. In fact, the diamond- (or double-triangle) frame bicycle of today's world, with its pneumatic tyres, has changed very little since the 1890s, save for the introduction of multi-gears in the early twentieth century and slight variations in design, such as the mountain bike which now accounts for around 95 per cent of adult bicycle sales in the USA.

Rolling through the years

The steel-tubed diamond-frame bike with its two wheels of equal diameter was a revolution. This design by Englishman H.J. Lawson made its appearance in 1874, and had cyclists leaping from its more dangerous predecessor, the *penny-farthing*, with its gigantic front wheel and small rear wheel. The diamond-frame bicycle had a rear wheel driven by pedals, chain and sprockets, similar to today's bike designs; its shape and design so brilliant that nobody has been able to better it in over 130 years. The only significant improvements over the course of its evolution have been John Boyd Dunlop's addition of pneumatic tyres in 1888, the implementation of gears in 1901 and derailleurs a few years later, and improvements in the materials used to construct the bicycle to make it lighter and stiffer.

To examine the issue of cycling economics in greater detail, Manchester Metropolitan University and Universitá degli Studi di Udine (Italy) combined biomechanical forces to quantify how the everyday bicycle had evolved to become the most energetically efficient mode of getting from point A to point B. The bikes that were studied marked the major milestones in frame and mechanical design, spanning almost two centuries.

The scientists began with the brake-less, pedal-less *Hobby Horse* of the 1820s, where the rider pushed their feet against the ground to start (and keep) its wooden wheels turning over – and to stop them! In fact, a German inventor, Karl von Drais, is credited with designing the world's first bike in 1817, which was named the *Swiftwalker*, similar in design to the Hobby Horse.

The next leap in bicycle design came in the 1860s with the revelation that the feet need not contact the ground! This prompted the invention of the *velocipede* bike design, with its pedals and cranks. The early velocipede soon gained the nickname 'the boneshaker' because of its wooden wheels, but along with the addition of pedals and cranks to the front wheel, it also had brakes on the rear.

A major evolutionary step then took place with the *penny-farthing* (1870s), with its solid rubber wheels and an enlarged front wheel so that with each pedal stroke came an increase in forward movement. In the 1880s, the *Rover* not only introduced the diamond-frame design to the cycling world but, as already mentioned, also sported a chain-driven rear wheel. By this time, most bikes had done away with wood or cast-iron frames and were now made of steel tubing. Inflatable pneumatic tyres on the diamond-frame design, now referred to as the *Safety* cycle, helped absorb the bumps and vibrations of a cycling trip and this model is also celebrated as making cycling more available to women.

Finally, the research team used the *mountain bike* (1980s) as its example of current-day cycle transport in their comparative study of cycling energetics through the ages. The *Superbike* technology was ignored in the study because these bike designs have not crossed over to become the common mode of cycling transport for the general public.

In their analysis, riders piloted each bike around a rough concrete path wearing a facemask attached to a portable metabolic analysis system. The metabolic system collected the air breathed out by the riders in order to understand how much oxygen was being used whilst cycling on the different bicycle designs. This allowed the scientists to calculate the energy requirements for riding each model at various speeds.

The Hobby Horse, even with its foot-to-ground power source (it is sometimes referred to as a 'running machine'), showed that there is nothing silly about the wheel. Its simple design reduced the energy required to transport oneself to half that of walking or running, when moving at its optimum speed. This improvement was due in great part to the seat supporting around 65 per cent of the body's weight.

The idea that the feet need not contact the ground spurred an increase in forward motion. The pedals and cranks of the boneshaker lowered the energy cost of moving about, being on average 15 per cent less than the Hobby Horse. The mechanical advantage of the big-wheeled penny-farthing, combined with solid rubber tyres and long spokes that lowered its rolling resistance, accelerated the evolving economy of the bicycle, with its energy cost being half that of its bone-shaking predecessor.

Interestingly, the ensuing appearance of the Rover did not provide for an enhanced economy over the penny-farthing. In actual fact, the energy cost of riding it was only 20 per cent less than that of the ancient boneshaker, compared to the 50 per cent improvement afforded by the penny-farthing. However, as the research team expressed in their analysis, the high-wheeled penny-farthing bicycles 'were difficult machines to ride, requiring great courage and good physical condition'. With the rider having to sit around 1.3 metres from the ground atop a great wheel, safety was of constant concern. The diamond-frame Rover may not have been as energetically efficient as the penny-farthing, but from an evolutionary standpoint, it represented a significant improvement in safety because its seat was now less than a metre from the ground, similar to today's mountain bike.

Finally, the pneumatic tyres and smaller mass of the Safety bicycle of the 1890s lowered both the rolling resistance and pedalling rate for the same forward speed, thereby achieving a new high in cycling efficiency. And to highlight the brilliance of the diamond-frame design of the late nineteenth century, today's bikes like the mountain bike vary little from their 1890s counterpart in the energy requirements for riding at various speeds. An interesting aside was that the pedalling frequency where the riders were most mechanically efficient was similar for *all* the bicycles studied – around 60 revolutions per minute.

Throughout the history of cycling innovation, the design changes from 1820 to 1890 speeded up the pace at which people could move by around 0.5 metres per second per decade. So, using the same measure of the energy required when walking at an average pace, the evolving bicycle designs resulted in a threefold increase in the speed of motion.

FIG. 3.2 EVOLUTION OF THE BICYCLE

1820s		*Hobby Horse* (or *Swiftwalker*) Wooden wheels/tyres No pedals and no brakes The feet were used to push along the ground
1860s		*Velocipede* (or *boneshaker*) Wooden/iron wheels/tyres Front-wheel pedals and cranks Rear brakes
1870s		*Penny-farthing* Solid rubber tyres Enlarged front wheel for more distance per pedal stroke
1874		H.J. Lawson invents the first diamond-frame bicycle with chain-driven rear wheel with pedals, chain and sprockets.
1880s		*Rover* Diamond-frame design Chain-driven rear wheel with pedals, chain and sprockets
1890s		*Safety* Diamond-frame design Inflatable pneumatic tyres
1980s		*Moutain bike* Current-day cycle design
1992	See Figs. J & K Illustrated section	*Lotus Superbike* Carbon fibre monocoque frame Disc and bladed-spoke wheels, tri-handlebars Weight of 9 kilograms

Superbike technology

Even though it appears that not much has changed by way of the energy requirements for getting about on a bike, we are ignoring the extraordinary reductions in aerodynamic drag, rolling resistance and bike weight that high-tech cycling science has produced over recent decades. Scientists have gone to great lengths in their laboratories to study the different factors that act to slow our forward motion when pushing the pedals. From this work, more efficient ways of directing rider effort into forward motion as well as streamlining both rider and bike have led to amazing improvements in professional cycling performances.

The fact that Chris Boardman could cover 49.441 kilometres in one hour on a standard-design bicycle but covered 56.375 kilometres in the same time on his Lotus-built Superbike (designed by Mike Burrows) in 1996 emphasises the incredible improvements that science has added to cycling economy at the elite level over recent decades. In fact, four years earlier, at the 1992 Barcelona Olympics, Boardman appeared with his first Lotus Superbike (now housed at the Imperial Science Museum in London).

The Lotus Superbike was constructed from carbon fibre moulded into a monocoque frame, complete with disc and bladed-spoke wheels, aerodynamic helmet, and special tri-handlebars to place Boardman in an aerodynamically optimal position – and it weighed just on nine kilograms! In the preliminary rounds of the 4000 metres individual pursuit in Barcelona, Boardman and his Superbike smashed the world record by close to four seconds. He then again cruised under this newly set mark in a following race (even before the medal rounds had begun), lowering the pre-Olympic world record by almost seven seconds. In an unprecedented effort in the final of the event, he actually lapped his opponent, the then world champion Jens Lehmann of Germany, and in so doing, Chris Boardman captured Britain's first Olympic cycling gold medal in 72 years.

The Australian Institute of Sport and RMIT University developed their own Superbike in the mid-1990s, having incredible success at World Championship and Olympic level (see Fig. K, illustrated section). These bike frames were made from a one-piece carbon fibre embedded with epoxy resin, making them some 50 per cent stiffer than normal. The rigidity of such bikes meant that less energy was wasted in the bending of the bike frame, so that more of the rider's energy was transferred to forward momentum. These bikes also utilised similar aerodynamic features as the Lotus Superbike, such as variations in fork design, tube angles and shapes, wheel design, and the use of tri-handle-bars and aerodynamic helmets.

High-tech testing

Cycle ergometers (see Fig. L, illustrated section), wind tunnels, power-monitoring devices and mathematical modelling are just a few of the techniques that researchers have utilised in attempts to minimise the resistive forces acting on riders. A myriad of mechanical and environmental factors slow us down as we roll onward and forward. Some of the techniques aimed at reducing the drag forces may be adopted easily by cyclists of all levels, others may require specialist expertise ... and money.

When flying along at 40 km/h, aerodynamic drag represents more than 80 per cent of the total resistance experienced by cycle and rider. The actual rider represents the greatest proportion of the total drag, with body size, riding position and clothing all playing a part in slowing us down. To a lesser – yet very significant – degree, the bicycle itself has much to answer for, with factors such as frame design, bicycle mass, wheel construction and its other componentry contributing to the resistance of forward motion. But that's not all – wind conditions, air density, gravity, rolling resistance, bearing friction, and the rider's mechanical efficiency all inhibit our perpetual motion. So which of these factors has the greatest impact on cycling performance, and importantly, what can we do to overcome, or at least reduce, the forces acting against us?

The standard racing bicycle itself is responsible for around 35 per cent of the total aerodynamic drag slowing us down. This contribution may fall to around 20 per cent when riding an aerodynamically stream-lined time trial bicycle, such as the Lotus or the Australian or US Superbikes. Alterations to the shape and configuration of the major structural elements are stand-out features of these high-tech bicycles.

Recent mathematical modelling of the resistive forces experienced by cyclists addressed the impact that aerodynamic time trial bicycle design alone would have over regular racing frames. One overt feature of these aerodynamically designed bikes is that their construction does not resemble the double-diamond design of conventional bicycles. The double-diamond design comprises four points where the airflow may be disrupted, as it crosses the forks, the down tube, the seat tube and the rear seat stays. Elite time trial bicycles are designed to reduce the number of these separate air-to-frame interactions. When assuming that the rider's position was standard on both types of bicycles, the mathematical modelling showed that for a 40-kilometre time trial the decrease in the drag area of the time trial bicycle resulted in predicted time improvements of 104 seconds and 77 seconds for a novice and elite cyclist, respectively.

However, the move away from the conventional double-diamond design is far from the only structural alteration that bicycles have undergone in an attempt to reduce the energy required by riders to maintain a specific speed. The circular nature of the tubing and spokes of regular racing bicycles has been replaced by ovalised structures on the aerodynamic bikes.

The more aerodynamic nature of these oval structures allows oncoming air to flow across the bicycle more easily, thereby reducing the drag that slows the cyclist down. The head tubes, down tubes, seat tubes and top tubes of the aerodynamic time trial bicycles, when taking a cross-sectional view of their oval nature, sometimes exhibit a side-to-side diameter that is only one-fifth of its front-to-back diameter. In other words, the cross-sectional view looks something like an elongated, pointed teardrop. This shape allows air to flow past the tubing with as little turbulence as possible. The spokes themselves have also been developed to have the same air foil characteristics, which have been found to decrease the trailing drag by one-tenth or more of that of normal cylindrical spokes.

Wheel design, however, is not limited to changes in spoke characteristics alone. Wheels now come in many forms, including disc wheels, three-spoke composite wheels, 16-blade aero-spoked wheels, and wheels with aero rims. Mathematical modelling has been used to predict the improvements in 40-kilometre time trial performance when comparing a conventional wheel set (with 36 round wire spokes) to that of an aerodynamic wheel set. The conventional wheel set was estimated to add 82 seconds and 60 seconds to the 40-kilometre times of novice and elite cyclists, respectively.

Wind tunnel experiments have provided some of the most practical data for reducing aerodynamic drag across the wheels. In headwinds, disc wheels and three-spoke composite wheels are most effective in lowering air resistance, with the general rule that drag is decreased with lower numbers of spokes. Smaller-diameter wheels also produce less drag for the cyclist, explaining one of the reasons why time trial bicycles often have a smaller front wheel. Both narrow tyres (for example, 18 millimetres) and aero-blades also help to reduce the energy expended by a rider when spinning the wheels to maintain speed. Interestingly, wind tunnel tests demonstrated that mild crosswinds actually produce a lift effect when cycling with disc wheels or three-spoke composite wheels.

However, aerodynamic wheels are heavier than conventional wheels. Therefore, the terrain of a specific event must be considered with respect to wheel choice. To examine this interaction, a mathematical predictive equation was used, and assumed that the conventional wheels were 500 grams lighter but had a greater drag area of 0.0063 m^2. On a road modelled with a 3 per cent grade, novice through to elite level cyclists were predicted to produce faster times over 40 kilometres with an aerodynamic wheel set. On a road with a 6 per cent grade, only elite cyclists would benefit from using aerodynamic wheels due to their greater fitness levels. On a steeper 12 per cent grade, all cyclists would perform better with the lighter non-aerodynamic wheels. As such, wheel choice must take into account both the grade of the course and the power output capabilities of the individual rider.

Aerodynamic advantages may even be gained by cyclists through some simple innovations such as clipless pedals instead of pedals, toe clips and straps; using an 'aero' water bottle and cage; and by placing the water bottle behind the seat instead of on the down tube of the bike.

Batman returns

Robert Sabin from Long Island believes that cyclists make bicycles inefficient and contribute to 64 per cent of the aerodynamic drag. To combat this, Sabin has developed a tunic, which clings tightly to the rider's stomach and has two triangular wings attached extending from the shoulder blades. The cyclists look like Batman.

BMX terminology
BERM: Banked mound used for turn
DROP-OFF: A step drop in the race track
ENDO: End over end crack-up
GATE: The thing riders line up against for the start of the race, you go when it drops
HOLE SHOT: Taking lead position out of gate
JOFA: Plastic mouth protector that snaps onto open-faced helmet
MOTO: A group of up to eight riders of the same class who will race each other
RAD: Wild, Insane, Crazy
RACE FACE: Goggles attached to a jofa-like mouth piece
ROLLERS: A series of bumps – 3, 4, 6, and 8 packs of them
SLINGSHOT: An illegal gate start that helps you get out of the gate faster (don't get caught)
SPEED JUMP: A little jump on the track that is faster to ride over
SQUIRRELY: Not in control, wobbly
SWEEPER: A flat curve on a track
SWEET: Something that is Very Nice
SWOOP: To pass someone in a turn
TABLETOP: A jump with a long flat top. Some are as low as 2 or 3 feet (60 or 90 centimetres) while others are as high as 6 feet (1.8 metres).
WHOOP-DE-DOOS: Three or more short jumps placed one after the other

Source: <http://www.cvworld.net/idahofalls/bmx/bmxterms.htm>

The bicycle and the body

The cyclist's body position also plays a very significant role in the resistance that the rider must overcome to propel the bicycle forward. As mentioned earlier, aerodynamic drag represents more than 80 per cent of the total resistance experienced when cycling at 40 km/h. Of this drag, depending on the bicycle's aerodynamic set-up, it is estimated that 45 to 60 per cent is due to the rider's body. However, this resistance can be dramatically reduced by lowering the body surface area that is exposed to the oncoming airflow and by providing a smoother passage for air streaming past the body.

The ideal position to reduce aerodynamic drag is that of a flat back, head lowered and forearms parallel to the bicycle frame. Wind tunnel experiments have reported that extending the aerodynamic handlebars and dropping the handlebar stem both by 20 millimetres (mm) may improve 4000-metre time trial times by around 4 seconds (or approximately 60 metres).

Modelling experiments also compared the aerodynamic effects of riding with (1) hands on the brake hoods, (2) hands on the drops of road handle bars, (3) elbows on time trial bars, and (4) in a wind tunnel optimised position (where the handlebars were lowered by 18 mm, elbow pads moved back 190 mm, and the hands moved upwards by 60 mm). Over 40 kilometres, performances were predicted to improve by 120 to 150 seconds in the wind tunnel position as compared to the time trial bar position. The other two riding postures significantly increased the time to finish by 2 to 7 minutes compared with the time trial bar position, with the hands on brake hoods being by far the least aerodynamic position.

It must be noted, however, that while changes in body position may reduce aerodynamic drag, these positions may negatively impact on overall power production. Cyclists must be careful that posture changes do not produce suboptimal joint angles that compromise power generation or interfere with the coordination of different body structures (for example, between the thigh and chest during pedalling).

Finally, never forget the joy of drafting when riding in a pack. One study reported that a Tour rider who completed a 6-hour stage at an average speed of 40 km/h, with little wind and on level road, did so with an average power output of just 98 watts by spending most of his time in the pack. According to mathematical models, to maintain such a speed out on your own in these conditions you require an average power output of around 275 watts! So energy conservation is not only about your body and the bike bits, but also about brains.

During the 2004 Tour de France,
Lance Armstrong's suggestion to his team-mate
Floyd Landis that he should go for the stage win
'Run like you stole something, Floyd.'

Bicycles for running

The Olympic distance triathlon comprises a 1.5-kilometre swim, a 40-kilometre cycle and a final 10-kilometre run. Numerous preparation strategies have been proposed to maximise performance in the cycle–run transition, with triathletes seeking to minimise the physiological impact that cycling has on subsequent running performance. If you have ever ridden 10 kilometres (let alone 40 kilometres), jumped off your bike, and then immediately started to run, you'll realise that this is no easy feat!

In an attempt to optimise the movement economy of the cycle-to-run transition, triathlon-specific cycle frames with altered geometric configurations have entered the sport. These bicycle designs are proposed to enhance running performance. Specifically, the seat tube angle (that is, the position of the seat relative to the crank axis on the bike) has been increased from a shallow (less than 76°) to a steeper (greater than 76°) angle. The idea for this alteration is that the further forward the seat tube angle is, the more closely the cyclist's posture resembles a running movement pattern.

Until recently, the benefits of this configuration on running performance have been anecdotal, but English researchers have now backed up these claims with science. By examining 10-kilometre running performances after 40 kilometres of cycling, the scientists demonstrated that both the 10-kilometre running performance and the combined cycle–run times were enhanced when the seat tube angle was increased from the standard 73° shallow frame shape to an 81° steep frame configuration. Specifically, improvements were observed in the stride length and stride frequency of triathletes during the first 5 kilometres of running. It was hypothesised that the steeper tube angle of the bikes shifts the hips further forward, thereby altering muscle group recruitment and allowing running speed to be maximised during the first 5 kilometres of the run leg.

WILL NASAL STRIPS PUT
YOU A NOSE AHEAD?

Back in 1996, a slew of athletes (from soccer to American football to cycling to motor racing) began sporting a white strip across the bridge of their noses – the so-called *nasal strip* – with Australian tennis player Pat Cash even decorating his strip with the black-and-white check-pattern of his matching headband. Then at the 2000 Olympics, a fair percentage of runners in the men's marathon wore the funny-looking adhesive across the nose, indicating a resurgence in acceptance. But despite its ebb-and-flow popularity, its merits as a performance-enhancing device have always been questioned.

Initially developed to assist people with snoring problems, the nasal strip is a like a miniature Band-Aid with a flexible backbone. When fixed across the nose, it acts to hold the nostrils open; the result of which is nasal dilatation, and hence, a reduction in airflow resistance through the nose. The manufacturer's claims that the strip can improve sports performance are debatable. The manufacturer argues that because there is less resistance when breathing, more oxygen reaches the lungs. Interestingly, the manufacturer relies heavily on testimonials from satisfied athletes rather than any hard physiological evidence.

A summary of physiological research investigating the impact of nasal strips on sports performance is relatively clear. The most common finding is that the nasal strips do not improve oxygen consumption or actual sports performance in relation to repeated sprinting efforts, cycling to exhaustion, treadmill running at a variety of intensities or recovery from maximal efforts. Basically, small alterations to normal airway resistance will have a minuscule effect on the oxygen saturation levels of the blood. In fact, one study reports that nasal airflow is unaffected by nasal splinting.

Therefore, the bottom line is that healthy athletes don't stand to gain any performance advantage from nasal strips. Although the wearer may feel like they can breathe more fully, the ability to breathe a higher volume of oxygen is unchanged. However, further research is warranted in relation to athletes suffering from asthma, allergies or other pathologies that result in blocked nasal passages.

Big nose
Between 30 and 70 years of age, your nose may lengthen and widen by as much as 1.3 centimetres due to the presence of ever-growing cartilage.

So why have so many athletes embraced the nasal strip over the years? Well, the answer may well lie between the athletes' ears. There is debate as to whether the nasal strip may assist with brain cooling. Nasal dilatation seems to assist with the removal of heat from the head due to increased airflow in the cranial sinuses. Therefore, athletes in endurance sports such as road cycling or the marathon, where large increases in body temperature can occur, may benefit from nasal dilatation, particularly if competing in hot environments. Alternatively, from a psychological perspective, it may simply be a placebo effect whereby the athlete has the perception of a performance advantage over a fellow competitor due to the nasal strip, even if the reality is quite different.

After examining all the available evidence, perhaps lawn bowls is the only sport capable of reaping the benefits of the nasal strip: as a courtesy to fellow competitors, bowlers wearing a nasal strip will be able to nod off between ends without disturbing others with their snoring.

FORMULA ONE RACING – A CHALLENGE TO SPEED AS WELL AS SAFETY

Motor racing proper began in the late nineteenth century, when in 1894, a motor race on the roads between Paris and Rouen saw the winner average a speed of 16.4 km/h. Then in 1895, the winner of a 1200-kilometre road race from Paris to Bordeaux reportedly took 48 hours to complete the distance. These days in Formula One (F1) Grand Prix racing, drivers can cover their 300-kilometre events in around an hour and a half, depending on the track. In the 2004 season, Michael Schumacher covered the 307-kilometre Albert Park course in Melbourne in one hour and 25 minutes.

In 1899, the Paris–Bordeaux race was won with an average speed of 29.9 miles per hour (mph) but by 1901, when the term *Grand Prix* was first used, the winner of the French Grand Prix at Le Mans covered the 700-mile race distance at a speed of 63.0 miles per hour. The *average*

Top ten Latin phrases for the sportsperson

Around the greens
This is a gimme, isn't it?
Nonne hoc mihi conceditur?

Isn't that lucky? My ball just rolled out of the rough
and onto the fairway!
*Fortunatus sum! Pila mea de gramine horrido in pratum
lene recta modo volvit!*

At the baseline
It's just out!
Paulo excessit!

It was just a hair long!
Longius capillo fuit!

In the ski suit
Boy, I hate lift lines.
Heu, odi manere in agmine pro sellis volatilibus.

Let's get in the hot tub.
In thermulam intremus.

In the rigging
Is there supposed to be a lot of water down here?
Oportetne multum aquae hic in ima nave esse?

All of a sudden I'm not feeling so good.
Subito minime valeo.

In the cheap seats
These are great seats, aren't they?
Nonne praestant haec sedilia?

God, these halftime shows are boring.
*Hercle, haec ludicra inter dimidia muneris
intercedentia insulsa sunt.*

Source: H. Beard, *Latin For All Occasions*, Gotham Books, New York, 2004

speed for the fastest lap in Melbourne in 2004 was set by Schumacher at 226.9 km/h, whilst at Monza in Italy, Rubens Barrichello clocked an average speed of 257.3 km/h for his fastest lap. The Italian Grand Prix is where F1 cars achieve their highest speeds, these days approaching 370 km/h down Monza's long straight!

The modern era of Formula One racing began in 1950, and ever since, technology has taken a front seat in the sport as racing car manufacturers experiment with new materials and old physics to eke a little extra horsepower from their cars. Nowadays, an F1 car is composed of about 9000 separate components. Its body and chassis are made of carbon fibre – a material that is five times stronger than steel and some four times stiffer. Whilst staying within the regulations set out by car racing's governing body, Federation Internationale de l'Automobile (FIA), this ultra-light material allows F1 cars to weigh as little as 600 kilograms.

The engines themselves weigh about 100 kilograms and, in the past, have had a life expectancy of no more than 800 kilometres, but continual changes to the F1 Grand Prix rulebook mean that engines will have to become more durable in the future. As opposed to the average (larger) domestic car generating 150 kilowatts of power at 5000 revs per minute (rpm), F1 engines rev over 18,000 rpm, sucking up 650 litres of air per second at this rate.

Most F1 cars now have a seven-speed gearbox, with some 120 sensors spread about the car to monitor everything from tyre pressure to brake temperature to the rear wing angle. With race positions often decided by a good or bad pit stop, 60 litres of fuel can be pumped into the tank in as little as five seconds (and it's full service!). Unfortunately, these cars need around 75 litres of fuel to travel just 100 kilometres – no wonder the budget of the top teams is around $400–500 million each season.

The fundamental principle in the evolution of the racing car is that its performance should never exceed safety standards or the human capacities of the driver. When you consider that during the 1950s and 1960s, 50 F1 drivers lost their lives whilst racing or testing, and in the

Formula One drivers killed during racing or qualifying

1954	Onofre Marimon	Argentinian
1958	Luigi Musso	Italian
1958	Peter Collins	British
1958	Stuart Lewis-Evans	British
1960	Chris Bristow	British
1960	Alan Stacey	British
1961	Wolfgang Von Trips	German
1964	Carel Godin de Beaufort	Dutch
1966	John Taylor	British
1967	Lorenzo Bandini	Italian
1968	Jo Schlesser	French
1969	Gerhard Mitter	German
1970	Piers Courage	British
1970	Jochen Rindt	Austrian
1973	Roger Williamson	British
1973	Francois Cevert	French
1974	Helmuth Koinigg	Austrian
1975	Mark Donahue	American
1977	Tom Pryce	British
1978	Ronnie Peterson	Swedish
1982	Gilles Villeneuve	Canadian
1982	Ricardo Paletti	Italian
1994	Roland Ratzenberger	Austrian
1994	Ayrton Senna	Brazilian

1970s and 1980s, 24 drivers were killed, it is understandable that many of the technical advances created for Grand Prix racing have been limited, and even banned, in order to protect the drivers and spectators. In the last decade and a half, only two drivers have had fatal accidents, both on the same weekend at Imola in 1994 – Roland Ratzenberger and the triple world champion Ayrton Senna.

Racing car driver Mario Andretti
**'If everything seems under control, you're just
not going fast enough.'**

Cars with wings

Midway through the 1968 racing season, *aerofoils* (or 'wings') appeared on F1 cars. This design addition acts in the same manner as wings on an aeroplane but in reverse. Therefore, as aeroplane wings are shaped to provide lift, the wings of an F1 car are inverted to create *downforce* so that the car grips to the road. The improved traction provided by the inverted aerofoils also allows the car to take corners at greater speeds. Due to some major teething problems in their first few years of use that resulted in some major accidents, the size and location of the wings had to be regulated, but they are still an integral component of the F1 machine.

The dimensions of the primary wings on the front and back of the car are altered from race to race, depending on the circuit's layout. On fast circuits with long straights like Monza, the wing size is minimised as much as possible to reduce drag on the car so as to attain the highest possible speeds. On the other hand, the street racing of the Monaco Grand Prix demands that the downforce is maximised to deal with the circuit's tight corners. For this race, teams even mount two separate blades on the rear wings for maximal effect. In fact, at 160 km/h, an F1 car is producing enough downward force that it could drive upside down in a tunnel. However, no driver has been brave enough yet to try such a passing manoeuvre in the tunnel at the Monaco Grand Prix!

The sudden changes in momentum during accelerating, decelerating and cornering, thanks in large part to the massive downward forces produced by the car's design, means drivers often experience g-forces in the order of 3.5 *g*s, and in some cases, as high as 5 *g*s. At 3.5 *g*s, a driver who weighs 70 kilograms would experience his weight rise to 245 kilograms during cornering, and his neck musculature would have to support a head and helmet that may suddenly weigh near 28 kilograms. To lessen this stress on the neck during racing, a compulsory head and neck support system was installed in cars, reducing these forces by 86 per cent.

Under pressure

A Formula One racing driver's blood pressure can increase by as much as 50 per cent throughout the race whilst noise levels in the cockpit can reach in the order of 125 decibels.

The ground effect

In the mid-1970s, airboxes were installed behind the driver's cockpit to increase the airflow to the rear-positioned engine, and these continued experiments into airflow and aerodynamics soon led to an enormous change in car design – *ground effects*. The ground effect is a phenomenon that also ultimately creates downforce for the racing car, literally sucking the car to the ground (hence the term), providing unprecedented cornering abilities.

In the mid-1970s, Lotus engineers embraced the ground effect idea and began work on a design that would basically make the car act like one large wing. In 1977, Lotus released their *Wing car* (also known as the Lotus 78), with its sidings shaped like inverted aerofoils. It won five championship races that year despite its poor engine reliability.

Ground effect technology worked by producing a volume of low pressure under the car that effectively sucked the car to the road. Lotus designers did this by curving the underbelly and skirts of their cars like an inverted aerofoil so that large volumes of air rushed underneath these structures as well as through a narrow slot (*venturi tunnels*) between the car and road, lowering the pressure beneath the car.

In 1978, these improvements led to the Lotus 79 winning eight of the 16 races and the World Drivers Championship for Mario Andretti (despite the car not being ready until round six of that year's championship). Andretti said that the installation of ground effect technology made his car 'feel like it's painted to the road'. The Brabham team went another step with their BT46B model by installing a fan that drew air out from under the car to further lower the car's underside pressure.

After protests from other teams, it was removed from competition after only one race.

As ground effect technology was taken up by other teams and further improvements were made, racing speeds continued to increase. But small miscalculations in the car's set-up due to the extremely low clearance heights needed between car and road for an effective ground effect, and the inability to handle bumps and curbs well due to this, could make these cars extremely unstable. In 1981, restrictions to ground effect technology began with bans on the skirts that contained a low-pressure zone, followed by a ban on the venturi tunnels of the underbody in 1983; ground effect technology had made racing too unsafe.

FIG. 3.3 GROUND EFFECT CAR

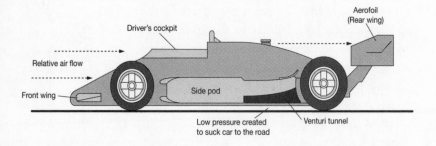

Turbocharged racing

In 1977, Renault brought forward another great technical revolution – *turbocharging* – but its development moved at a slower pace. The early turbocharged cars were extremely quick but notoriously unreliable, and it took Renault a year to make the design adjustments that would enable one of its turbocharged cars to finish a Grand Prix.

A turbocharger uses the waste energy from exhaust gases to drive a turbine that in turn drives a compressor unit that compresses incoming air to the engine. The increased mass of oxygen in compressed air allows more fuel to be burned, thereby having greater efficiency than uncompressed air. Because the compressor unit is driven by waste exhaust energy, there is little cost in attaining the improved engine performance.

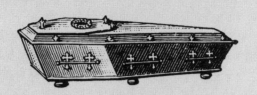

Deadly race

Seven-time Winston Cup stock-car champion Dale Earnhardt turned
down a request from a fan to drive the hearse at the fan's funeral.

In 1983, with gradual improvements in the technology, a turbocharged car finally won a World Drivers Championship, the driver being Nelson Piquet. In 1984, the McLaren team, now with a turbocharged engine, won 12 of that season's 16 races to take the Constructor's Championship (setting a new record points total) and give Niki Lauda the World Drivers Championship. With their turbocharged engines, McLaren continued to dominate the remainder of the decade, and in 1988, the team won 15 of the 16 championship races, smashing their 1984 Constructor's Championship points total. But by the time the 1989 season came around, turbocharging was banned and cars had to return to using normally aspirated engines.

Active cars

In 1987, Lotus again proved revolutionary in their thinking when they raced the first F1 car with a computer-controlled *active suspension* system. With active suspension, the balance and ride height of the cars could be held constant so as to improve their handling over bumps and curbs. This also helped with optimising traction and maximising downforce. Other automatic car adjustment mechanisms were to follow, and in 1991, Patrick Head of the Williams Team designed the first F1 car with a semi-automatic gearbox and traction control. But fearing that driver skill was being overshadowed by technological advances, many of these 'driver aids' were banned by the FIA before the commencement of the 1994 season.

However, traction control was back in racing in 2002. It works by using a host of electronic sensors to gather data about wheel and track speeds – if the wheel is spinning too fast for the road surface, the car automatically throttles back to prevent 'wheel spin'.

Launch control systems were also used up until the 2004 season. This active system automates many of the processes necessary for a good start from the grid, meaning that cars could go from zero to 100 km/h in 3.0 seconds. The 2004 banning of launch control meant that starting times increased by as much as half a second in some instances. With these systems, F1 cars could often hit 160 km/h in around 3.5 seconds; a high-powered sports car would be just clocking 60 km/h in that same period of time.

Anti-skid braking systems were also developed for F1 cars but were banned during the 1990s. These days, F1 cars carry disc brakes made of a carbon fibre material that is light but can operate at temperatures as high as 750° Celsius, capable of going from 180 km/h to a dead stop in a distance of 80 metres.

McLaren boss Ron Dennis on criticism
of his F1 team's two-pedal braking system
'Some teams complain they do not have the money to develop something like this, but it's more accurate for them to say "We do not have the brains".'

Racing in drag

Downforce is not the only aerodynamic principle that engineers strive to optimise when designing an F1 car. Any reduction in *drag* will also improve the chances of winning. Drag, which slows the car down, is created when air separates from the body of the car and becomes turbulent. As such, a design that enhances the flow of air about the car will improve driving speed.

Recently, Ferrari has opted for a 'narrow-waisted' chassis – the rear of the car being as narrow and as low to the ground as possible. This acts to minimise drag whilst also maximising the airflow reaching the rear wing. Also, low at the rear of the car are diffuser plates that act to re-equalise the pressure of fast-flowing air emerging from under the car. 'Barge boards' at the sides of the cars also act to reduce turbulent air flow.

Slick and groovy

The single biggest performance variable on an F1 machine is its tyres. Whereas a conventional car tyre lasts around 16,000 kilometres, the life span of an F1 car tyre is about 200 kilometres tops. But that's not so bad when you consider the racing machines of the early twentieth century. These beasts were far too heavy for the tyres of the time, and the ever-increasing motoring speeds ripped the rubber to shreds. Christian Lauteschalnger apparently destroyed 10 tyres in winning the 1908 French Grand Prix in his Mercedes.

Current-day F1 tyres are made of soft rubber compounds to deliver maximum grip. This idea is exemplified in the development of the *slick* tyre in the 1960s, where all tread was removed so that more tyre surface would be in contact with the racetrack, but *slicks* were banned in 1998 in order to slow cornering speeds. *Grooved* tyres, with four continuous grooves 2.5 millimetres deep and 50 millimetres apart, are now standard under F1 regulations.

F1 car tyres are designed to work best at high temperatures. Grooved tyres for dry circuits operate best at 90–110 °Celsius. These tyres are not inflated with ordinary air but contain a special low-density, nitrogen-rich gas mixture that helps to maintain a constant tyre pressure despite fluctuations in operating temperature. In wet conditions, *intermediate* and *wet* tyres have full tread patterns, mathematically designed to remove as much water as possible from the track so that tyre–road contact is again maximised.

Street drag
The French police pulled over British F1 driver Jenson Button for speeding. He was fined $1320 for going 228 km/h and admitted he was surprised to have reached such a speed.

TECHNICAL TALES: BROOMSTICK PUTTING

While golf is a game built on tradition, this is not the case when it comes to equipment design. Over the last few decades, the speed of change in club and ball design has been breathless. In 2002, the worlds of technological development and tradition collided when golf's law-makers, *The Royal and Ancient*, were forced to officially legalise the broomstick put-

Helping hand

Three-times world rally champion Tommi Makinen
did everything to win back-to-back titles in the Safari
Rally and, despite his efforts, he still came in second –
but the judges would not even allow him to keep that.
Twice during the race he was spotted breaching the tyre-
changing rules: instead of changing the tyres himself,
he got together a few locals to do it
for him.

ter – the long-shafted saviour to golfers with the putting yips.

Concerns about the broomstick in regard to the spirit of golf can be traced to the biomechanical changes in technique that the club causes. The shaft of a broomstick putter is designed so that the handle is aligned with either the chest/belly or chin of the player. The player is able to grasp the club at either of these two points, which allows a pendulum motion to be created, eliminating much of the movement and jerkiness that can accompany the use of a traditional-length putter. It is argued by the traditionalists that a pendulum motion is not a true golf-stroke action; for example, you could not use the same grip to hit a drive.

Biomechanically, the main advantage of any broomstick putter is that it reduces the unwanted involvement of the wrists – the source of most golfers' *yips* (a jerk, spasm or freezing of the hands while putting). When considering the mechanics of using a chest- or belly-length broomstick putter, an advantage is that the player remains in a posture that is close to the ideal as taught when using a conventional putter. Because belly-putters are longer than conventional putters, and generally have a thicker grip, the feel and subsequent distance control can be reduced. When the chin-length putter is considered, the putting stroke becomes a true pendulum swing, totally eliminating wrist hinge. Golfers adopt a more upright stance, and the even longer shaft of the belly- or chest-putter creates even less feel and distance control. As many golf pros suggest: this putter is a golfer's last resort; if this doesn't cure the yips, take up tennis!

Golfer and part-time comedian Lee Trevino
'I had a titanium shaft put in my driver to
swing faster and a titanium plate put in my throat
so I could talk faster.'

UPDATE FROM THE LAB:
CYCLING'S ONE-HOUR RECORD

One of the great pursuits on the track, somewhat unique given that it has been held by both track and road specialists through the years, is the *One-Hour Cycling World Record* – the furthest distance ridden in a 60-minute period. In 1967, Ferdinand Bracke covered 48.093 kilometres (km) in an hour. In 1972, Eddy Merckx powered to a 49.431-km record, whilst in 1994, both Miguel Indurain and Tony Rominger set new world marks by exceeding 53 km. The current record is now held by Chris Boardman, covering 56.375 km in 1996.

With a history dating back to Dodds's 1876 penny-farthing distance of 25.508 km, the One-Hour Record gives cycling enthusiasts the chance to undertake their own form of the ultimate in sporting debates – comparing performances across eras. Cycling, however, throws an extra spanner in the 'comparative' works, due to the incredible impact that science has had on bicycle and clothing design over the past 30 years. Despite such technological advances, two research teams in recent years have attempted to bring the great rides to a common baseline to ascertain who is in fact the most-travelled cyclist in a one-hour period.

In *Run Like You Stole Something*, we featured work by a collective of scientists from American and Scottish universities who analysed the One-Hour Record from Bracke's 1967 ride through to Boardman's effort in 1996, developing a mathematical equation that brought all the cyclists to the same theoretical conditions. The model was used to estimate the average power output of each cyclist during their record attempts, taking into account variables such as the cycling equipment and clothing worn, the altitude, circumference and surface characteristics of each track, the riding (body) position of each rider, and their height and weight.

Furious cyclist declines to pay fine

A British speed cyclist training for a world record refused to pay a $270 fine after being stopped by police for pedalling 'furiously' in Cambridge. Anthony Adams, training for an attempt at the One-Hour Record was found guilty of breaking a 150-year-old law that 'he did in a public place drive or ride furiously to the annoyance, obstruction or danger of any resident or passenger' during a midnight ride through the city.

The research team estimated that Switzerland's Tony Rominger would be the rider out in front when the stopwatch clicked over 60 minutes. This was based on his 1994 Bordeaux attempt where he covered 55.291 km. For the conditions of that particular ride, he was estimated to have produced an average power output of 460 watts. Boardman's 1996 ride had him in second place with an estimated average power output of 442 watts. Corrections for the Mexican altitude at which Merckx set the 1972 record ranked him third, whilst Indurain's 1994 ride in Bordeaux had him rolling into fourth spot.

But like all great scientific (and sporting) debates, not everyone agreed. The following year, a team of Basque and Spanish researchers, using their own predictive mathematical model for estimating power output, published findings putting Indurain on the highest step of the podium. The average power output for Indurain's 1994 record was estimated at 510 watts. Boardman's 1996 ride was second with 462 watts, with Rominger coming in third, predicted at 456 watts.

Of interest was that this research team worked closely with Indurain during the lead-up to his 1994 ride, to describe the physiological, aerodynamic and training characteristics required to break the One-Hour Record – which Indurain ultimately did. This provided the scientists with the unique opportunity to precisely measure (for their model) some of the important variables that determine cycling speed, by testing Indurain on the track, in the lab, and in a wind tunnel (see also page 194). The 1999 report, on the other hand, had to rely on estimations and assumptions for the same variables. We now await the next rebuttal!

Poker hands in order of winning power

Hand	Description of cards	Odds
Royal flush	Five-card sequence of the same suit comprising 10, jack, queen, king and ace	1 in 649,740
Straight flush	A five-card sequence in the same suit (e.g. 4, 5, 7, 8, 9 of clubs)	1 in 64,974
Four of a kind	Any four cards of the same value (e.g. fourjacks)	1 in 3914
Full house	Three of a kind plus a pair (e.g. three jacks and two 7s)	1 in 586.1
Flush	Five cards of the same suit (e.g. 2, 4, 7, 9 and jack of hearts)	1 in 273.1
Straight	Any five cards in consecutive order (suit not important)	1 in 131.8
Three of a kind	Any three cards of the same value (e.g. three queens)	1 in 34.8
Two pairs	Two pairs each consisting of two cards of the same value (e.g. two aces and two 10s)	1 in 13.11
Pair	Any two cards of the same value (e.g. two 4s)	1 in 2

Source: C. Wilson, 'Raise you 50', *New Scientist*, 180 (2426), 64, 2003

Despite the vast array of body shapes and sizes that compete in any given sport, it is true that certain physiques and physiological characteristics can signify the probability for success in certain sports. In this chapter, we discuss the emergence, and the development through training, of the specific body types that tend to confer to the athlete a greater chance of making it to the elite level.

The Sumo supposition: Despite looking the part, no amount of hair grooming and appropriate mawashi (white sumo belt) placement can replace training – and muscles – for wrestling success.

THE TALE OF THE TAPE

4

Have you got the perfect sporting body?

RECORD BREAKERS
Swimming superpowers

Swimming has a number of blue riband events, with time barriers made to be broken. In 1902, Australian Richard Cavill became the first man to swim 100 yards in under a minute using the revolutionary *Australian crawl* stroke. However, if we focus our attention on modern distances, it was the 100 metres freestyle for women where the one-minute barrier was the benchmark to be beaten. Not surprisingly, it took none other than Dawn Fraser to beat it. In October 1962 at the Empire Games (now called the Commonwealth Games) trials, she clocked 59.9 seconds. In the men's event, the elusive barrier was 50 seconds. On this occasion, it was American James Montgomery who swam a 49.99-second world record in the 1976 Montreal Olympics final. Interestingly, for both Fraser and then Montgomery, the records tumbled after near-misses in a preceding heat swim.

At the other end of the distance spectrum lurks the 1500 metres freestyle, with 15 minutes being the magic mark. The 1500-metre event was present at the 1896 Athens Olympics where competitors were confronted with exceptionally cold weather and 12-foot waves. Race winner Hungarian Arnold Guttmann was quoted as saying, 'I must say I shivered from the thought of what would happen if I got cramp from the cold water. My will to live completely overcame my desire to win.' Guttmann won the first event in 18 minutes 22.2 seconds; the 15-minute barrier was to become the objective of modern-era swimmers. Despite most Australians presuming that Kieren Perkins would have been the man to break it first, it was in fact Russian legend Vladimir Salnikov who swam

The big men fly

In the AFL, the same researchers collated four decades of data relating to the average physical characteristics of the players. The most interesting finding was that the average height amongst the tallest players is increasing at a significantly faster rate than the rate of height increase amongst the shortest players. If their respective growth rates continue, the three tallest players in a team will average 2.13 metres (7 foot) by the year 2050.

14 minutes and 58.27 seconds in the 1980 Moscow Olympics final. Salnikov was a deserving record breaker, having won 61 consecutive 1500 metres finals between 1977 and 1986. We now wait for Grant Hackett to set his sights on breaking the 14-minute barrier – again, a time that many current-day experts think impossible to better.

FOOTY PHYSIQUES

The sporting physique required for successful performance in the different football codes is often very plastic. The optimal body dimensions of footballers do evolve over the years as the demands of each sport change. Researchers from the University of South Australia and the South Australian Institute of Sport have highlighted just how the ever-evolving patterns of play on football grounds can dictate a change in the body proportions of the players as the years roll by.

Power in the union

Firstly, the researchers examined data on 1420 rugby union players representing international, national and state levels of performance between 1905 and 1999. Of particular interest was the evolution of anthropometric variables such as height, body mass and physique. The elite international group consisted of senior national teams representing their country in the Tri-Nations competition (Australia, New Zealand and South Africa) and the former Five Nations competitions (England, France, Ireland, Scotland and Wales). National level included other World Cup countries, while state level referred to other national teams and regional teams.

This combination of data revealed large changes over time in the physique of rugby players. In general, they have become taller, heavier and more mesomorphic (muscular). Interestingly, in the last 25 years, their body mass has increased at a rate twice that of the average increase over the century, and five times the rate of changes in the general population of young males over the same time period. For example, the average mass of players in the period 1905–74 was 87.8 kilograms while their height was 1.804 metres. In the period 1975–99, the mass of players has jumped to 95.1 kilograms and height to 1.840 metres.

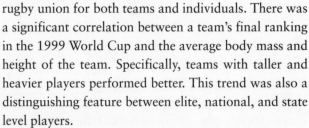

Too fat to score

Belgian football players at Standard Luik were being fined $1000 for every kilogram they were overweight. The players are considering legal action as their contracts stipulated that they only had to pay $20 per kilogram. The team director, however, said that they were 'just too fat', and that he was justified because, at the time, the first division team had not scored in their last nine matches.

Not surprisingly, the build of the players has changed significantly, with players' body shapes looking more like Hulk Hogan than the ex-Wallaby known simply as Buddha. The backs are the only positional group of players who seem to have resisted the urge to 'muscle up' and generally remain quite lean.

A strong relationship was identified between body size and success in rugby union for both teams and individuals. There was a significant correlation between a team's final ranking in the 1999 World Cup and the average body mass and height of the team. Specifically, teams with taller and heavier players performed better. This trend was also a distinguishing feature between elite, national, and state level players.

The researchers argue that the change in morphology of current rugby union players is a result of Darwinian influences. Specifically, the long process of competition has created a natural selection system where players' builds have become more specific to their sport, and in turn, unique. This has impacted on the game in numerous ways, including an increased use of performance-enhancing drugs to improve growth. This may in turn affect injury rates and characteristics, and will most likely continue to create a more distinctive physique.

Scary body

Rugby fan, Mr Ed Cliff, uses seven inflatable balloons of England skipper Martin Johnson to frighten birds off his vegetable patch. The balloons are life-sized and apparently work better than scarecrows.

Weight divisions in professional boxing

Weight division	Weight range	
Strawweight	up to 105 lb	~47.5 kg
Junior Flyweight	105 to 108 lb	~47.5 to 49 kg
Flyweight	108 to 112 lb	~49 to 51 kg
Super Flyweight / Jnr Bantamweight	112 to 115 lb	~51 to 52 kg
Bantamweight	115 to 118 lb	~52 to 53.5 kg
Super Bantamweight / Jnr Featherweight	118 to 122 lb	~53.5 to 55 kg
Featherweight	122 to 126 lb	~55 to 57 kg
Super Featherweight / Jnr Lightweight	126 to 130 lb	~57 to 59 kg
Lightweight	130 to 135 lb	~59 to 61 kg
Super Lightweight / Jnr Welterweight	135 to 140 lb	~61 to 63.5 kg
Welterweight	140 to 147 lb	~63.5 to 66.5 kg
Super Welterweight / Jnr Middleweight	147 to 154 lb	~66.5 to 70 kg
Middleweight	154 to 160 lb	~70 to 72.5 kg
Super Middleweight	160 to 168 lb	~72.5 to 76 kg
Light Heavyweight	168 to 175 lb	~76 to 79 kg
Cruiserweight	175 to 200 lb	~79 to 91 kg
Heavyweight	over 200 lb	over 91 kg

Weight Divisions in Olympic Boxing

Weight division	Maximum weight	
Light Flyweight	48 kg	~105 lb
Flyweight	51 kg	~112 lb
Bantamweight	54 kg	~119 lb
Featherweight	57 kg	~125 lb

Weight Divisions in Olympic Boxing (cont.)

Weight division	Maximum weight	
Lightweight	60 kg	~132 lb
Light Welterweight	63.5 kg	~140 lb
Welterweight	69 kg	~152 lb
Middleweight	75 kg	~165 lb
Light Heavyweight	81 kg	~178 lb
Heavyweight	91 kg	200 lb
Super Heavyweight	Unlimited	

Diego the divine

Maradona's fans, who set up their own church to worship their idol, have celebrated Christmas on his birthday. The group of 100 members celebrated the football player's forty-second birthday, telling the *Diario Ole* newspaper, 'We believe he is football's god. So, for us, this is the 42AD,' stating that AD stood for After Diego. The members call themselves Diegorian Brothers and use the book 'I Am Diego' as their bible. They recite their own Ten Commandments which include: 'You will be only a fan of Maradona, not any football club in particular.'

Barbie and Ken

Model agencies look for women with a 61-centimetre waist. If Barbie's waist was this size, what would her other dimensions be? Well, Barbie would be 218 centimetres (7 feet 3 inches), a bust size of 114 centimetres, 99-centimetre hips, an inside leg of 106 centimetres, whilst weighing an estimated 92 kilograms. Xena has met her match! Ken is not as out of proportion (or as scary) as Barbie. Most of his dimensions are actually much smaller and skinnier than the average Australian male. His head is also smaller than the average male, but larger than the average Australian Rules footballer. Does this tell us anything about some of Australia's highest-paid sportsmen?

BORN TO RUN – WHY SOME PEOPLE ARE FAST

Several studies have demonstrated that in the leg muscles of sprinters, there is a higher percentage of fast-twitch fibres; the proportion of slow-twitch to fast-twitch muscle fibres in specific groups of muscle can make a difference to athletic potential. Slow-twitch muscle fibres have characteristics desirable for an endurance athlete. For example, they take longer to fatigue. Fast-twitch fibres, on the other hand, confer certain advantages to sprint athletes. Fast-twitch fibres provide energy more rapidly for muscle contraction; they confer a greater velocity of contraction and power output; and they are related to maximum running speed and 100-metre performance. Research from Finland reported that the volume of the *vastus lateralis* muscle of the thigh in sprinters was comprised of 67 per cent fast-twitch muscle fibres, but only about 50 per cent in the normal population.

Muscle also contains an elastic property when it is stretched – somewhat like a rubber band. Research from Italy suggests that once a sprinter reaches a speed of 6 to 7 metres per second, this elastic property becomes important in providing extra energy for motion. Such speeds are attained by the 20-metre mark of a 100 metres race. When a muscle is rapidly stretched, elastic energy is stored within its structural units. This energy can then be released and added to the force generated when the muscle shortens for contraction.

Longer, thinner Achilles tendons may even confer an anatomical advantage for sprinters. The Achilles tendon is greatly stretched as a runner prepares for the foot to strike the ground. Once the runner contacts the ground and rolls from heel to toe, the Achilles tendon recoils, donating the stored elasticity to the push-off phase. Work from the University of Copenhagen reports that an Achilles tendon 10 per cent longer than normal increases running economy by 8 per cent, whilst a similarly shorter Achilles tendon will decrease economy by 6 per cent. Therefore, the greater the tendon length and hence stretch, the greater the energy returned when it recoils.

A relationship between sprint ability and fascicle (a bundle of muscle fibre) length in leg muscles has also been reported. A Japanese collaboration found that these fascicles were greater in length in faster sprinters.

Marsupial pogo stick

The idea of recycling stored elastic energy into the next stride is highlighted by the amazing efficiency of the hopping kangaroo. The kangaroo maintains a constant hopping rate when travelling between 10 to 35 km/h - that of two hops per second. It also expends less energy when travelling at 20 km/h as compared to 6 km/h. This ability is predominantly due to the kangaroo's ability to store energy in its very lengthy Achilles tendon. The calf muscle is also integral in storing energy; however, the tendon stores eight times more energy. The provision of this stored elasticity to the next leap requires no extra energy production.

Longer muscle fibre bundles may bestow to the muscle as a whole the ability to shorten (contract) more rapidly when running, resulting in greater power output and a quicker time to the tape.

Extra force may be further added from the 'stretch reflex' – a protective mechanism that kicks in when a muscle is stretched rapidly, as occurs when sprinting. This reflex forces the muscle to contract when the muscle is overstretched, thus guarding against injury. Training techniques such as *plyometrics* make use of both the stretch reflex and the elasticity of muscle to increase the power generated by the trained muscles.

TECHNICAL TALES: AUSSIE INVENTS STARTING BLOCKS

Australian icon, 102-year-old Charles Booth, is credited with inventing the starting blocks for sprinting. The convention in the 1920s was to dig holes in the track to place one's feet in, but to save his backyard from turning into a rabbit warren due to his son's training regime, Booth Snr placed some angled wooden board on the ground as a substitute. Young Charles, an engineer, realised the potential, and then configured a set of blocks out of angle iron. Ironically, after winning a club meet using the blocks, Booth was rubbed out for life by the Amateur Athletic Association because they did not want mechanical devices on running tracks. Then in the 1930s, American runner Eddie Tolan successfully

Artificial armoury

Paralympic skier Mathew Butson (NZ) used his artificial arm to beat off a wild monkey that invaded his hotel room near the Olympic city of Nagano. He feared the monkey was about to attack after it leapt through a window into his room. 'It was baring its teeth and snarling. It was about 1.2 metres high when it stood up,' he said. But when Mr Butson brandished his metallic artificial arm, the intruder fled.

used Booth's blocks and the world saw their potential. With the advent of aluminium, engineers overseas were able to develop the blocks further. Unfortunately for Booth, Australia did not manufacture aluminium at the time and the change from steel to aluminium was enough for Booth's patent to be considered 'altered'.

BUILT FOR DISTANCE, NOT FOR SPEED

There is no way that we two-legged creatures can keep up with many four-legged animals in a head-to-head sprint (see page 129), but in recent years, some anthropologists have suggested that the human species has evolved in such a way as to be built for marathon running. Researchers from Harvard University and the University of Utah point to our long legs and short arms as being suited to running – necessary for our early hunter–gatherer lifestyle on the African savannahs – as opposed to the body segment proportions of modern chimps. More specifically, the scientists highlight the abundance of tendons in our legs – used little in walking but essential for running; our large legs joints – for shock absorption; our large gluteal muscles – for trunk stability; and our relative lack of body hair combined with a high density of sweat glands – for minimising rises in body temperatures.

These characteristics demonstrate that the human body as a whole is comparatively well suited to endurance running compared to other animals. But within the human population, other bodily adaptations may help to explain why some people appear to be 'naturally suited' to certain sports.

The chosen few

Have you ever met a person who, despite having no history of training, can run like the wind without ever running out of puff? Well, a research group from York University in Toronto, Canada, may have found the reason why these frustrating people have this ability.

After two years of testing more than 1900 participants, the researchers were able to identify six young men in total who possessed excellent aerobic fitness without any history of training. These six men – which we will call the 'naturally fit six' – had VO_{2max} (oxygen utilisation at maximal effort) scores above 62.5 ml.kg^{-1}.min^{-1} (millilitres of oxygen used per kilogram of body weight): the average score for a sedentary male of age 19–22 years would normally fall between 40–50 ml.kg^{-1}.min^{-1}.

The study compared the 'naturally fit six' to a control group of men of similar age and weight, but with normal VO_{2max} scores; below 49 ml.kg^{-1}.min^{-1}. Firstly, the 'naturally fit six' had significantly greater *stroke volume* and *cardiac output* values than the control group. Stroke volume is the amount of blood that the heart muscle can pump per heartbeat, whilst cardiac output is the total volume of blood that can be pumped by the heart each minute; both are important determinants of cardiovascular fitness. In fact, the volumes achieved by the 'naturally fit six' were comparable to those observed in 'endurance-trained' men of similar age!

It was also found that the 'naturally fit six' had a genetically endowed blood volume that was significantly greater than that present in the control group participants. These levels again neared those reported in endurance-trained athletes. This expanded blood volume helps, in part, to explain the vast differences observed in aerobic fitness between two groups of men with no history of training.

Mountain fitness

As an athlete (trained at sea level) ascends a mountain to higher altitudes, his or her capacity to perform exercise steadily decreases. These reductions in working capacity start to become significant at an altitude around 1500 metres; they are dramatic at greater altitudes. In addition, many visitors to higher altitudes experience a condition known as 'altitude sickness'.

One well-established change observed in athletes, as a consequence of the lower amount of oxygen in a given volume of air at altitude, is a

Why do talented Kenyan athletes boast similar names?

According to Runner's World magazine, it's because three-quarters of Kenya's best runners come from the Kelanjin tribe, whose names are derived from a pool of only a few dozen. Coupled with this is the fact that a boy's first name is usually a derivative of the father's first name. Below is a list of some Kenyan athletes' names and an explanation of where they come from.

Name	Explanation
KIPKORIR	Born just before dawn
KIPKOECH	Born at dawn
KIPNGETICH	Born when cows are taken to pasture after morning
KIPNGENO	Born when goats are waking up
KIPKETER	Born on the verandah
KIPSANG	Born outdoors
KIPTANUI	Fainted, failed to cry or breathe at birth
KIGEN	A long-awaited son
KIMAIYO	Born when beer is being brewed or drunk
KIPLIMO	Born among grazing cattle

decline in maximal aerobic power (VO_{2max}). But natives of high-altitude environments, like Tibetan Sherpas, develop VO_{2max} levels similar to those of sea-level dwellers. Several research groups have studied the physiology and adaptive responses in various highlander races, in order to better understand how these people successfully function despite an ever-present reduction in oxygen availability.

Interestingly, the mechanisms by which altitude residents cope with the low-oxygen environment do not appear to be consistent across races. Residents living high in the Andes are reported to have more haemoglobin compared to their sea-level counterparts. With haemoglobin being the oxygen-transport protein in the blood, higher concentrations will subsequently enhance the delivery of oxygen to the tissues.

The Sherpas of Tibet, on the other hand, display similar haemoglobin concentrations to lowlanders, but the protein compensates by binding more oxygen than normal. And Ethiopian highlanders differ again. Compared to sea-level dwellers, these Ethiopians present no differences in haemoglobin levels or oxygen-binding capacity: the mechanism by which they live comfortably at altitude is still unknown.

A recent study from the University of Milan reported that Tibetan Sherpas, born and living at 2800–3500 metres, acclimatised faster and retained a greater proportion of their aerobic power when moving above 5000 metres for a month compared to sea-level Caucasians (both trained and untrained). Also included in this study was a group of second-generation Tibetans – born by Tibetan migrants but never having lived at high altitude. Interestingly, they also acclimatised to the high-altitude environment significantly faster than the Caucasian individuals, signalling the presence of a genetic disposition for altitude acclimatisation in the Tibetans, regardless of where they had lived their entire life.

DEFINITION
Altitude sickness

Also known as mountain illness, altitude sickness is experienced by around 40 per cent of climbers who ascend above 4000 metres. Despite the cause not being fully understood, it is thought that the low oxygen levels in the blood and its reduced acidity play an important role. Perhaps these factors produce body fluid shifts and mild cerebral oedema that lead to the characteristic symptoms of light-headedness progressing over hours to fatigue, dizziness, headache and nausea.

Another recent study used similar participants: (i) Tibetan Sherpas, born and living at 3500–4500 metres; (ii) second-generation Tibetans living at 1300 metres; (iii) a Nepalese control group who also lived at 1300 metres. It was demonstrated that the muscles of the Sherpas possessed four times the concentration of a specific enzyme, called glutathione-S-transferase p and known to defend against muscle damage, than in the Nepalese control group, and more than twice as much as the concentration in the second-generation Tibetans. This enzyme protects against a form of muscle deterioration that is stimulated in times of inhibited oxygen supply – as at extreme altitude. The increased activity

FIG. A
The development of the golf ball
From left to right: Wooden c. 1590; Feathery c. 1790;
Gutta percha c. 1850; Machine gutty c. 1880; Haskell c. 1900; Modern

FIG. B
The insides of balls
Top, left to right: Basketball; Soccer ball
Bottom, left to right: Golf ball; Hockey ball; Cricket ball;
Tennis ball; Squash ball

FIG. C
The evolution of the athletic shoe
1. Marjorie Jackson (100 m, 200 m gold medallist, 1952 Olympics); 2. Betty Cuthbert (100 m, 200 m, 4 x 100 m relay gold medallist, 1956 Olympics; 400 m gold medallist, 1964); 3. Maureen Cade (80 m hurdles gold medallist, 1968 Olympics); 4. Raelene Boyle (200 m silver medallist, 1968 Olympics; 100 m, 200 m silver medallist, 1972 Olympics); 5. Debbie Flintoff-King (400 m hurdles gold medallist, 1988 Olympics)

FIG. D
Canvas football boot (1900)

FIG. E
Leather football boot (1880)

FIG. F
The revolutionary clapskate
The clapskate (see Chapter 3) has a hinge at the toe to allow the heel to lift from the skate during each push-off phase. Note that the clear plastic wedge inserted at the heel is not part of the skate – it's inserted to hold the skate in position for this photo.

FIG. G
The swimsuit of Murray Rose
(4 gold, 1 silver, 1 bronze medals,
1956/1960 Olympics)

FIG. H (right)
The swimsuit of Dawn Fraser
(4 gold, 4 silver medals,
1956/1960/1964 Olympics)

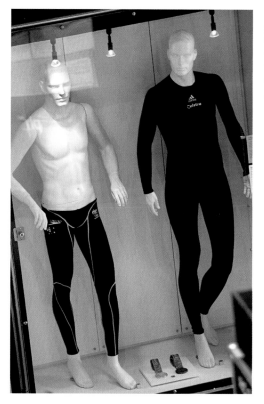

FIG. I
Modern swimsuits
The half bodysuit (also known as
the jammer), often worn by Grant
Hackett, and full bodysuit, often
worn by Ian Thorpe
(see Chapter 3)

FIG. J
Superbike
An Australian version
of track cycling's
Superbike

FIG. K
Superbike
The Australian
Superbike designed
at RMIT University in
Melbourne
(see Chapter 3)

FIG. L
Old Ergo
Australia's first
ergometer bike was
invented by Professor
Frank Cotton in 1946.
As athletes gained in
fitness, Cotton would
add more weight,
creating more drag on
the leather strap
against the wheel.

of another enzyme in the Sherpas' muscles also suggested that these native highlanders may revert to an enhanced fat utilisation in times of prolonged exercise (such as work or climbing); this may possibly improve body temperature regulation as well.

The unfortunate few

As you can see, some people are simply built better for endurance performance. However, for some unlucky few, the opposite is true: they simply do not respond to exercise. In a study from Louisiana State University, renowned geneticist Claude Bouchard put 742 volunteers through a 20-week training program; by the last six weeks, the participants were completing 50 minutes of exercise, three times per week.

At the study's completion, maximal oxygen utilisation (VO_{2max}) – the gold-standard measure of aerobic fitness – had increased by 17 per cent on average for the group. Whilst the best performers improved by over 40 per cent, a few exercisers showed no improvement, despite 20 weeks of training! Heart rate and blood pressure responses, along with other cardiovascular markers of fitness, showed similar outcomes; not very encouraging for the unlucky 'untrainable' few. (It should be noted, however, that everybody's health did improve in some way following the exercise training.) This highlights the incredible variation that exists

Too hot to trot

The story of Pheidippides – how, in 490 BC, he ran from Marathon to Athens with an important message, then dropped dead upon delivery – has always been subject to great debate: not about the first marathon run itself but the likelihood that a trained runner like Pheidippides could die after a 42-kilometre run. But researchers at Texas State University now believe the story to be less improbable than once thought. Originally, historians dated the run of Pheidippides to have taken place on 12 September 490 BC. This calculation was based on the Athenian calendar and Moon references in ancient texts. But using the Spartan calendar (which differs from that of the Athenians), the researchers re-calculated the date to be one month earlier: 12 August. The implications of this are great: temperatures generally hover around 28 OC in September; in August, however, 39 OC is commonplace. Therefore, if Pheidippides did in fact run to Athens at great speed under a hot August sun, it is entirely possible that heatstroke may have precipitated his untimely end.

in people's responsiveness to exercise; better known as their 'trainability'. Many of the so-called 'performance genes' being investigated today – that is, genes that appear to exist in higher proportions within a specific elite sporting population – are often hypothesised to confer greater trainability in those who possess them.

ULTRA-RUNNING: THE WESTFIELD SYDNEY TO MELBOURNE RACE

Phil Essam in his self-published book, *I Have Finally Found My Hero*, provides the history of the Westfield Sydney to Melbourne ultra-endurance run that was raced between 1983 and 1991. Essam reports that ultra-running was alive in Australia before the Westfield. The 1800s saw many people compete in the 'Pedestrian' races around the country. The 1900s saw many people attempt the highways between Australian capital cities. In the 1970s, ultra-running legends Tony Rafferty and George Perdon had many battles. As a result of this rivalry, sports promoter John Toleman put up a 'winner takes all' purse and the Westfield was born. To follow is a table listing the winners of this famous but short-lived event. Essam's book is freely available as an Adobe Acrobat PDF file at <www.ultraoz.com>

THE WEIGHTY ISSUE OF BEING A JOCKEY

Great expectations abound around a racetrack, with owners, trainers, and punters demanding that their investments have maximal potential for success. When considering the combined weight of all these interested parties and their fiscal contributions, a great amount of hope rides on a horse's back. As such, the area remain-

Endurance danger
A bacteria known as Bartonella has been blamed for the heart attack deaths of 16 elite orienteers in Sweden between 1979 and 1992. It is believed that the competitors were exposed to ticks or fleas that may have carried the bacteria. Bartonella has already been shown to damage the heart muscles of cats in the same way it did the orienteers. As a precautionary measure, competition was suspended for a period of six months and competitors were given antibiotics, which seemed to do the trick in preventing bacteria-related deaths.

Winners of the Sydney-Melbourne Westfield Ultra-Endurance Race

Year	Winner	Nationality
1983	Cliff Young	Australia
1984	Geoff Molloy	Australia
1985	Yiannis Kouros	Greece
1986	Dusan Mravlje	Slovenia
1987	Yiannis Kouros	Greece
1988	Yiannis Kouros	Greece
1989	Yiannis Kouros*	Greece
	David Standeven	Australia
1990	Yiannis Kouros	Greece
1991**	Bryan Smith	Australia

* Race winner on corrected time
** Kouros raced solo as a protest against Westfield.

ing vacant on the saddle to house the man of colours is only enough for one of diminutive ilk. It is little wonder that jockeys sit one, two, or more, standard deviations below the height and weight of the average twenty-first-century man.

Jockeys are under constant pressure to keep their body weight low for *every* race meeting. Riding weight restrictions demand that jockeys come in under a specific body weight for each race. If a jockey fails to attain the selected weight, then no ride – no ride, no pay packet. As such, most jockeys resort to varied and often extreme methods of weight reduction.

Interestingly, jockeys are not usually born 'light'. Research from the University of Stellenbosch in South Africa reported that the average birth weight for jockeys was 3 kilograms, with only 20 per cent being lighter than 2.5 kilograms. However the average adult body weight for the jockeys in the study was 52.9 kilograms, ranging from 44 to 60 kilograms. Of more concern are the rapid weight gains and losses that jockeys contend with on a weekly basis. In this study, 58 per cent of jockeys lost up to 2 kilograms on a weekly basis to make weight for race meetings, 33 per cent of them lost 2–4 kilograms, whilst 3 per cent of riders were losing 4–6 kilograms each week.

This constant yoyo-ing of body weight, often twice weekly, demands effective, but not always healthy, techniques to reduce the weight quickly. To do this, 77 per cent of the South African jockeys used dieting (by reducing or stopping food and fluid consumption), 70 per cent retreated to the sauna, 80 per cent exercised (often in heavy clothing or sweat suits to increase sweat losses), and 27 per cent took a hot bath. Moreover, 70 per cent of jockeys also reported using diuretics, 27 per cent used laxatives, and 48 per cent downed appetite suppressants. With riders obviously combining many – and sometimes all – of these practices, this cocktail is not without its side effects.

The jockeys reported that irritability, tiredness and dizziness often accompanied their rapid weight loss – not ideal when in control of an animal travelling at up to 60 km/h. When the jockeys were asked to perform a set of cognitive tasks designed to assess memory, recall identification and accuracy skills, as well as reaction and response time, they performed worse when tested prior to the first race of a meeting than their baseline data. In fact, their decline in performance for certain tasks was significantly correlated to the amount of weight lost prior to the race meeting. Furthermore, it is known that a 3 per cent loss of body weight due to fluid restriction can result in decreased muscular endurance, and possibly strength – side effects also not suited to handling half a tonne of racehorse.

Researchers from Liverpool John Moores University found similar practices when questioning 92 British jockeys. The jockeys regularly skipped meals; the percentages of riders who missed each meal were 49 per cent (breakfast), 47 per cent (lunch), 59 per cent (dinner) and 41 per cent (snacking) with 92 per cent of jockeys skipping lunch on race days. The most used methods to control their weight were sauna, exercise and fasting, with 2 per cent of jockeys reporting diuretic and laxative use.

Recent research from the University of Sydney analysed the diets of eight professional jockeys to assess their energy intake and compared it to their resting metabolic rate (RMR). RMR is the minimum amount of energy expenditure needed to support *basic* physiological processes –

this does not include exercising, or riding a racehorse. The jockeys' average daily energy intake from food was 5871 kilojoules, whilst their average RMR was 6190 kilojoules. This means that the jockeys expend more energy just lying about resting than they take in from their diet!

Whilst equine physiology has not changed significantly since the early days of modern horseracing (as highlighted by almost unchanging winning times), the human body has – average heights and weights have increased steadily over time. But unfortunately, the regulations governing present weight scales for racing are rooted in centuries of tradition. A century's worth of data shows that jockeys' weights have changed little: in 1900, their average riding weight was 49.2 kilograms; in 1925, 50.8 kilograms; in 1950, 49.2 kilograms; in 1975, 50.0 kilograms; and in 1998, 52.2 kilograms. As such, jockeys have been forced into a time warp, having to maintain the body weight of the petite nineteenth-century man (whilst also having to wear the clothing of the court jester).

Heavy hair
Fifteen minutes before his 1956 Olympic event, American weight-lifter Charles Vinci found himself 200 grams above the bantamweight limit – so he had a haircut. He went on to lift a world record and to take gold.

SUMO – SPORT'S BIGGEST MEN

Sumo has always been a sport of big men. But in recent years, concerns have been raised by sumo's governing body about the ballooning size of its kings of the dohyo (the fighting ring). The average weight of today's wrestlers in the upper echelon tips the scales past 150 kilograms!

In 1976, the body weight of elite *rikishi* (wrestlers) averaged 109.5 kilograms. These days, the average weight falls between 150 and 160 kilograms; the lightest sumo weigh in at around 100 kilograms, whilst the famous Hawaiian-born wrestlers Akebono and Konishiki had body weights that peaked at 233 and 275 kilograms, respectively.

At the college level, sumo are much lighter. One study reported that a group of 20-year-old wrestlers had an average body weight of 111 kilograms, with an average body fat of 24.8 per cent. Akebono's body fat percentage hovered between 34 and 36 per cent. Interestingly, in 1976, the average body fat level of the top sumo was reported to be only 18 per cent.

Increasing stature cannot explain why today's wrestlers are heavier. Current-day competitors have an average height of around six feet (~ 183 centimetres); this is similar to sumo 30 years ago and similar to college-level wrestlers. In fact, height is often considered a disadvantage, since a low centre of mass is perceived as a necessary component for success.

Akebono was extremely tall, standing at a height of 204 centimetres: he was considered too tall for success. But he worked heavily on his hip and lower torso strength so that the smaller, quicker and more technical wrestlers were not a threat to his stability. And he eventually became only the sixty-fourth wrestler in sumo's 2000-year history to be promoted to grand champion. He also perfected an open-handed slapping technique that, in its viciousness, would drive many opponents from the dohyo – and that always helps.

The sumo diet has much to do with the ballooning weight of competitors. Every day the wrestlers consume between 5500 and 6000 kilocalories. To put this into perspective, the average daily intake by Australian men is 2900 kilocalories, whilst cyclists during the Tour de France eat around 6000 kilocalories (but they are also expending ~6000 kilocalories per day on the bike). Akebono is even said to have once consumed 37 bottles of beer in one night.

But the increasing body weights are taking their toll on the competition. Most tournaments see a significant number of the top-level com-

Short stuff at shortstop

On 19 August 1951, 26-year-old Eddie Gaedel stepped up to the plate for his baseball team the St Louis Browns against the Detroit Tigers. That may not seem unusual except that Gaedel stood at a height of 3 feet 7 inches (108 centimetres) – he also wore a uniform numbered 1/8. He faced four pitches – all of them out of the strike zone – and received a walk to first base. He was immediately replaced by a new baserunner. St Louis Browns owner Bill Veeck, who had signed Gaedel in an attempt to increase attendance, received a telegram from the American League president the following day, condemning his 'stunt'.
Gaedel never played again.

FIG. 4.1 SELECTED SUMO MOVES

Sumo has 70 officially recognised wresting moves, and the degree of difficulty is classified according to how often they are seen in tournaments.

Move	Occurrence	Description
	**basic** seen several times a day during a tournament	**Oshi-dashi** Frontal push out The rikishi pushes his opponent in the side, chest or throat until he steps over the edge of the ring.
	**common** seen several times during a tournament	**Uchi-gake** Inner leg trip A foot move of tripping the opponent by putting one foot between his legs.
	**uncommon** seen once a year or so	**Nichoh-nage** Leg sweep throw The rikishi throws his opponent by tripping his pivot foot.
	**rare** seen once every few years	**Yagura-nage** Pendulum throw The rikishi pulls his opponent closely with one foot pressing against the thigh of his opponent, then throws him by lifting and swinging his body on this foot.
	**very rare** seen once about every ten years	**Koshi-nage** Hip lift throw The rikishi pulls his opponent's body tightly and throws him by bouncing off his hip.

Heavy impact

To give an idea of the power generated by sumo wrestlers, the impact force that Akebono could produce when crashing into a tackle bag was around 800 kilograms. This is equivalent to two small cars colliding at 60 km/h.

petitors sitting out due to injury. For example, after Akebono won three consecutive tournaments in 1993 and appeared to be a threat to the all-time winner's list, knee problems set in. In June of 1994, Akebono had operations on both knees. Over the next seven years, he battled persistent knee and back injuries: these injuries not only punctuated his dominance of the sport but they finally ended his fighting career in 2001.

PGA golfer Tim Herron in response to a query
about whether he was offended by his nickname, 'Lumpy'
'If I really got tired of it, I'd stop eating
and start exercising.'

A HEART THE SIZE OF PHAR LAP'S

What makes a great racehorse like Phar Lap or Makybe Diva? A correct answer would literally make it 64-million-dollar question. One key predictor of racing performance is a horse's maximal ability to use oxygen for energy production, known as VO_{2max}. This physiological parameter determines a horse's ability to take oxygen from the air, transport it via the bloodstream, and extract it from the blood once it reaches the exercising muscles. Studies at the University of Sydney have shown that training may increase a Thoroughbred's VO_{2max} by 20 per cent or more, with these improvements highly attributable to the racehorse's heart and its capacity to pump blood. VO_{2max} values in trained racehorses are reported to be around 160 millilitres of oxygen used per minute per kilogram of body weight; this is twice that of the most well-trained human endurance athletes.

A deep girth to house the heart and lungs that handle the acquisition and transport of oxygen to the working muscles is therefore imperative. The lungs play a primary role in equine racing performance, with a large lung capacity an essential criterion. At rest, horses breathe around 80 litres of air per minute (L/min), compared to only 6 L/min in humans. But at maximal exercise, a galloping racehorse may take close to 150 breaths each minute, moving an incredible 1800 litres of air in and out of the lungs in this time; the fittest humans are lucky to exceed 200 L/min.

But it seems that for as long as horseracing has existed, so too has the assumption that a horse with a 'big heart' provides a big purse for the owner. Much of the longevity of this fable can be attributed to Phar Lap – so much so that his large heart is part of Melbourne Museum's permanent collection. His heart weighed 6.25 kilograms whilst the average weight of a horse's heart is 4.2 kilograms. In fact, the great American horse and Triple Crown winner, Secretariat, had a heart nearing 10 kilograms in weight!

Recently, a British research team at the Animal Health Trust in Suffolk decided to test this longstanding belief. Firstly, using ultrasound scans they measured the heart sizes of 400 horses and correlated the measures with the official form ratings given by the British Racing Board for each horse. What they found will warm the cockles of any lover of equine folklore – the more successful horses did in fact have the bigger hearts.

The research team then delved a little deeper. Of 17 horses monitored for the amount of oxygen used whilst running on a treadmill, those horses with the larger hearts also possessed greater $VO_{2\,max}$ values. It is presumed that horses with a larger cardiac size can pump more blood per heartbeat, thereby supplying more oxygen to their exercising muscles per minute.

Two points are worthy of noting, however. Firstly, whether a big heart is the cause or the effect of winning remains unresolved. Perhaps the successful horse was *born* with a larger heart, or perhaps a bigger heart is just an *adaptation* to better, more intense training.

Divine intervention
Catholic nuns from a Los Angeles school took donations to the track, winning $200,000 by backing six straight winners.

Samurai spirit

Japanese racehorse Haruurara has become a cult figure after losing her first 105 starts. She is featured in a beer commercial and fans can buy Haruurara 'Never Give Up' shirts and lucky charms.

Secondly, and most importantly, the relationship between heart size and performance did not hold true for sprinters – it was only specific to steeplechasers that compete over 2 miles or more. But with the Melbourne Cup distance clocking in at 2 miles, it may be worth trying to smuggle a portable ultrasound scanner into the stables just prior to visiting the bookies.

Another possible indicator of equine performance is the amount of lactic acid formed for a given running intensity. Lactic acid (see Chapter 6) is a chemical that is produced in muscle particularly during intense exercise, and has been suggested to play a role in fatigue. The University of Sydney researchers ran Thoroughbreds on a treadmill in the laboratory, measured lactic acid responses after exercise and found that the superior horses had less lactic acid in their blood. However, when they tested horses after an 800-metre gallop on the track, the predictive relationship disappeared.

And with speed on the track being the all-important factor, consideration must be given to the notion that speed is the product of stride frequency and stride length. Between ordinary and elite horses, there is very little difference in the time taken to complete a stride. As such, to increase speed, a horse must increase the length of its stride. Two factors may play a major role in the length of a Thoroughbred's stride. Firstly, a horse with an ability to change its leading leg when it gets tired is a good bet. As one leading side gets tired and stride length starts to fall, the other leg can take over. Secondly, a physically big (tall) horse will usually have a naturally longer stride length – Phar Lap stood at a massive 17.1 hands high.

However, the victor will need more than just good physiology. A winner needs attitude. Researchers at the University of Melbourne described certain behavioural characteristics that tend to help predict the success of a horse in an upcoming race. In the mounting yard, check the angle of the horse's head – it should be about 45°. Look to see if the strapper needs to hold the horse tightly or loosely. And does the horse need handling by the course clerks at the starting gate? Basically, the more relaxed the horse, the better the chance of redeeming some cash.

The animal Olympics		
Event	**Human**	**Animal**
100 metres sprint (top speed)	Asafa Powell ~ 43.38 km/h	Cheetah ~ 114 km/h
800 metres run (min:sec)	Wilson Kipketer 1:41.11	Cheetah ~ 0:32
5000 metres run (min:sec)	Kenenisa Bekele 12:37.35	Pronghorn antelope ~ 3:00
Marathon (hr:min:sec)	Paul Tergat 2:04:55	Pronghorn antelope ~ 0:42.12
200 metres swim (average speed)	Ian Thorpe 6.92 km/h	Tuna ~ 72 km/h
Gymnastics Floor Routine	Olga Korbut Cannot change direction 25 times/sec	Cockroach Can change direction 25 times/sec
Gymnastics Uneven bars	Nadia Comaneci Perfect 10.0	Gibbon Extra 900 rotation in the wrist and thumb joints
High jump (Jump height)	Javier Sotomayor (1.95 m tall) 2.45 m (1.256 x body length)	Froghopper insect (6 mm long) 700 m (116 x body length)

DO YOU HAVE THE BODY FOR A LIFE ON TWO WHEELS?

Anyone who has spent some time in the cycling world will know that road riders and track cyclists are not of the same breed. Whereas most road competitions are performed at submaximal intensities and power outputs, track events usually demand the riders to perform at maximal effort. As such, anatomical and physiological differences exist between the road-loving endurance riders and the bank-loving track power-houses.

Air resistance nothing

An Italian mountain biker wearing a wetsuit and diving gear managed to pedal 30 metres under sea in Portofino. His tyres were pumped up with water and the bike was weighed down with lead.

Life on the road

One enthralling aspect of road cycling, and particularly tour events, is the variation in the terrain that riders must endure. Taking the Tour de France as an example, the 3500–4000-kilometre route each year offers new daily challenges to every rider, with flat terrain stages, uphill days in the Alps and the Pyrenees, and time trials on the flat and in the mountains. These ever-changing environments mean that very different riders may excel on different days, with flat terrain specialists struggling up the hills, and climbing specialists struggling to keep pace on the flats.

By grouping these professionals into four categories depending on their preferred stage conditions – uphill, flat terrain, time trial and all-terrain specialists – we begin to get an understanding of what advantages and disadvantages body size provides on the road. Unlike most endurance sports, professional road cyclists come in various shapes and sizes. Depending on the daily topography, a road cyclist's success is greatly determined by their morphology. The average height of professional road riders is 180 cm, but ranges from 160 to 190 cm. Average body mass is 69 kg, ranging from 53 to 80 kg, whilst the frontal area of cyclists (that which will meet oncoming airflow) ranges from 0.28 to 0.38 m^2.

Body mass plays a major role during uphill stages, as cyclists must overcome the force of gravity when pushing towards mountain summits. Not surprising, uphill specialists are significantly lighter than the flat terrain, all-terrain and time trial riders, thereby reducing the gravity-dependent resistance when ascending along alpine roads. Combined with the fact that these hill climbers have both the greatest power-to-weight ratios and the highest oxygen utilisation for body size of all four riding specialities, it is little wonder that they appear to glide away from the group on winding mountain roads.

On the other hand, success on the flat and in time trials is greatly affected by air resistance. Therefore, the cyclist's frontal area that is exposed to the oncoming air plays a dominant role in the aerodynamics of the ride. Despite climbers having the smallest frontal area, it is the flat terrain and time trial experts which have the greatest power-to-frontal area ratio. This lower ratio in climbers is not a major factor when ascending hills at low speeds, but when pushing the cranks at high speeds on level ground, the flat specialists excel.

However, for a road race comprising all terrains, the overall physical characteristics of time trial specialists, when considered in both absolute terms and relative to maximal power output and oxygen consumption, provide the best balance for attacking both the countryside and mountains. It is little wonder that over the past decade, Lance Armstrong and Miguel Indurain have not only dominated the time trial stages of the Tour de France, but also the yellow jersey in Paris.

Moving in circles

The variance observed in the physical characteristics of professional road cyclists is similarly present in the track cycling world. With events ranging from a 200-metre flying sprint (~ 10 seconds) to an hour-long 50-kilometre points race, it is little wonder that track riders are also a heterogenous group. A study of Australian track cyclists found that sprinters were significantly heavier and stronger than the endurance track cyclists. Sprinters (< 1000 metres) tend to be shorter and more muscular, whereas the time triallists (1000 metres) and pursuit riders (4000 metres) are taller and leaner. This leanness helps reduce the aerodynamic drag of the upper body over these longer distances. These riders also have longer leg-to-height ratios than sprinters, which allows them to use higher gear ratios.

At the Sydney Olympic Games, the average body mass characteristics of track cyclists demonstrated a definite trend. For body weight and the body mass index (a weight-to-height measure), sprint cyclists were heaviest, and these measures decreased progressively through the 1-kilometre time trial and the 4-kilometre pursuit, with the lightest riders being those of the 50-kilometre points race. This was true for both the female and male competitors. Interestingly, the top four placegetters for each Olympic track event were usually larger versions of their competitors in the same event, being heavier and taller, with greater body mass indexes.

Wheelie worlds collide

So how do road and track riders match up? What similarities do they share, and importantly, what makes them different? Beginning with morphological characteristics, professional road riders (as mentioned above) average 69 kg and 180 cm in weight and height, respectively. Track cyclists are heavier, with sprinters weighing 83 kg on average and endurance track riders around 75 kg. A small amount of variance in height exists on the track, with sprinters standing just below the 180 cm mark (~178 cm on average), with 1-km time trial and 4-km pursuit riders being a little taller than 180 cm (~ 182 cm).

The body fat carried by cyclists can also impact on performance. High body fat levels can be detrimental to performance as fat adds to the body weight but contributes little in the way of energy utilisation for muscle contraction for powering the bicycle. For road cyclists climbing those hills, it becomes dead weight to be carried up the mountain. The percentage of body fat in male road cyclists does not tend to differ much between the different terrain specialists. Their values range between 6 per cent and 11 per cent, with average levels falling to around 8 per cent during three-week tour races. These values tend to be higher than those of marathon runners but lower than in distance swimmers. Women road cyclists tend to have average values between 12 per cent and 16 per cent.

With respect to track cycling, increased body fat levels also adversely affect riding performance, with the resulting heavier body mass acting to increase the cost of acceleration, increase the rolling resistance experienced by the rider, and increase the frontal body area exposed to oncoming airflow. In consequence, track cyclists have some of the lowest body fat percentages reported across all sports.

A look at some physiological characteristics between the two cycling styles not only highlights some important differences, but reveals some surprising similarities. Firstly, track cycling is known for its high power outputs. As such, efficient anaerobic energy production is a track cycling imperative, especially in the shorter events. Lactic acid, a by-product and indicator of carbohydrate breakdown under anaerobic conditions, can rise in the blood ten- to 20-fold during an all-out effort for these riders. Comparatively, the anaerobic capacity of track sprinters has been reported to be around 15 per cent greater than endurance track cyclists, and higher again than road riders.

The ability of the body to deliver oxygen from the atmosphere to working muscles in large quantities for energy production is vital to all cyclists. The road races, with their major endurance component, obviously require the riders to have an efficient supply and utilisation of oxygen for successful performance. And this is indeed the case. Male professional road cyclists demonstrate maximal oxygen uptake (VO_{2max}) values of 70 to 80 ml.kg^{-1}.min^{-1}. This means that 70–80 millilitres of oxygen are utilised for aerobic energy production per minute for each kilogram of body weight when working at maximal exertion. Elite women road cyclists demonstrate scores between 57 and 64 ml.kg^{-1}.min^{-1}. The hill climbers usually have the highest VO_{2max} values, with the males around 80 ml.kg^{-1}.min^{-1}, largely due to their lighter body weights. These results compare well with other endurance athletes such as runners and cross-country skiers. Amateur cyclists in good condition would likely record values around 55–60 ml.kg^{-1}.min^{-1}.

Interestingly, however, track cyclists are also reported to have an extremely high aerobic power. VO_{2max} values greater than 90 ml.kg^{-1}.min^{-1} have been recorded in two champion male pursuit cyclists. Miguel Indurain only demonstrated a score of 88 ml.kg^{-1}.min^{-1}! This clearly demonstrates the importance that aerobic energy production plays in successful track cycling. In fact, peak VO_{2max} values greater than 80 ml.kg^{-1}.min^{-1} for men and 70 ml.kg^{-1}.min^{-1} for women are considered prerequisites for success on the track at the elite level.

Rapidly evolving bodies

Two men had their arms torn from their bodies as a result of a tug-of-war contest in Taipei. Both men wrapped the rope around their left arm in an attempt to have a better grip but their limbs were torn when the rope snapped. Doctors performed a seven-hour reattachment operation and are hopeful that the men will recover up to 70 per cent of the use of their arms.

Multi-disciplinary events

Decathlon

100 metres

Long jump

Shot put

High jump

400 metres

110-metre hurdles

Discus throw

Pole vault

Javelin

1500 metres

Heptathlon

Javelin

200 metres

100-metre hurdles

Shot put

High jump

Long jump

800 metres

Modern pentathlon

Horseriding

Fencing

Pistol shooting

Swimming

Running

Triathlon

Swimming

Cycling

Running

Biathlon

Cross-country skiing

Rifle shooting

Duathlon

Running

Cycling

Aquatic engineering

British scientists believe that the winning formula for the perfect sandcastle is one part water to eight parts sand. They say that too much water makes the sand liquefy, but if there's too little water, the sand won't bind.

Running mad

At the 1928 Amsterdam Olympics, several women in the 800 metres final collapsed from exhaustion. The IAAF then made the ridiculous decision to ban all women's events longer than 200 metres, because women who ran 800 metres would 'become old too soon'. It was not until 1960 that the 400-metre and 800-metre races were reinstated at Olympic level. It took a further 12 years before women were permitted to compete over 1500 metres!

UPDATE FROM THE LAB: CAN WOMEN OUTRUN THE MEN?

When examining performances in individual sports that involve running, jumping, throwing, swimming and cycling, men hold all the world's greatest marks. Due to various genetic differences between the sexes, men have evolved in such a way that they can perform these physical feats higher, faster and stronger than women. However, in many of the long-distance swimming events women like Australia's Tammy Van Wisse and Susie Maroney are record-setters. In *Run Like You Stole Something* we discussed the possible reasons.

And for a few decades now, scientists and athletes alike have contemplated the possibility that women may match, and even exceed, the performances of men in endurance running races. Predictions have been made by several research groups as to the likelihood of women catching up to men in terms of running records. Most famed (and often criticised) are the predictions of Brian Whipp and Susan Ward in the prestigious scientific publication *Nature*. In 1992, they predicted that women would hold all the Olympic marks from 100 metres through to the marathon by the middle of the twenty-first century. More boldly, they predicted that women would surpass men in the marathon by 1998! Ten years on, we know this not to be true. The rapid improvements observed in women's running performances prior to the 1990s have started to plateau over the past decade such that the possibility of women outpacing the men on the track now seems unlikely.

However, some irregularities do exist. In 1989, American ultra-distance great, Ann Trason, finished more than four miles ahead of her nearest male rival in the USA 24-hour Championships. Since that time, women have conquered their male counterparts in many other ultra-running events, despite their significantly lower participation rates in these races. Could it be that women are turning the tables when it comes to the genuinely tough events – that of the ultra-marathons?

The ultra-endurance edge

Support for the suitability of the female body for ultra-endurance running comes from the swimming fraternity. Tammy Van Wisse holds several ultra-distance swimming world records, including her 2438-kilometre Murray River paddle in 2000/2001 which took 103 days, smashing the 138-day effort set by Graham Middleton in 1991. She also entered the *Guinness Book of Records* as the first person to swim across Bass Strait. Susie Maroney has also done her fair share of record-breaking ultra-swims, covering the 107 miles from Cuba to the USA, and completing the longest non-stop open water swim of 128 miles. However, the nature of swimming differs in many ways to that of pounding the pavements, and some of the advantages enjoyed by women in the water may be a hindrance when covering long distances by land.

Interestingly, very little research has been conducted in the area of gender differences and their impact on athletic performance. Much of the work has examined the gender variation in body composition and the differences in fuel stores between the sexes. Of particular interest is women's greater storage of fat as a potential source of energy. Work from MacMaster University in Canada has examined the ways in which female and male runners utilise the energy stores in their respective bodies. Importantly, the researchers matched the runners for training status, racing experience and dietary intake.

Spring in her step

Norwegian police mistook a 94-year-old female jogger as having escaped from a nursing home. Police were alerted to a strange lady running down the street. The woman said, 'I said [to the police] there was nothing wrong with my head or legs. He [the policeman] had to check that I lived at the address I gave him. When that was all clear, I could continue my jogging.'

Firstly, the Canadian scientists found that during endurance exercise, women used more fat as an energy source than their male counterparts. The majority of well-controlled studies from other laboratories support this observation. In actual fact, it appears that women may use around 70 per cent more fat than men in supplying the energy required when running at a moderate intensity. What this also means is that by using a greater proportion of fat for energy, women use comparatively less carbohydrate for the same running speed, thereby sparing more of this valuable fuel source. With the muscle and liver storage of carbohydrate being very small in comparison to our bodies' fat stores, this sparing effect may help women maintain higher running speeds later in an ultra-run as the male's carbohydrates begin to deplete.

Women may have larger fat stores immediately beneath the skin than men, but they also tend to have greater amounts of fat stored within the muscles themselves. This likely plays a big part in women's ability to better utilise fat for energy. Fat stored within the muscle can be directly used by the muscle fibres for energy without having to wait for fat stored underneath the skin to be broken down, transported through the blood to the muscle, and then transported into the fibres for energy release. As a result, the rate at which energy can be made available from fat to the contracting muscle fibres may be more rapid in women.

The Canadian scientists have also reported that, at a moderate running pace, women are also less dependent on using protein as an energy source. This effect, once again, can be traced to the female's ability to use more fat as an energy source. As carbohydrate stores start to fall, the body may increase its use of protein as an energy source. However, since women spare more carbohydrate, their protein dependence (protein

Devil's design

Reebok had to do some major back-pedalling after naming a women's shoe after the mythical demon Incubus. It was later revealed that Incubus's main claim to fame was having sex with women in their sleep.

being the major structural component of many tissues, including muscle) will be lower. As such, the accumulated muscle damage from an ultra-endurance run may be lower in women due to their lower rate of protein breakdown for energy.

At the muscle level, the individual muscle fibres that make up the muscle as a whole play a major role in one's endurance capabilities. A comprehensive study of 418 women and men reported that in the *vastus lateralis* muscle of the thigh (that is one of the quadriceps muscles), women had a higher slow-twitch fibre percentage. On average, 51 per cent of the female muscle was composed of slow-twitch fibres, whilst men had only 46 per cent slow-twitch fibres. This higher percentage of slow-twitch, 'more fatigue-resistant' fibres in women would prove advantageous for an ultra-marathon where the same muscle fibres are repeatedly recruited to contract, mile after mile. Several studies have also demonstrated that females may be better able to maintain maximal force outputs over many repetitions in muscle tests when compared with men – just another example of the hypothesised enhanced fatigue resistance in the muscles of women. Interestingly, in a study that examined muscle responses to eccentric exercise, the body's inflammatory response to the damaging workout was lower in the women participants. Once again, could this mean that female muscle is more suited to coping with the rigours of extreme exercise?

However, when you look at the men's and women's records for the marathon through to 100 miles, men still cover these distances at significantly higher speeds. In fact, men are 10–20 per cent quicker than the fastest women over these ultra-runs. Unfortunately, some of the female advantages discussed above have the potential to be disadvantageous as well. For example, the metabolic benefits of greater fat storage may be negated by having to carry this non-force producing tissue over long distances. Another report suggests that women may also exhibit greater vertical displacement of their body mass with each stride. These two factors alone may decrease the running efficiency of women. And men themselves enjoy certain physiological advantages that aid their endurance running potential.

But debate still runs high on this issue. Research groups in South Africa have compared female and male runners matched for training status and, importantly, similar 42-km and 56-km performance times. Over a longer 90-km race, the women in both studies maintained higher running speeds and subsequently completed the distance much faster than the men. Therefore, it may be that when women and men are matched for their shorter endurance personal-best times, the women will then have the edge in the ultra-runs.

The pain barrier

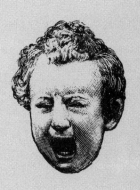

At a psychological level, it is often suggested that women are more resistant to pain – helpful over many hours of physical exertion. Many athletic mothers have proclaimed that no amount of discomfort or pain experienced on the road or track can match that of childbirth. When Kerryn McCann was asked after finishing the London marathon in 2:28:44 whether the race was harder than giving birth to her son, she replied, 'Having a baby. There's nothing worse. There couldn't be anything as painful as labour.'

The word 'doping' goes back way before the days of Ben Johnson or the East German drug programs of past decades. The word itself is thought to derive from the Dutch word 'dop' – an alcoholic beverage taken by Zulu warriors prior to battle. Stories from the Ancient Olympic Games and Roman gladiatorial events indicate a long history of drug use in physical competition. In this chapter, we discuss the performance-enhancing substances and methods that current-day athletes have at their disposal if they wish to cheat the system and their fellow competitors.

The Elvis effect:
A cocktail of muscle-building drugs like steroids and growth hormones may have a profound impact on physique. During a brief stint as a professional wrestler, Elvis experimented with such a mix. At his peak, he stood at 9 feet, 3 inches (282 centimetres).

BEATING THE CHEATS

5

The battleground of performance-enhancing drugs

RECORD BREAKER
James Hines breaks the 10-second barrier

The very first race of the modern Olympics was the opening heat of the 100 metre dash. It was won by Frank Lane of Princeton in a time of 12.20 seconds. The American sprinters captivated the crowd with their 'crouch' start and the orchestrated cheering of team-mates with chants such as 'B.A.! Rah! Rah! Rah!' Fast-forward a century or so and not much is different. The 100 metres sprinters are still regarded as the entertainers on the track and seats are at a premium for the final of this blue-riband event.

Much of the general public's interest in the 100 m sprint for males is whether an athlete can break 10 seconds. The honour of being the first to break this barrier was afforded to American James Hines in 1968 – but not without a fight. The magical moment was not an Olympic final but the Amateur Athletic Union (AAU) races in Sacramento earlier in the year where in the first semi-final Hines ran 9.90 seconds. Amazingly, 5 minutes later in the second semi-final Charlie Greene equalled Hines's record time. In the final, Greene defeated Hines with both men running 10 seconds.

FROM STRYCHNINE TO STEROIDS –
A BRIEF HISTORY OF DRUGS IN SPORT

Most athletic drug abuse in the nineteenth and early twentieth centuries involved the use of alcohol, strychnine, caffeine and cocaine for their stimulant and fatigue-relieving effects. In 1904, Thomas Hicks won the Olympic marathon by having strychnine and brandy administered throughout the race, but by the 1930s, amphetamines were in production and quickly superseded strychnine as the potent stimulant.

Synthetic hormones were soon on the market, and by the 1950s, power athletes were beginning to experiment with testosterone and steroids. At the 1960 Rome Games, Danish Knud Enemark Jensen, suffering from heat exhaustion, fell from his bike in the team time trial event in 34 °C temperatures, fracturing his skull as he hit the road surface. At his autopsy, the blood vessel dilator drug, Ronicol, was discovered in his system.

Evolution of the men's 100 metres world record

Time	Athlete	Nationality	Year
Manual timing			
10.6	Donald Lippincott	American	1912
10.4	Charles Paddock	American	1921
10.3	Percy Williams	Canadian	1930
10.2	Jesse Owens	American	1936
10.1	Willie Williams	American	1956
10.0	Armin Hary	German	1960
9.9	James Hines	American	1968
Electronic timing			
9.95	James Hines	American	1968
9.93	Calvin Smith	American	1983
9.92	Carl Lewis	American	1988
9.90	Leroy Burrell	American	1991
9.86	Carl Lewis	American	1991
9.85	Leroy Burrell	American	1994
9.84	Donovan Bailey	Canadian	1996
9.79	Maurice Greene	American	1999
9.77	Asafa Powell	Jamaican	2005

Note: An athlete is only listed if they were the first to set the listed time.

At the following Olympics, the team time trial became the first event to experiment with pre- and post-race drug tests. It was not until the televised death of the great British cyclist Tommy Simpson in the 1967 Tour de France that sporting bodies began to take serious steps in the fight against drug use – Simpson was found with amphetamines in his system and his riding jersey.

Coffee and colds

Caffeine and pseudoephedrine (an ingredient in many over-the-counter cold medicines) were removed from the World Anti-Doping Agency's list of banned substances in 2003. This decision was taken in order to save athletes from being disqualified for innocently taking medicine for a runny nose or having one too many cold Colas or hot coffees.

In 1928, the International Amateur Athletic Federation (IAAF) was the first sporting body to ban athletes from using stimulants, but procedures to tackle the problem were ineffective. In 1966, the governing bodies of cycling (UCI) and soccer (FIFA) introduced drug tests at their World Championship events. In 1968, both the Winter and Summer Olympic Games began mandatory anti-doping measures which gave Swedish modern pentathlete, Hans-Gunnar Liljenwall, the dubious honour of becoming the first Olympian to be labelled a drug cheat, for his use of alcohol. By the 1972 Games, drug testing was fully instituted.

Following the collapse of Europe's Communist Bloc, secret documents found their way to the German weekly magazine *Stern* outlining two decades of pro-grammed drug administration. It was reported that every elite athlete in the country (bar sailing) was receiving anabolic steroids. Many pre-pubescent girls were even given steroids unknowingly, and in 1976, evidence of the drugs' effectiveness was demonstrated when East German women won 11 of the 13 swimming events at the Montreal Olympics, despite not winning a single gold medal at the 1972 Games. In 1980, the women's swim team again backed up with 11 victories from 13 events, whilst every one of 54 East German rowers went home with a medal in hand!

Of note, serving on many international drug com-missions was the deputy director of the East German Sports Medical Service, Manfred Höppner. Having access to information concerning new drug testing analyses, Höppner would take this knowledge back to East Germany where methods could be devised to ensure that their drug program remained undetected. When a reliable method for detecting anabolic steroid abuse was introduced in 1974, East German athletes had no problems escaping detection.

Four days before the 1998 Tour de France, a masseur for the Festina cycling team was caught with a reported 400 vials of performance-enhancing drugs, including recombinant erythropoietin (EPO), a synthetic version of the hormone that stimulates red blood cell production. This discovery highlighted that systematic drug administration had not disappeared with the disintegration of the East German program, and in 1999, the IOC-initiated World Conference on Doping in Sport proposed the establishment of the World Anti-Doping Agency (WADA).

GETTING STRONG WITH STEROIDS

Anabolic steroids (as they are discussed in relation to performance enhancement) are a family of synthetic hormones designed to mimic natural male hormones such as testosterone. All anabolic steroids feature a similar chemical backbone (see page 146), but small modifications made to the molecular groups that attach to their core fragment produce new derivatives of the original hormone. These minor variations in the periphery of the molecule do not inhibit the steroid's anabolic activity, but they do make its detection very difficult – until some hint of its existence is discovered.

After testosterone was first isolated in 1935, weightlifters in the 1950s began injecting themselves with the hormone. Later that decade, a synthetic anabolic steroid that could be taken orally, called Dianabol (methandrostenolone), was released onto the market. Since then, many other synthetic versions of testosterone have been created, each varying slightly in their chemical structure to that of the naturally occurring testosterone. The steroid Stanozolol became famous when Ben Johnson tested positive for its use immediately after capturing the100 metres gold at the 1988 Seoul Olympics.

In 2003, tetrahydrogestrinone (THG) became the newest derivative of testosterone to be exposed in the world of elite sport when Bay Area Laboratory Co-operative (BALCO) hit the headlines as a producer and supplier of the performance-enhancing drug. The chemical structure of THG arose from that of another banned anabolic steroid, gestrinone. BALCO added four hydrogen atoms to gestrinone to create THG, and

Irish whizzkey
Athletes undergoing doping tests must provide a urine sample of at least 100 millilitres. Two years after winning four medals at the 1996 Atlanta Olympics, Irish swimmer Michelle Smith was found guilty of manipulating a urine sample for an out-of-competition test. Smith was banned from competition for four years.

due to its new composition, it tended to break down during standard drug testing analyses – hence, it escaped detection. It took a tip-off and a move to a more sensitive method of analysis to finally isolate THG's trademark structure. Immediately, a test was developed for detecting its presence in urine, and some of the world's most prominent athletes then became embroiled in the scandal.

FIG. 5.1 STEROID CHEMISTRY

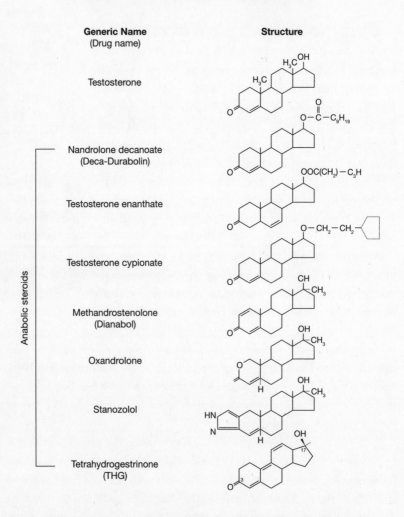

Source: Brooks, G.A., Fahey, T.D., & Baldwin, K.M. (2005). *Exercise Physiology: Human Bioenergetics and Its Applications* (4th Ed.). Boston: McGraw-Hill.

Hot dog

The Irish greyhound racing board has banned Viagra because it is said to make the dogs run faster by increasing their heart rates. The Irish Independent newspaper reported a racing source, stating that in greyhound racing Viagra was 'the greatest thing since sliced pan (bread)'.

The ups and downs of steroids

Steroids are often divided into two classes – *endogenous* steroids and *exogenous* steroids. *Endogenous* steroids are produced naturally within the body, which means that detecting their abuse carries the problem of trying to determine what has been administered and what is natural to the athlete. Testosterone is one commonly used endogenous steroid, whilst two endogenous testosterone precursor compounds used by the body to produce testosterone, namely androstenedione and dehydroepiandrosterone (DHEA), are also used by athletes. DHEA was the drug used by Brisbane Lions player Alistair Lynch in his battle with the chronic fatigue syndrome. *Exogenous* steroids are laboratory-produced steroids and these artificial derivatives include Dianabol, Stanozolol, Nandrolone and THG.

Anabolic steroids bring about muscle growth by increasing the synthesis of proteins within muscle cells. To reap the greatest gains, their use should be accompanied by heavy resistance training. In a recent study conducted by Southern Cross University in New South Wales, athletes injected with testosterone enanthate for only six weeks demonstrated significant improvements in muscle size and power, with the most dramatic gains occurring in the first three weeks. Previously it was thought that prolonged use (for example, at least 10 weeks) was required to achieve substantial gains in muscle size and performance.

It is believed that these drugs may not only produce an *anabolic* (tissue building) effect but may also reduce the *catabolic* (tissue breakdown) response experienced by muscles undergoing intense training. As such, it is hypothesised that the increased muscle protein synthesis, stimulated by anabolic steroids, not only helps to accelerate gains in muscle strength but also enables power athletes to recover more quickly.

Technically, anabolic steroids are termed *anabolic-androgenic* steroids. The *anabolic* nature of these drugs is responsible for increases in muscle and bone growth, improved nerve conduction and reduced body fat. The *androgenic* effects of these steroids lead to the development of the male sex characteristics like genital growth, facial hair and a deepening voice. In refining the techniques used for synthesising these drugs, scientists have attempted to maximise their *anabolic* effects whilst minimising the *androgenic* impact. However, because the androgenic responses produced by these male hormones are primarily anabolic effects in sex-linked cells, no synthetic steroids have been created that produce only anabolic changes for the athlete without some associated androgenic outcome. In fact, the more potent the anabolic nature of the drug, the greater the androgenic response.

These androgenic outcomes are most prominent in female athletes. Because women naturally have low levels of such hormones circulating in their body, anabolic steroid use not only produces relatively greater muscle growth compared to that of men, but the side effects can include the growth of extra body hair, deepening voice, clitoral enlargement, acne and disrupted menstrual function.

However, for women or men, other severe side effects also accompany the use of anabolic steroids. Finnish researchers examined the mortality rate of 62 high-level powerlifters from 1977–82, who were suspected to be anabolic steroid users. After a 12-year period, 12.9 per cent of the powerlifters had died compared to only 3.1 per cent in a control group comprised of the general populace, equating to a death risk some 4.6 times higher for the suspected steroid users.

High blood pressure, increased total cholesterol and blood fat levels, and decreased high-density lipoprotein cholesterol (often termed 'good cholesterol' because of its ability to remove cholesterol from the system) make steroid users prime candidates for coronary heart disease. Liver toxicity is also of concern (especially when taking the drug orally as opposed to injecting it) because these drugs are synthesised in a way to make them more biologically active, which results in the hormone accumulating in greater than normal concentrations in the liver. Many reports also exist of increased aggressiveness when on such drugs, and cases of depression, irritability and paranoia when off them, indicating that prolonged use of anabolic steroids can have profound psychological outcomes.

World records

In the power events of women's athletics – the sprint and throwing events – the world records (as at October 2005) for the 100 m, 200 m, 400 m, 800 m, 100 m hurdles, high jump, long jump, shot put, discus, 4 x 100 m relay and 4 x 400 m relay were all set prior to 1989.

Testing the limits

Because most anabolic steroids are broken down by the body and their breakdown products appear in urine, exogenous steroid abuse can be detected once an athlete has given a urine sample. By comparing the compounds in the urine to samples of known chemical composition, testers can discover the presence of any breakdown products from known synthetic steroids and thus point the finger at drug cheats.

Urine samples are also required when testing for endogenous steroid abuse but the detection technique differs from that used for revealing the presence of synthetic hormones. The test involves comparing the concentration of testosterone (T) in the urine to that of its inactive form known as epitestosterone (E). On average, the normal ratio for these two molecules is 1, but if an athlete has administered testosterone, the T/E ratio increases, sometimes to a value of 10 or more. Traditionally, if an athlete presented a T/E ratio in the urine above 6, eyebrows would be raised and more rigorous tests would be applied to the sample. But as of 2004, the World Anti-Doping Agency recommended that any sample with an elevated T/E ratio, no matter how small, should be considered suspicious.

Running rife

In 1983, 17 athletes tested positive for anabolic steroids at the Pan American Games. At the 1984 Los Angeles Olympics, 12 athletes were disqualified from competition – and the Eastern Bloc was boycotting! At the 2004 Olympics, 24 doping violations were exposed, whilst many other athletes had already received bans in the lead-up to the event. Notably, three athletes were stripped of gold medals in Athens.

An extremely precise procedure for detecting illicit steroid use involves analysing the urine for the proportions of two naturally occurring atomic forms of carbon, known as carbon-12 (C12) and carbon-13 (C13), which exist in different ratios in the natural and the administered steroid. An abnormal C12:C13 ratio ultimately confirms the taking of an illegal steroid. The C12:C13 method is not used routinely due to the expensive nature of the instrumentation, but is used when a urine sample presents a suspicious result.

Push-up rules for world record attempts
What counts as a push-up? The palms must be at shoulder-width. The body must remain straight throughout (i.e. no bending at knees or waist). The body must be lowered until at least a 90 degree angle is attained at the elbow and the body is parallel to the ground. The body must then be raised until the arms are straight. This equals one push-up. All push-ups should be made on a hard surface. This basic principle applies to all our push-up entries with minor modifications:
Finger tip: instead of the palm of both hands touching the floor, only the finger tips (including the tip of the thumb) may touch.
One arm: Only one arm may be used and the same arm must be used throughout the attempt. In this attempt, the hand is placed flat on the floor.
One finger: Only one finger of one hand may be used. The thumb may not be used. The record is for the number of repetitions; no rest breaks are permitted. The one-finger position must be maintained throughout. The side of the index finger must not be used, as this means other parts of the hand will come in contact with the ground and therefore invalidate the attempt.

Source: World Records for Push-Ups (Press-Ups)
<http://www.recordholders.org/en/list/pushups.html>

KEEP GOING WITH BLOOD DOPING

The Tour de France began in 1903 as both a dream and a publicity stunt, organised by newspaper mogul and former cyclist Henri Desgrange. The first stage rolled along unpaved roads between Paris

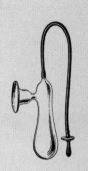

The whizzinator

The World Anti-Doping Agency has reported that some athletes have used prosthetic devices in an attempt to fool drug testers. One gadget is a tube that attaches to the underside of the penis and inserts into the rectum where a small reservoir of 'clean' urine is housed. Another involves a prosthetic penis, mounted on a jockstrap, that releases a 'clean' sample at the press of a button. This tool comes in a range of colours, including white, tan, brown, black and Latino.

and Lyon on 1 July, its field comprising 60 amateur cyclists. Maurice Garin won this inaugural 467-km stage in a time of 17 hours, averaging 27 km/h for the distance. Garin would go on to win the overall race in 1903 – a six-stage event over 2428 km – in 94 hours and 33 minutes. Only 21 of the original 60 riders eventually reached Paris to complete the first Tour, with the final finisher spending 160 hours in the saddle.

The following year, the Tour took place over the same distance. But its distance rapidly grew in subsequent years, peaking at 5745 km in 1926, with this race referred to as *le Tour de la souffrance* – the Tour of Suffering. Over the subsequent decades, the distance demands placed on the riders have progressively decreased, with the centenary race in 2003 spanning 3361 km. On average, for each year of the Tour's first hundred, cyclists would spend the month of July travelling approximately 4339 km over the rough and smooth of French roadways.

With such extreme physiological (as well as psychological, and management) demands placed on Tour competitors, one can somewhat understand why these athletes, at times, have sought pharmacological aid in an attempt not only to win the race but more so, perhaps, to deal with the gruelling daily stress of the race and to survive the distance into Paris.

Anecdotal reports from the early years tell of cyclists undertaking some remarkable methods to alleviate feelings of fatigue and to dull the pain. Sniffing ether-soaked handkerchiefs, rubbing their gums with chloroform, downing a glass of strychnine-laced wine, or the taking of cocaine and other sympathomimetic drugs were all means that riders found themselves using to get from one French town to the next. This problem of drugs use first came to cycling's world stage when Knud

A glass of bubbly

In 1994, shot-putter Paul Edwards drank a whole bottle of shampoo before a drug test in an attempt to destroy the results.

Enemark Jensen dropped dead during the road race at the 1960 Olympic Games with a blood vessel dilator drug circulating through his bloodstream. But drug use really hit the headlines (and live television coverage) for the Tour on Friday 13 July 1967.

In oppressive temperatures exceeding 40 °C and at an altitude nearing 1700 metres, British cycling legend Tommy Simpson toppled from his bike some three kilometres from the summit of Mont Ventoux. What happened next has gone down in cycling lore, where he is rumoured to have muttered to roadside spectators to 'Put me back on my bike.' Being helped back into the saddle, he turned the pedals over for another 200 metres before collapsing again, this time never to recover. He died on the way to hospital. His jersey was said to have carried a pocketful of amphetamines and the autopsy showed a mixture of cognac and amphetamines in his system.

Around this time, interest was growing concerning *blood boosting* – that is, methods that increase the blood's capacity to carry oxygen. This interest hit high gear in 1968 when, at the Mexico City Olympic Games (held at an altitude of 2340 metres), virtually all endurance running races were won by competitors from mountain homelands; the scientific notion was that these athletes possessed physiological adaptations from living at altitude – including more haemoglobin in the blood – that gave them an endurance advantage.

In 1972, a technique referred to as *blood packing* (a form of *autologous* blood transfusion – see page XX) was investigated in Sweden, whereby an athlete's blood was removed, its concentration of red blood cells increased by centrifugation, then later reinfused into the athlete. This form of blood boosting increased aerobic power (VO_{2max}) by 9 per cent and running time to exhaustion by 23 per cent – *blood doping* had well and truly arrived.

Erythropoietin – the endurance hormone

Over recent decades, haematological techniques for improving endurance performance have grown considerably. The practice of blood transfusions (see page 156), and in more recent times, the use of erythropoietin (EPO) has pervaded elite endurance sports like cycling, cross-country skiing, distance running and triathlon. In 1998, the Tour de France received a severe puncture when a Festina Team support vehicle was found to be carrying vials of EPO, along with drugs of the nature of anabolic steroids and growth hormone.

Erythropoietin is a natural hormone synthesised predominantly by the kidneys (with up to 10 per cent of its production achieved by the liver). It acts to stimulate bone marrow to produce new red blood cells – and housed within red blood cells is haemoglobin, the oxygen carrier of the blood. Red blood cells (and more specifically haemoglobin) play the primary role in carrying oxygen from the lungs to the exercising muscles.

The explosion of DNA technology meant that in 1985, the human EPO gene was cloned. This allowed for the production of recombinant (non-natural) human EPO (rHuEPO), with its development aimed at clinical use for patients suffering anaemia due to kidney damage. But rHuEPO worked well – and light globes starting flashing in sports science laboratories.

By 1987, EPO had emerged as a new doping agent for increasing the oxygen-carrying capacity of the body. Subsequently, elite endurance athletes began to experiment with it. Research has since found that rHuEPO can increase haemoglobin mass by 7–12 per cent in athletes, with the body's ability to utilise oxygen at maximal exertion rising by 6–7 per cent. But EPO use is not without risk.

By 1990, at least seventeen Dutch and Belgian professional cyclists had died, some in circumstances suspiciously linked to EPO abuse. Extra EPO circulating around the blood causes great increases in red blood cell numbers, resulting in thickened blood (hyperviscosity) and high blood pressure. Accompanying these changes is an increased risk of blood clotting. But the problems can really set in when the cyclist ends a day of racing. Firstly, the sweat losses resulting from exercise make the hyperviscous blood of the rider even more so, like a 'thick' red soup. Secondly, when the rider steps from the bike, the rhythmic contractions of the exercising muscles that helped squeeze the thick blood back to the heart whilst pedalling now no longer perform this role. Therefore such, there is a heightened risk of thrombosis. Most of the professional cyclists mentioned above were reported to have died from

cardio-respiratory failure or stroke – not a problem generally associated with elite endurance athletes – and some of these deaths occurred
in the hours or days following competition – once again, very unusual
for such heart problems to be exacerbated by rest, not by exercise. In
1990, EPO was added to the International Olympic Committee's list of
banned substances.

EPO is all the go

Due to its stimulatory role on bone marrow for red blood cell production, EPO also causes a rise in the *haematocrit* of the blood. The haematocrit is simply the percentage of red blood cells in the whole blood.
Whole blood consists of red blood cells, white blood cells, various other
proteins, and fluid (known as plasma). A normal haematocrit for an
adult male is around 42–46 per cent; for females it is usually in the
range of 38–42 per cent.

Interestingly, endurance training usually decreases an athlete's
haematocrit, despite an overall growth in red blood cell numbers. This
may sound paradoxical, but plasma volume also increases with
endurance training, and to a greater extent than red blood cells, such
that, in sum, the percentage of red blood cells to total blood volume
decreases. In the blood samples of 353 riders in Tours de France
between 1980 and 1986, the average haematocrit level was reported at
43 per cent, ranging from 39–48 per cent.

Therefore, in an initial attempt to combat the rise in EPO use, governing bodies like the Union Cycliste Internationale (UCI) and the
Federation of International Skiing (FIS) implemented an indirect
method of 'somewhat implied' detection, whereby athletes with haematocrit levels exceeding 50 per cent were not permitted to race. This technique does not point the finger *per se* to EPO misuse, but does prevent
an athlete from participating on the grounds of 'health risk'.

In 1998, Marco Pantani became the first cyclist since 1952 to win both
the Giro d'Italia and the Tour de France in the same year. But the following year, he displayed elevated haematocrit levels during the Giro d'Italia
and was barred from finishing. This was the first of two incidents where
he fell under the suspicion of doping, though it was never substantiated.
These ordeals irrevocably tarnished his image, and in 2003, suffering
from depression, Pantani committed suicide at 34 years of age.

Leading up to the 2000 Sydney Olympics, several laboratories worldwide strove to develop detection practices that would definitively identify EPO use by athletes. The National Anti-Doping Laboratory in France used a technique based on the analysis of proteins in urine. When examined in a specific manner, peculiar protein patterns were observed in the urine samples of individuals injected with recombinant EPO that differed from their 'clean' samples. This method was then tested on frozen urine samples acquired from cyclists during the infamous 1998 Tour de France. When the samples with the highest EPO levels were investigated, they all demonstrated the same peculiar protein pattern that was seen in the urine of known EPO users. This technique has now been systematically employed in the Tour de France since 2001.

Just prior to the 2000 Games, the Australian Institute of Sport also established a series of techniques, this time based on blood sampling, that identified 94–100 per cent of athletes who volunteered to use recombinant EPO as part of the research. Importantly, these methods continued to identify 67–72 per cent of users for up to three weeks following the termination of EPO injections. This was significant because EPO benefits disappear within 2–4 weeks, and so athletes must maintain the boosting to near competition. Therefore, even if athletes discontinue use in the few weeks leading up to an event, there is still the chance to trace its use.

I'm trying!

Perth rugby league player Nick Jenkins, playing professionally in Europe, came off the pitch dehydrated after a game in 30o C temperatures. He was targeted for a random drug test, but despite downing litres of juice, he was unable to produce a urine sample. At 11.45 pm, three hours after the game, Nick still hadn't provided a drop, so the drug officer had to accompany Nick on his drive home. It was not until 1.30 am that Nick, with drug official in tow, pulled into a petrol station for the long-awaited pit stop.

Swapping blood for gold

Prior to erythropoietin abuse as a means of illegally enhancing endurance performance, another form of blood doping existed – that of blood transfusions. This more primitive technique is said to have been used in sports like distance running, cycling and Nordic skiing as far back as the 1960s. However, this method of boosting the oxygen-carrying capacity of the blood went on the decline in the mid-1980s when recombinant erythropoietin (EPO) hit the market. Simply, erythropoietin injections were far more convenient than blood transfusions.

After the emergence at the 2000 Sydney Olympics of a test that could detect the illegal use of EPO, rumours circulated concerning the potential return by some athletes to the old-fashioned technique of transfusing blood. Then midway through the Vuelta España (Tour of Spain) in 2004, American cyclist Tyler Hamilton was prohibited from continuing because he tested positive to receiving an illegal blood transfusion. This came as a surprise to many, not only for the fact that blood transfusions were indeed back on the doping landscape, but more so that a testing method now existed that could detect their use. Interestingly, in the month prior to the Vuelta España, Hamilton won Olympic gold in the road time trial. At these Games, his first blood sample also proved positive for blood doping, but his 'B' sample was mistakenly frozen, leaving too few red blood cells remaining for analysis to confirm the doping; he retained the gold.

With respect to blood transfusions, two techniques are used by endurance athletes. The first, called *autologous* transfusion, involves withdrawing one's own blood (often 500–1000 millilitres), freezing it for a period of time (such as for 4–6 weeks), then reinfusing it just prior to a major competition. The extended time between removal and reinfusion allows the blood volume and red blood cell count of the circulating blood to return to normal. Reinfusion of 900–1350 millilitres of stored blood has been shown to dramatically increase the oxygen-carrying capacity of the blood by 10–20 per cent in some instances, whilst enhancing the maximal amount of oxygen utilised by exercising muscles (VO_{2max}) by 4–9 per cent.

Reinfusing one's own blood carries a lower risk of infection than using somebody else's blood, but the removal of a half or a full litre or more of blood reduces the athlete's ability to train at high intensities for the period of time the body takes to return its blood volume to normal. However, if the timing of the blood removal is well planned within a training program, the physiological benefits at competition time outweigh any short-term training decrements.

Blood doping came to the fore in 1976 at the Montreal Olympics when Finnish distance runner Lasse Viren won gold in both the 5000 metres and 10,000 metres events, repeating his 1972 Munich Games performances. With his performances often sub-par outside of Olympic competition, many in the Athletics world suspected Viren of employing autologous transfusions prior to major events. Viren himself always denied the accusations, claiming that his training schedules were devised so as to peak at the Games. It should be noted that despite being frowned upon for many great reasons, blood doping was not legally prohibited in 1976.

The second blood infusion method is called *homologous* transfusion, where an athlete immediately receives a volume of blood drawn from another individual. This process carries with it greater health risks than autologous infusions due to the potential for the athlete to produce an unfavourable immune reaction to the foreign blood cells or any other components contained in the donor's blood. Its advantage, however, lies in its ability to provide an immediate boost in blood volume and red blood cells.

In the 1984 Olympic Games, it was reported that seven members of the US cycling team called upon relatives and others to provide *homologous* blood transfusions in the week leading up to competition. One of these riders, Steve Hegg, won the 4000 metres individual pursuit at the Games, with another American cyclist, Leonard Harvey Nitz, taking bronze. However, two other team members fell ill after the transfusions. This prompted the International Olympic Committee to finally ban the practice of blood doping prior to the 1988 Games.

Despite the ban, detecting autologous or homologous blood doping has proved impossible ... until now. A collaborative pursuit between the Royal Prince Alfred Hospital in Sydney and an organisation known as Science and Industry Against Blood Doping (SIAB) has developed an analysis technique that can expose an athlete using homologous transfusions to improve their performances. So how does it work?

The blood of a particular person has its own fingerprint – a unique and identical spectrum of proteins on the surface of each red blood cell. If foreign blood is injected into an athlete, the protein profile on the donor's red blood cells will differ from that of the recipient, and is therefore detectable. The new antibody-based test can examine 15 various proteins on red blood cells, being capable of detecting any cells that are either expressing or missing the specific proteins of interest. If different sets of proteins exist, it signals that the analysed blood has come from more than one person. And this is how Tyler Hamilton was busted in Spain.

The development team claims that this new detection method can identify as little as one teaspoon of foreign blood, and importantly, can still catch a cheat using an homologous transfusion in weeks or months after the doping took place. With respect to the practice of autologous transfusions, as yet there is no technique capable of identifying its exploitation; however, research groups are quietly working on the problem.

HBOC to beat the clock

The newest form of blood doping is that of using blood substitutes, also known as haemoglobin-based oxygen carriers (HBOCs). The development of this form of blood substitute has important clinical implications, particularly in easing the burden of the donor supply of blood for transfusions. However, some endurance athletes have realised the potential for this technology to enhance their own oxygen transport capacity by increasing the total amount of haemoglobin circulating through their system.

Addicted to golf

Actor Dennis Hopper, who had a previous addiction to drugs and alcohol, has admitted he is now addicted to golf. Hopper told magazine Maximum Golf, 'Golf is addictive. It replaces the drugs. It replaces the alcohol.' He was also reported as saying, 'I see it as a natural progression. I suppose if you survive your drug days, you have golf ahead of you. That is, if you have any brain left.'

Top ten sporting excuses when failing a dope test

1. When U.S. sprinter Dennis Mitchell was caught using the anabolic steroid nandrolone in 1988, he claimed that a large consumption of beer combined with four hours of intense sex the previous night had caused the high nandrolon levels in his blood.

2. When Cuban high jumper Javier Sotomayor was tested positive for cocaine in 1999, Cuba claimed that the CIA had put cocaine in his food.

3. Swedish (former Russian) 100-metre hurdler Ludmilla Engquist was caught for anabolic steroid abuse in 1996 and promptly shifted full responsibility onto her husband; she claimed that he had put anabolic steroids in her food because he wanted a divorce.

4. When American cyclist Tyler Hamilton was caught for blood doping during the 2004 Vuelta d'Espana (Tour of Spain), his wife explained that 'his dog died from a blood transfusion and therefore Tyler would never do such a thing'.

5. Ross Rebagliatti had a sense of humour when he tested positive for marijuana following his 1988 Olympic gold medal performance in snowboarding, by saying that 'there is no fire without a smoke'.

6. Italian cyclist Dario Frigo defended drug allegations by saying, 'they found (the drugs) in my luggage and not in my blood', claiming that the banned drugs were for only for 'security' purposes, in case he needed them later at the Giro d'Italia (Tour of Italy).

7. Two-time Giro d'Italia winner Gilberto Simoni has also twice tested positive for cocaine – the first time due to a visit to the dentist and the second time due to a throat tablet.

8. German distance runner Dieter Bauman claimed that someone had put nandrolone in his toothpaste.

9. After steroid allegations, bobsledder Lenny Paul claimed: 'I have eaten spaghetti Bolognese; there must have been hormones in the meat.'

10. When Australian cricketer Shane Warne was caught using a banned diuretic, his excuse was the most shameful of all — he blamed his mother!

Flying for the basket

A US high school basketball player dropped a small bag of marijuana during a scuffle for the ball. A press photographer pointed it out to the referee, thinking it was litter. County prosecutors are still deciding whether to press criminal charges.

Haemoglobin molecules exist within red blood cells. However, with HBOC biotechnology, haemoglobin molecules are removed from red blood cells and then linked together so that these HBOCs can circulate harmlessly but effectively throughout the recipient's bloodstream. And because HBOCs consist of several haemoglobin molecules linked together, their molecular size is larger than a normal haemoglobin unit, and as such, they are relatively easy to distinguish from normal human haemoglobin.

However, catching an athlete who is abusing HBOCs is not so simple. The modification and binding of haemoglobin units to form an HBOC molecule can be achieved by various means and therefore a test to detect the presence of HBOCs in the circulation of an athlete would need to be able to identify all existing forms of HBOCs. The life span of HBOCs is also very short; consequently, a sample for analysis would need to be obtained within 12–24 hours of HBOC use. Finally, HBOCs do not appear in the urine. This means that blood sampling is needed for analysis, and to date, many sports do not require their athletes to provide blood samples for drug testing.

TECHNICAL TALES: TESTING FOR PERFORMANCE-ENHANCING DRUGS

- Athletes may be asked to provide a urine and/or blood sample.
- Athletes will provide a urine sample in the presence of a chaperone who is the same gender as the athlete. The chaperone will directly witness the provision of the urine sample from the athlete's body into the beaker.
- Athletes will provide a blood sample, collected by the phlebotomist, in the presence of a Drug Control Official and the athlete representative (if present).
- Athletes are responsible for controlling their sample (urine and/or blood) until it is sealed in a sample collection kit.

- After collecting a blood sample (in full view of the athlete, the athlete representative and the Drug Control Official) the phlebotomist will remove the blood collection equipment from the athlete's body, thereby sealing the collection equipment containers. The athlete is then responsible for controlling the sample until it is sealed in a sample collection kit.
- The athlete will pour a measured amount of urine sample into each of the 'A' and 'B' labeled containers and then secure the kits.
- The athlete will place and secure their blood test sample collection equipment (tubes) in the relevant labeled containers.
- The laboratory will analyse part 'A' of an athlete's urine sample for the presence of prohibited substances or doping methods.
- If part 'A' of a urine sample returns a positive test result, the athlete has the right to have part 'B' of their urine sample analysed to confirm the positive test result.
- The laboratory will analyse an athlete's blood sample for the purpose of detecting the use of prohibited substances and/or methods.

Source: Australian Sports Drug Agency (ASDA), Drug testing procedure
(*Note*: This is an abridged version of what appears on the Australian Sports Drug Agency: Drug testing procedure web page; for full details, please refer directly to the ASDA website <http://www.asda.org.au/athletes/testing.htm>.)

FATIGUE AND HEAT

The heat and humidity of an Athens summer was one worry in the forefront of the minds of many Olympic athletes leading up to the 2004 Games. Some famous incidents at these Games subsequently ensued where the heat appeared to strip athletes of their ability to go on. The women's marathon world record holder, Briton Paula Radcliffe, stopped running near the 36-kilometre mark of the 42-kilometre race, crumpling into the gutter by the side of the road. Australian Loretta Harrop, after leading for most of the Olympic triathlon, had nothing left to give when she was run down by Austrian Kate Allen in the last few hundred metres of the race. And whether the moment in the

Women's rowing eights final, where Australian Sally Robbins lay flat on her back with a few hundred metres still remaining of the 2000-metre race, had much to do with the Athens heat or with some other fatigue-inducing mechanisms, the incident was a wondrous example of how a fatiguing body sometimes says 'enough is enough'.

It is well known that rising body temperatures during intense exercise in a hot environment adversely affect sports performance, and for those competing in endurance events, hyperthermia-induced fatigue was of particular concern at the 2004 Athens Games. In order to best prepare themselves for the tough conditions ahead, most athletes underwent some form of heat acclimatisation training in the weeks and months leading up to the competition.

Raising the body core temperature is the major stimulus for inducing beneficial changes in the heat-coping mechanisms of the body. This can be achieved by moving to a hot environment, using a laboratory heat chamber, or simply through intense exercise. The physiological adjustments induced by heat acclimatisation occur very rapidly when moving to a hot environment, especially if athletes combine this with high-intensity training. In fact, the majority of the adaptations develop in as short as a week, with full acclimatisation complete within a fortnight.

These adaptations include an increased plasma volume, an earlier onset of sweating, greater sweat rates, a more even distribution of sweat over the skin, reduced salt losses in the sweat itself, and reduced blood flow to the skin. Overall, these changes not only maintain body temperature nearer our normal resting value of 37 $^{\circ}$C for longer, but they also provide a larger reserve volume of blood available to the exercising muscles.

Recent research has shown that when the body core reaches temperatures around 40°C, the brain may step in to reduce an athlete's work rate. When changes in the activity levels of the brain and nerves result in a lowering of the power output during exercise, this is termed *central nervous system fatigue*. Reaching this critical temperature of near 40 $^{\circ}$C does not appear to impair a muscle's maximal ability to produce force, but it does seem to inhibit the amount of sustained force that it can generate – thereby possibly having greater implications to the endurance athlete. Importantly, this reduction in performance occurs irrespective of whether moderate or intense exercise is used to raise the body core to 40 $^{\circ}$C, or whether this critical temperature is reached more rapidly by exercising in a hot environment.

Some hypotheses concerning central nervous system fatigue have centred on alterations to the body's neurotransmitters during an exercise bout. Neurotransmitters are chemical messengers (molecules) used by nerves to communicate with each other and with other tissues of the body. Dopamine and noradrenaline are two neurotransmitters that, when their levels are decreased, reduce arousal and motivation. These two chemicals are also thought to influence the initiation and control of movement and therefore positively effect exercise performance. Interestingly, these two hormones (particularly dopamine) also appear to play a role in the control of body temperature and heat loss. As such, they have become major suspects in the apparent *hyperthermia-induced central nervous system fatigue* that takes place when an athlete suddenly becomes reluctant to continue exercising in hot conditions. That is, if the levels of these two hormones decrease in specific areas of the brain, performance may be adversely affected.

Bupropion: A drug that plays with fire

Bupropion is a drug that inhibits the re-uptake of dopamine and noradrenaline, meaning that the two hormones stay active for longer. Recent work has investigated whether Bupropion may be a drug that can increase endurance in athletes. Initial reports showed that the drug did not improve time trial performance when cycling to fatigue in 90 minutes. In fact, the Union Cycliste Internationale (UCI) even removed Bupropion from their list of banned substances due to its apparent benign impact on performance. However, there is a new twist to the Bupropion story.

Belgian researchers continued to examine the effect that Bupropion may have on long-term exercise by giving the drug or a placebo to volunteers and then asking

Roman acclimatisation
To acclimatise to the predicted heat at the 1960 Rome Olympics, Briton Don Walker exercised in his bathroom with heaters turned on and kettles on the boil – he won the 50-km race walk.

Cool running
Mizuno has designed underwear, made of cotton and PVA, that keep your privates cool. The undies, called Icetouch, keep the groin 10 C cooler than normal cotton undies by radiating the body heat and sweat away from the wearer.

Keep cool

To illustrate the importance of thermoregulation for health and human performance, consider this: an elite marathon runner is able to sustain an oxygen consumption of about 4 litres per minute and therefore produce a power output of about 1200 watts for the entire race. The heat capacity of human tissue is about 3.5 kilojoules per °C per kilogram of body weight. Therefore, for a runnner weighing 65 kilograms, the rate of heat production for 2100 watts would cause the the body temperature to rise approximately 1°C every three minutes. This means that without normal heat loss taking place (for example, by sweating), the athlete could only exercise for a little over ten minutes before their body core temperature would have risen to the upper limit of tolerance. At the completion of the race, the body temperature would have hit about 80°C!

them to cycle for 60 minutes at a moderate intensity. Then, immediately following the 60-minute bout, participants completed an intensive 30-kilometre time trial. What they discovered may make the UCI and other sport-governing bodies rethink the acceptance of Bupropion.

When working in temperate conditions, Bupropion had no effect on exercise performance, just like in the earlier study. But when participants were forced to cycle in hot and humid conditions, the drug produced a 10 per cent increase in time-trial performance – almost three and a half minutes quicker over 30 kilometres!

Relating this back to the earlier discussions about hyperthermia-induced central nervous system fatigue, it appears that Bupropion allowed core temperatures to rise to critically high levels (such as above 40 °C) by blocking the natural removal of dopamine and noradrenaline from the system. Consequently, the normal perception of fatigue did not take place to the expected degree – the result being an improvement in cycling endurance. This may sound good for the endurance athlete – that is, better performance times – but uncontrolled body temperatures are extremely dangerous, and even fatal at times.

Ecstasy and amphetamines are other examples of drugs that interfere with dopamine and noradrenaline re-uptake, and it is well known that several fatalities caused by ecstasy and amphetamines have been linked to hyperthermia. The combination of intense exercise, blazing heat, and amphetamine use could result in an athlete's core temperature exceeding critical levels where the body would normally slow down or stop, instead moving into a temperature range of grave danger. This cocktail may well explain how an elite cyclist might collapse to his death during a race. As mentioned on page 152, during a stage of the Tour de France, on a day where temperatures exceeded 40 $^{\circ}$C, the great British rider Tommy Simpson toppled from his bike to the road below, dying on the way to hospital. Reports since claim that amphetamines were discovered in his riding jersey.

DEFINITION
Malignant hyperthermia

A genetic disease experienced by one in 20 000 people. An attack can be triggered by anaesthetic gases (like halothane), by amphetamine-based drugs (like ecstasy), or in some cases, by the heat induced by exercise. These triggers cause spontaneous muscle contractions (like shivering) and the body temperature starts to rise very rapidly – in serious cases, by as much as 10 C every five minutes. This condition can be fatal if not immediately treated because the massive build-up of heat causes muscle tissue to literally 'melt down'.

Interleukin-6

A messenger molecule, called interleukin-6 (IL-6), fulfils many physiological functions, including some within the central nervous system. Injecting people with recombinant (artificial) IL-6 brings on feelings of fatigue, whilst IL-6 receptor antibodies (that block the effects of IL-6) have shown positive signs for chronic fatigue sufferers. It has also been noted that IL-6 levels in the blood can increase by 60 to 100 times during long-term exercise. At the University of Cape Town, researchers assessed the 10-kilometre performance in runners injected with recombinant IL-6 or a placebo, demonstrating that the IL-6 trial extended run times by almost an extra minute. This effect appears to be independent of increases in body temperature. But IL-6 plays numerous roles within the body so, once again, the blocking of its action may have serious consequences to the overall health of the athlete.

Performance-enhancing (ergogenic) substances

Substance	Action	Proven or proposed exercise effect
Human growth hormone (hGH)	1. Facilitates transport of amino acids intocells 2. Anabolic hormone 3. Stimulates IGF-I	1. Increases muscle mass 2. Increases strength 3. Reduces body fat 4. Cartilage growth effect
Insulin-like growth factor I (IGF-I)	1. Anabolic hormone 2. Facilitates amino acid	1. Increases muscle mass 2. Bone and cartilage growth and glucose transport into cells 3. Glycogen synthesis
Caffeine	1. Central nervous system stimulant 2. Increases fatty acid breakdown and availability	1. Lowers reliance on carbohydrate during endurance exercise
Sodium bicarbonate		1. Buffers metabolic acidosis 1. Delays fatigue in events of 1 to 7 mins duration
Amphetamines	1. Central nervous system stimulant	1. Increases fatigue tolerance 2. Increases strength
Beta blockers	1. Decreases the rate and force of heart contractions	1. Decreases heart rate and blood pressure
Dehydroepiandro-sterone (DHEA)	1. Increases testosterone levels	1. Increases muscle mass
Creatine monohydrate	1. Increases total muscle creatine (*phosphocreatine* is an important short-term energy source)	1. Maintains power output in short-term exercise 2. Increases in body mass due to: - water retention - anabolic effect
Diuretics	1. Increases the amount of urine produced by the body	1. Helps athletes 'make weight' in weight division sports 2. Used as a 'masking agent' to dilute urine to avoid steroid detection

Note: **Not all the substances listed in the table are 'banned'.** For prohibited status, refer to:
1. World Anti-Doping Agency, (2005), Prohibited list. <http://www.wada-ama.org/en/dynamic.ch2?pageCategory_id=47>
2. Australian Sports Drug Agency, (2005), Prohibited substances and methods. <http://www.asda.org.au/athletes/banned.htm>

THE SEX TEST CONTROVERSY

At the 1932 Los Angeles Olympics, Stanislawa Walasiewicz won the women's 100 metres sprint, equalling the world record of 11.9 seconds. Walasiewicz was born in Poland but grew up in the United States, adopting the name Stella Walsh. In 1930, she became the first woman to break 11 seconds for the 100-yard dash, but due to issues outside of athletics, she decided to compete for her native Poland at the 1932 Games. When the 1936 Berlin Games came around, American Helen Stephens ran a wind-assisted 11.5 seconds to win the final of the 100 metres, with Walasiewicz winning silver, 2 metres behind. A Polish journalist actually accused the American Stephens of being a man and Olympic officials were forced to validate her femininity. But in a bizarre twist some 44 years later in 1980, Walasiewicz was an accidental bystander at a robbery in Cleveland and was shot dead. During her autopsy, she was in fact discovered to have male genitalia!

Sex testing for female athletes was first introduced at the Summer Olympics in 1968. This followed the controversial ejection of Polish sprinter Ewa Klobukowska from international competition after she failed a sex test. Klobukowska, who captured the 100 metres bronze at the 1964 Olympics, failed a sex chromosome test in 1967, despite having passed a visual examination. It is said that Princess Anne, who competed in equestrian events at Olympic level, is the only woman to have been spared from sex testing during those times.

In 2004, the International Olympic Committee (IOC) approved the recommendation that individuals who have undergone sex reassign-

Don't mess with her

Parinya Kiatbussaba's dreams of becoming a famous kickboxer went pear-shaped after having a sex change – because, in Bangkok, women are banned from the ring. Rather than giving up her dream, she moved to Japan where their laws are more flexible. 'It's better money than in Thailand, so it's worth it, even if it hurts,' Kiatbussaba said.

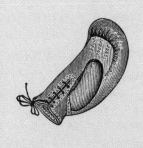

ment of male to female or female to male be eligible for participation in female or male competitions, respectively. The IOC stated that eligibility should begin no sooner than two years after gonadectomy and that a case-by-case evaluation process would take place.

> **Psych drug**
>
> The Cameroon national goalkeeping coach Thomas Nkono was arrested over allegations of practising black magic during the African Cup of Nations semi-final against Mali. Nkono dropped a charm on the pitch, and the object was supposedly a black magic talisman aimed at helping Cameroon's chances. A policeman retrieved the charm and Nkono was taken away in handcuffs before the start of the game. Cameroon beat Mali 3-0 and Nkono was banned for a year.

GENE DOPING – THE HIDDEN ENHANCEMENT

With the mapping of the human genome and the refinement of technologies aimed at working with, and even manipulating, genetic material, concerns have been raised (with good reason) that gene therapy may soon be used for the engineering of athletic prowess.

On an annual basis, a special report called 'The Human Gene Map for Performance and Health-related Fitness Phenotypes' is published by collaborating scientists. This paper outlines all known potential genetic markers that may be associated with exercise performance, highlighting the current search for so-called 'performance genes'.

To date, only a couple of genes have been identified that appear to play a direct role in either power performance – the *a-actinin-3* (*ACTN3*) gene – or endurance ability – the *angiotensin converting enzyme* (*ACE*) gene. However, other ongoing research efforts have already posited other candidate genes likely to be linked to sporting potential.

Knowledge of such genes is one thing; being able to play with these genes is something quite different. The sporting community is now facing the possibility that, as gene therapy skills are refined, *gene doping* will soon become the newest form of high-tech cheating. Whilst the ability to safely manipulate an athlete's genetic make-up is still a way off, many scientists fear that the practice is inevitable.

Switching 'on' a gene leads to the production of a specific protein. The process of muscle growth and repair, for example, is regulated by certain chemical signals controlled by the activity of certain genes. A protein called *insulin-like growth factor I (IGF-I)* is a potent growth factor for stimulating muscle growth; if the IGF-I *gene* is switched 'on', then the resultant production of the IGF-I *protein* will signal muscle to grow. When scientists at the University of Pennsylvania School of Medicine inserted a synthetic gene, that would overproduce IGF-I, into skeletal muscles of sedentary mice, they reported 15 per cent to 30 per cent increases in muscle size and rates of growth. This type of work is aimed at addressing potential therapies to help people with muscle-wasting diseases – but the athletic implications are obvious.

This same research team also injected the synthetic IGF-I gene into single legs of rats, using the contralateral legs (the legs on the opposite side of the body) as the *control* condition. After putting the rats through eight weeks of weight training, they reported that the legs that housed the inserted gene could develop almost twice the amount of strength as the un-injected (control) legs.

The suppression of a gene may act in much the same way. For example, the protein *myostatin* acts to inhibit muscle growth; that is, it stops our muscles growing too large and becoming dysfunctional. However, blocking the action of the gene that produces myostatin (or even knocking out the gene) results in monstrous muscle growth.

There are other genes in the human genome that lie dormant; never being switched 'on' because we lack the appropriate signals. One such gene is that which produces a protein called *type IIb myosin heavy chain (MHC IIb)*. MHC IIb is the motor protein in super-fast skeletal muscle fibres of small mammals; it helps them move super-fast to escape predators. But what if we could switch our dormant MHC IIb gene 'on' within our bodies? What a boon that would be for sprinters – extra-fast muscle fibres, contracting at greater rates than ever before, to power them to the tape in record time.

Gene doping may eventually take many forms:

(1) enhancing or suppressing the activity of a gene, so as to manipulate the production rate of a specific protein (e.g. IGF-I or myostatin genes)

(2) injecting a missing gene variant to adjust the protein composition of a tissue (e.g. ACTN3 or ACE genes; see page 168)

(3) activating a previously dormant gene (e.g. MHC IIb gene).

It is believed that gene therapy has the ability to perform all these tasks, but augmenting or altering sporting potential is not the only potential benefit to the athlete. Genetic engineering demonstrates great potency within the field of sports injury and rehabilitation; that is, genetic manipulation will also lead to improvements in the rate and extent of tissue repair following sporting injury. Gene therapy offers promising avenues for stimulating cell repair and growth at injured sites where blood supply is limited (for example, ligaments, tendons and cartilage), or in tissue engineering for the creation of biomaterials and scaffolding necessary in the healing of musculoskeletal injuries.

Gene doping is an ethical minefield. Not only is the human body being tampered with, it is also considered a form of cheating (akin to performance-enhancing drug abuse). But the fact that it may also help athletes recover from injuries adds a dimension to healthy living. For organisations like the World Anti-Doping Agency (WADA) and the Australian Sports Drug Agency (ASDA), gene doping is of great concern. The chemicals used to switch genes 'on' or 'off', and even the synthetic genes themselves, will be located within the muscle tissue, not floating about in the blood or urine. This means that the present testing procedures used for detecting athletic doping will be powerless against the gene-doped athlete.

Unearthly enhancement

Chilean football team Deportes Arica hired a witch to cast out evil spirits from the dressing room, stadium and even the players' kits. Before games, the witch would perform a ritual with candles and smoke to 'purify the team'. The team believed it worked, as they won two games after her visits. The only time she didn't come, the team drew.

UPDATE FROM THE LAB: THE POWER GENE

In *Run Like You Stole Something*, we discussed a gene known as the *ACE* gene – responsible for a protein called the *angiotensin converting enzyme* – because it appeared to impact directly on endurance ability. Now, a second gene has been identified that appears to be directly linked to elite power performance – the a-*actinin-3 (ACTN3)* gene.

A research group comprising scientists from Sydney's Institute of Neuromuscular Research at the Children's Hospital (Westmead), University of Sydney, Australian National University, Children's Hospital (Boston) and the Australian Institute of Sport have discovered that one variant (called the R allele) of the ACTN3 gene is responsible for producing a protein called a-actinin-3 – this protein is found only in fast-twitch muscle fibres. The second variant (called the X allele) of the ACTN3 gene does not produce a-actinin-3.

Our DNA contains two copies of the ACTN3 gene – a copy inherited from each parent – which means that each person either possesses two R alleles, two X alleles, or one R and one X allele. In a large cohort of elite sprint athletes, the research team found that 95 per cent of elite Australian sprinters possessed at least one copy of the R allele, whilst 50 per cent of the sprinters had two copies of the R allele. When compared to elite endurance athletes and the general population, only 31 per cent and 30 per cent, respectively, had two copies of the R allele.

On the other side of the coin, only 5 per cent of the elite Australian sprinters had two X alleles, compared to 18 per cent in the general population. Interestingly, no Olympic-class sprinters or any of the female sprinters had the XX characteristic. Meanwhile, 24 per cent of the endurance runners had two XX alleles.

The family of proteins known as a-actinins help maintain muscle structure, aiding with the efficient contraction of muscle fibres. The fact that the R allele of the ACTN3 gene signals the production of a-actinin-3 – and this protein is only produced in fast-twitch fibres – may provide sprinters' muscles with an enhanced ability to generate force at high velocities. Meanwhile, the higher incidence of the XX allele combination in endurance athletes may confer greater 'slow' characteristics to their muscles – important for resisting fatigue over long periods.

The job of a sports scientist is now a full-time profession and its aim is simple: discover new and innovative ways to improve athletic performance. Increasingly, the sporting feats that we marvel at are not just the products of an athlete's raw talent and hard work – they are also the result of systematic contributions from a team of scientists. This chapter will take you into the laboratory to explain how the life of an athlete is supported by sports science.

The Frankenstein hypothesis: Due to their midnight ravings and maniacal laughter, mad scientists have been effectively removed from sports science laboratories. These traits were disturbing the sleep patterns of athletes and hence their recovery from training.

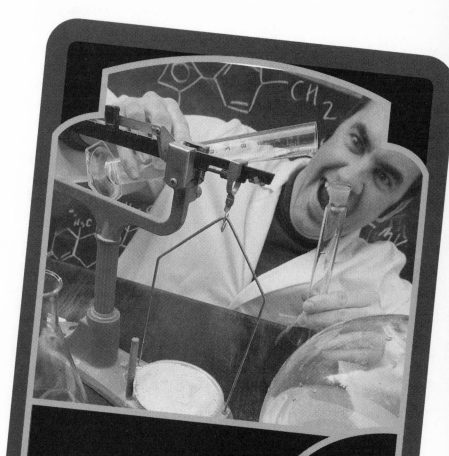

IN THE LAB

6

The science behind the
superathlete

RECORD BREAKER
Roger Bannister – the four-minute mile

The four-minute mile – four laps in four minutes – one minute per lap. Simple.

In 1886, W.G. George set a mile record of 4 minutes, 12.75 seconds (4:12.75). This record may have only been 12.75 seconds outside of the magical four-minute mark, but the fact that it stood for 37 years added great strength to the idea that a four-minute mile was unattainable.

Most experts in the sports sciences believed that the human body was not capable of running four laps of a track in four minutes. When the 'Flying Finn' Paavo Nurmi (winner of nine gold and three silver Olympic medals) broke George's record in 1923 by setting a new mark of 4:10.4, few believed still that sub-four minutes was possible, but by 1937, S.C. Wooderson had lowered the time to 4:06.4. Then World War II broke out.

Unlike most sporting endeavours, the chase for the four minute mile was not halted by the war. With Sweden remaining essentially neutral, two of its countrymen continued to pursue athletics's Holy Grail. From 1941 to 1945, an intense rivalry between Arne Andersson and Gundar Haegg drove the two men ever closer to sub-four minutes, with each man twice setting new world marks. The challenge culminated in Malmo, Sweden, on 17 July 1945, where one of the all-time great races took place. Haegg won the mile duel that day, getting within 8 yards of the goal, but his time of 4:01.4 was not enough. Andersson came in 0.8 of a second later.

At this time, many still felt that a mile in four minutes was beyond reach – an effort at the absolute limit of human performance. Those who did believe in the possibility reasoned that it could only be achieved under specific 'perfect' conditions. A group of sports-minded scientists from the fields of physiology, psychology, meteorology, medicine and athletics put forward what those conditions must be.

1. The race would have to take place in Scandinavia, where the presence of higher ozone levels might provide benefits to the runner.
2. The environmental conditions would include a day of moderate temperature and calm air.

3. The track would have to be dry.
4. A large, noisy, supportive crowd would need to be on hand to provide a psychological lift.
5. Other runners would be required to provide pacing.
6. Lap times would be slower initially and the pace would have to gradually increase over the four laps.

History tells us that at 6 pm on 6 May 1954, Roger Bannister set out on a sub-four minute journey on a cold, wet day (rain having fallen all afternoon) with a 15 miles per hour wind (and gusts of 25 mph at times), over a rain-soaked cinder track at Oxford University's Iffley Road grounds, in front of a small crowd of only 1000 to 3000 people. His two pacemakers, Chris Brasher and Chris Chataway, took him out hard, covering the first two laps in 1:58.0; the third lap was slower, taking the bell at 3:00.7; and Bannister then stormed home for a final lap of 58.7 seconds. Bannister broke the tape in a time of 3:59.4 – the miracle mile had been achieved.

Food for sport

Even though Australian John Landy's first sub-four-minute mile only took 3:58.0 (a world record at the time), this effort on 21 June 1954 was too late – Roger Bannister had already broken the four-minute barrier 45 days earlier. On the day Landy set this record, he ate a couple of pies and an ice-cream sundae.

AUSTRALIA'S FATHER OF SPORTS SCIENCE

Professor Frank Cotton is known as 'the father of sports science' in Australia. Many of the approaches to measuring athletic performance, and indeed enhancing it, have come from Professor Cotton's initiatives back in the 1940s and early 1950s when he teamed up with a willing assistant in Forbes Carlile – now renowned as one of Australia's foremost swimming coaches. Cotton, a well-known exercise physiologist working at the University of Sydney, applied his knowledge to the refinement of sports training approaches due to his own athletic ambitions – he narrowly missed qualifying for the 1920 Olympic Games as a relay swimmer – and general interest in sport. Using his academic background where he viewed the body as a machine, he attempted to quantify aspects of an athlete's performance that at the time were simply considered not measurable due to the chaotic nature of the sports environment.

A scientific adviser at the 1952 Olympics in Helsinki – probably the first sports scientist to advise an Australian sporting team – Cotton is regarded as the first to apply the concept of *tapering*. Conventional wisdom suggested that athletes should train hard right up to a major event if they wanted to maintain peak condition; but Cotton and Carlile insisted that an 'easing off' in training was important in the last two to three weeks before competition, and coined the term tapering to describe this process (see page 203).

Another first related to the use of active and passive warm-ups. Carlile would put his swimming group into a hot bath (44° C) at the North Sydney pool, and after 12 painstaking minutes, the swimmers would exit the bath to compete with their core body temperatures raised by about 2° C. Much to the swimmers' surprise, they would swim personal best times because the muscles worked more efficiently after they had been heated. It's now common practice that many swimmers passively warm up under a hot shower in addition to the usual active swimming warm-up.

Cotton and Carlile's interest in swimming had them on a search to improve swim times. Having already applied their physiological knowledge to training principles, the pair set their minds to coming up with an approach to minimise drag through the water. Initially looking to clothe swimmers in drag-resistant material, they were unsuccessful until they turned their attention to the swimmers' skin – or more specifically, their hair – requesting that Australian swimmers 'shave down'. The 1956 Olympics are recognised as the first time that swimmers shaved the hair off their bodies – a practice still employed today.

Another first for Cotton was his pioneering work in the development of rowing and cycling ergometers for use in training, testing and talent identification of athletes. In 1950, he received worldwide press when his 'guinea-pigs' – a crew of novice oarsmen selected on ergometer scores – narrowly missed Australian selection for the Empire Games (now the Commonwealth Games). This was possibly a world first in the use of talent identification, as well as a forerunner to the success most famously achieved by Professor Allan Hahn at the Australian

Institute of Sport some thirty years later. On the basis of physiological profiling, Hahn and his team fast-tracked non-rowers to the 1992 and 1996 Olympic Games, culminating in a gold-medal performance for Megan Still.

Monkey see, monkey do
Danny the chimpanzee from Twycross Zoo in England has taken up the sport of tennis. After Danny watched Wimbledon on a keeper's TV, zoo staff gave him a racquet and were shocked when Danny started hitting forehands against a wall.

THE PROCESS OF TALENT IDENTIFICATION

The implementation of a scientific, evidence-based program to assess the potential for success in any given sport (known as *talent detection*) is an increasingly vital strand of high-performance sport. With the aim of unearthing potential Olympians, the *Talent Search* program was established in 1994 as a part of the build up to the 2000 Sydney Olympic Games. The aim was for the program to identify talent and fast-track athletes to the Sydney Games within the sports of athletics, cycling, canoeing, swimming, rowing, triathlon, water polo and weight-lifting. Children aged between 14–16 years were selected for testing because this age bracket represented potential performers who would be 20–22 years at the time of the Games.

Identification consisted of three phases:

1. *School screening*: A battery of eight physical and physiological tests, including the measurement of height, body mass and arm span, and the performance of a basketball throw for distance, a vertical jump for leg power, a 40-metre sprint, and a shuttle run for aerobic endurance were implemented by school physical education teachers. Student results were then compared with a

national database and some students who were in the top 2 per cent on any of the eight tests were invited to the second stage.

2. *Sport-specific testing*: This phase refined some of the previous tests and added some sport-specific laboratory testing, such as aerobic power (VO_{2max}) tests for cycling.

3. *Training*: students demonstrating the desired talent after phase 2 were then invited to join a 'talented athlete program' organised by the relevant sport or a state-based institute or academy of sport.

While the above model has obviously been successful, its overall efficiency is less clear. The contemporary approach to talent identification has adopted a number of new initiatives to maximise the talent harvest for sports. In particular, older and more experienced athletes are now considered a rich source of talent. Ex-athletes with a particular quality (such as speed and power) may be invited to try a sport they may have never heard of. Two examples of this current approach include the identification of potential Olympians for the sports of slalom canoeing and the winter sport of Skeleton. In sum, modern talent identification is not just occurring in the school system but also through capturing talent hiding out there in the general public – you could be next!

Did You Know?

You can find out more about talent identification, current and previous initiatives, or how your child may be tested at the National Talent Search Program webpage: <http://www.ais.org.au/talent/index.asp>

You chews, you lose

Phil Jackson, the LA Lakers coach, monitors the gum-chewing intensity of his players. He says it indicates how much pressure they are experiencing. 'If I see players chewing gum too hard and getting their jaws tight, I'll ask them to take the gum out or stop chewing for a while so they don't create tension. It all flows, all that is connected.'

Talent ID success stories

Athlete	B/gnd	Year identified	Sport / Success
Alayna Burns	Schoolgirl Netball	1993	Track Cycling 1998 Commonwealth Games gold 2000 Olympic Games 7th and 9th
Megan Still		1988	Rowing 1996 Olympic Games gold
Alisa Camplin	Retired gymnast		Aerial skiing 2002 Winter Olympics gold
Lydia Ierodiaconou	Retired gymnast		Aerial skiing Current World Cup Star
Kate Barclay	Basketball	1996	Kayaking LK4500 m 2004 Olympic Games 6th
Janelle Lindsay	Road cycling	2002	Track cycling 2004 Paralympics 1st and 3rd

PRECISION TIMING IS A SPORTING MEASURE

The 1912 Stockholm Olympics saw the first use of electronic timers to back up the times displayed by stopwatches in track events. The public address system was also first used at these games. But it wasn't until 20 years later that official automatic timing devices and the photo-finish camera was introduced at the 1932 Olympics for track events. Jack Keller of the US was possibly the first athlete to experience the consequences of great measurement precision. He won the bronze medal for the 110 metres hurdles, but after the film was reviewed, the result was changed in favour of Great Britain's Donald Finley. Keller, who had already been awarded the bronze, took off to the Olympic village, found Finley and handed him the medal. We wonder if things would be so simple today.

High-tech trophy

A Colorado bar owner hung his laptop on the wall of his sportsman's bar as his latest hunting trophy, after he shot it four times. The laptop had apparently crashed too many times.

While the use of reliable and more precise timing approaches will always be vital in deciding winners and losers on race day, time in the hands of scientists and coaches can be used to optimise their athletes' chances of walking away with a medal. The use of split times for sections of a race or components of a movement allows scientists and coaches to study an event in greater detail than ever before. Even for an event such as the 100 metres sprint that is completed in the course of a few breaths, the use of timing measures has provided greater insight into how the all-important finishing time can be further improved.

In simple terms, running speed is the product of stride length and stride frequency. If sprinters can improve one or both, they will reach the finish-line faster. However, stride length usually falls when stride rate increases (and vice versa). Thus, the big question is which one of the two aspects should be improved more to achieve the greatest increases in speed?

Stride length can be separated into two phases – ground contact and flight. Ground contact is the only time that an athlete can impart force to increase speed. Top sprinters take 4.5 to 5 strides per second, with each ground contact lasting around 0.1 second. As such, an essential characteristic of the great sprinters is the ability to apply large forces very rapidly. This is particularly important in the first 30 metres; it has been found that the greater the acceleration to maximum speed, the better the outcome at the tape.

Most athletes reach top speed within 30 to 60 metres. The top speed for men is around 12 metres per second, whilst for women it's nearer 11. At this point, sprinters cover between 2 and 2.5 metres per stride. At top speed, 50–60 per cent of the race is spent in the air – an interesting paradox where more time is actually spent airborne and, therefore, 'slowing down'.

However, stride rate (the speed at which an athlete can turn the legs over) tends to be the factor that increases when a sprinter sets a personal best time. In 1936, to exaggerate his leg speed, Jesse Owens was told to run like he was on a hot tin roof. Many experts suggest that stride rate is an innate ability possessed by the great sprinters and difficult to teach effectively – even talent scouts take great notice of the leg speed of potential sprint champions.

A matter of centimetres

At the 1993 world championships in Falun, Sweden, the 50-km cross-country skiing event was decided in sensational fashion when Vladimir Smirnov and Bjorn Daehlie crossed the finish-line in a dead heat. Smirnov was initially given the win because his body reached the line first, but upon review, officials reversed the decision: Daehlie's foot had actually breached the finish-line first. In cross-country skiing, events are decided by the breaking of an electronic beam 25 centimetres above the ground.

Dashing dasslers

Shoes are an integral part of one's ability to break running records. Adidas was the first major manufacturer to make shoes for athletes, when Adi Dassler and his brother Rudi ran the German-based company. After a time, however, Rudi decided to cross the river in their small town and start his own shoe company, which he named Puma.

Did you know?

To break the 10-second barrier for 100 metres, runners take between 43 and 47.5 strides.

TIMING IN TEAM SPORTS

The application of time measures is not just useful in track and field events but can also provide valuable information when attempting to analyse the skills of team-sport athletes. A hallmark of elite team sport is the frenetic pace at which games are played. For instance, analysis of the volume, intensity and variety of movement demands on netball players during a match reinforces the idea that netball is a game played at high speed with many sudden changes of direction. Players can spend up to 13 per cent of a match shuffling in a sideways direction at full pace and effort. The time spent shuffling ranged from 1.3–1.9 seconds depending on the position played, with an average over 300 shuffle movements performed per game.

The ability to change direction at speed is called agility. Incredibly, netball players may change direction over 2000 times per game. Historically, agility has been assessed by measuring the time an athlete takes to run around a series of cones in a pre-determined movement pattern. For example, a netball player may be required to sprint 5 metres in a straight direction, then turn and sprint back the other way. This type of test usually reflects the movements of an attacker who knows where they want to run, and measures the player's ability to accelerate and decelerate quickly whilst changing direction. When elite athletes are compared to less-skilled players, elite players are found to be faster in completing the movement pattern.

However, one only has to watch team sport to realise that most agility patterns in a game are not pre-planned, but rather, a player's agility relies on reacting to the movements of the opposition and the calls of team-mates. In recent times, sports scientists have tried to replicate this type of agility to better reflect the qualities of a real game.

Through the use of near-life-size video projections of a virtual opponent, netballers at the Australian Institute of Sport have had their reactive agility examined. The players are required to complete a shuffling pattern as if defending an opponent. While completing this movement, the players are also watching their life-size virtual opponent receive a ball and prepare to pass it off to a team-mate. The player being tested is required to intercept the ball by changing their direction and sprinting in the anticipated pass direction.

Upsetting the locals

Prostitutes are outraged at a comment made by
German football coach Eduard Geyer, likening
his underperforming players to prostitutes.
Geyer said his players drink and smoke too
much and sleep around all day. Local prostitutes
are insulted at the comparison, saying they
work up to 14 hours a day.

Results of such testing have revealed that the more agile players
really stand out on this reactive type of agility test more so than on a
pre-determined agility test. The reason for the clearer differences
between the skill levels on the reactive test can be attributed to the
anticipatory ability of the players. While less skilled players waited
approximately 20 milliseconds after the ball had been released by the
virtual opponent before changing direction, the elite players were able
to anticipate the pass direction based on the posture of the player, and
hence, change direction approximately 110 milliseconds *before* the ball
had been released. This quick decision allowed them to get the jump on
their opponent.

MEASURING THE IMPORTANT DECISIONS

Often, the focus in sports like netball is on the goal-shooting percentages when identifying why one team defeated another. However, there
is also a less obvious quality that can often separate the teams and their
players – the ability to *read the play*. Some coaches describe this as the
player who is 'a good driver in heavy traffic'; that is, the player who
seemingly knows what will occur two passes before it happens. Despite
such players often not being the fastest around the court, their ability to
accurately forecast a game's future means that they always appear to
have all the time in the world. Whilst reading the play is akin to reading

Latin for us mere mortals, for many players, like Australian wing attack Natalie Avelino or AFL footballer James Hird, it is second nature and makes them fast processors of their game's dynamics.

Adopting sports science terminology, 'reading the play' is related to pattern recall or recognition. Watching a team sport like netball is a classic example of watching a continuously changing pattern. Interestingly, while the pattern may look meaningless to the untrained eye – 14 players sprinting and dodging in all directions – to an expert player (or coach), it can look completely logical and can inform them in advance as to where the ball is about to be passed. This is quite a handy skill if your job requires you to intercept as many opposition passes as possible.

Pattern recall was first investigated back in the 1960s in the game of chess. Research was able to demonstrate that Grandmasters were able to sum up a board in one quick glance. Provided with 5 or 10 seconds to look over a specific chess situation, the best players could accurately recall the exact location of 90 per cent of the pieces. Less skilled players could only remember 50 per cent. The researchers concluded that the Grandmasters could 'chunk' the chess piece positions into fewer, larger chunks of information that were more easily remembered and subsequently recalled to re-create the required pattern; this is similar to the manner in which we remember frequently-used telephone numbers, as one block of numbers rather than eight individual digits.

In more recent times, sports science has applied the chess approach to team sports and has demonstrated that elite team-sport players also possess the analytical minds of chess masters. Australian netball team members were presented with video footage of netball game situations for approximately 10 seconds before the footage was occluded. They were then required to recall the attacking and defensive structures of the two teams by plotting on a blank diagram of a netball court the location of each player at the point of occlusion. On average, the netballers were able to accurately recall 70 per cent of the player positions. In comparison, club-level players had a recall ability of no more than 60 per cent.

Importantly, this capability to recognise opposition attacking or defensive patterns is not innate. Elite players don't possess a bigger-than-normal memory capacity. Rather their memory of sport-specific attack and defence strategies is predominantly acquired through years of game-specific experience and clever training approaches.

Knowing where 70 per cent of the players are positioned at any given instant allows a smart player to predict and move to where the ball is likely to be passed, increasing their speed of response and the chance of a turnover. So next time you dissect your favourite team sport's stats, consider who were more accurate in reading the play – it's usually the winning team.

Writing the play

In 1940, a football match between Scottish teams Hibs and Hearts was to be broadcast to soldiers overseas. However, the field became covered in heavy fog and the commentator could not see anything. To prevent the Nazis from finding out that there was heavy fog over the country, the BBC was told to provide full commentary. A system of runners and information chains was set up so that the commentator could mention all goals and corner kicks. However, he still had to make up the highlights for the rest of the match. The final score was a Hearts win, 6–5. The story has been made into a play called Playing a Blinder.

TRYING TO MAKE THE RIGHT DECISION

As revealed earlier, expert team-sport players demonstrate fast and accurate recognition of relevant patterns of play as they unfold during a game, allowing players to move into the correct position to receive or intercept a ball (see page 182). Likewise, players in one-on-one reactive situations, like a soccer penalty kick or tennis return of serve, can predict in advance where the ball will go on the basis of their opponent's movement pattern, without needing to see the ball's flight. Over the last decade in particular, scientists have explored whether these anticipatory qualities (or good decision-making skills) of the expert players is trainable.

Called *perceptual training*, in this training method scientists have focused on the use of video-based simulations which attempt to put a learner in the shoes of a player being forced to make a fast decision. Generally, perceptual training involves the use of a video presentation of a player performing a particular action or a pattern of play from a team perspective. This presentation is then edited at a point just before the occurrence of an important decision-making cue. The training task for the player completing the simulation is to predict the direction of the ball, even though they may have to base their decision only on the movement pattern of their video-based opponent – for example, imagine having to face a ball from Brett Lee without seeing any of the flight of his delivery. There is evidence of improvements in the speed and/or accuracy of players' decision-making capabilities after repeated exposure to this type of training.

Perceptual training of this kind initially started back in 1965 with tennis players having to predict the serve directions of a player on a film strip. By the early 1980s, players were reacting to footage played by video on small television monitors, having to verbally call out their decision or write it down on a piece of paper. However, as technology has developed, scientists have sought greater fidelity; simulations that can imitate reality ever more closely. As a result, near-life-size video projections were utilised at first, so that the players on the video display looked more life-like. Further improvements in the simulation followed when players were required to physically respond or interact with the vision. Hence, like the agility test described earlier (see page 182), performance measures such as a player's decision time and movement accuracy could be examined.

As we progress into the twenty-first century, two further innovations are apparent. First, the use of three-dimensional (3D) projections is becoming more widespread. In this case, the viewer watches the action with customised glasses to create a three-dimensional image. Again the scientists are simply attempting to create greater realism, as 3D displays provide a player with depth information – vital for good decision-making in a team-sport environment.

However, perhaps the most exciting development is the application of *Virtual Reality* (VR). Based on principles seen in many video games, a viewer can be fully immersed into a game from any on-field player's perspective. For example, the University of Michigan Virtual Reality Laboratory has developed the 'Virtual Football Trainer', where a player is placed into a CAVE (Cave Automatic Virtual Environment), which is a room-sized cube consisting of three walls and a floor that creates an illusion of being immersed in a 3D world. These four surfaces then serve as projection screens as computer-generated images of a football field, with virtual players and a crowd, surround the viewer. The player is then presented with specific situations that may arise in a game of American football, in order to improve his reaction speed. While evidence of the transfer of this training from the CAVE to the field of play is minimal at this stage, logic would suggest that it has potential, despite the use of animation rather than real-life figures (as in video-based training).

Ten Olympic medallists to gain film fame

Athlete	Event	Film fame
Johnny Weissmuller	5 gold – swimming (1924; 1928) 1 bronze – water polo (1924)	*Tarzan* (12 films)
Carol Heiss	1 gold – figure skating (1960)	*Snow White and the Three Stooges*
Buster Crabbe	1 gold – swimming (1932)	*Tarzan* *Buck Rogers* *Flash Gordon*
Harold Sakata	1 silver – weight-lifting (1948)	*Goldfinger* (played 'Oddjob')
Sonja Henie	3 gold – figure skating (1928; 1932; 1936)	*One In A Million* *Sun Valley Serenade* *Thin Ice*
Bruce Jenner	1 gold – decathlon (1976)	*Can't Stop The Music*
Herman Brix	1 silver – shot put (1932)	*Tarzan* *The Treasure of the Sierra Madre*
Mitch Gaylord	1 gold; 1 silver; 2 bronze – gymnastics (1984)	*Batman Forever* (stunt double for 'Robin the Boy Wonder')
Lee Barnes	1 gold – pole vault (1924)	*College* (stunt double for Buster Keaton)
Cornishman V	2 gold – equestrian (1972)	*Dead Cert* *International Velvet*

TECHNICAL TALES:
ICE JACKETS ARE A COOL INVESTMENT

The idea of pre-cooling the body to lessen the deleterious effects of a hot and/or humid environment on exercise performance has found its way into professional sports – via the use by athletes of *ice vests*. First developed by the Australian Institute of Sport prior to the 1996 Atlanta Olympics, ice vests are now commonplace. Ice vests come in various styles: as the vest; with sleeves; or with a hood (due to the head's crucial role in temperature regulation). Some vests, for example, house 10 ice packs in front and eight in back so that the majority of the torso is cooled; others may contain specially designed coolant materials.

By wearing an ice vest for up to an hour before competition, the goal is to lower the skin temperature to provide a larger heat gradient between the body core and the skin, thus improving heat removal for the athlete and increasing the time it takes for an athlete's body temperature to reach 40 °C – a critical temperature point that some scientists believe plays a large role in the onset of fatigue.

Despite claims that these pre-cool vests delay, by 19 per cent, the time that it takes for the body temperature to reach the critical threshold of 40° C, the jury is still out on the effectiveness of the ice vests on actual physical performance. One review suggests that pre-cooling may improve power output by as much as 7 per cent in continuous exercise of up to an hour, but some studies also report that ice vests failed to improve performance in intermittent activities (such as team sports). However, any small improvement at the elite level can make a big difference at the end of the day.

> **The Matrix is old hat**
>
> A head-mounted display as seen in many modern-day sci-fi movies such as The Matrix was first developed back in 1965. However, it took more than 20 years before it became commercially available.

TURNING TO THE INSIDE TO
MEASURE LACTIC ACID

During the 2004 Olympic Games, the newspapers ran daily headlines extolling the great athletic achievements. But at times, the impact of performance stress knocked these triumphs from the front page: the collapse of Australian eights rower Sally Robbins before the finish line and the disintegration of the women's marathon favourite Paula Radcliffe spring to mind. In the aftermath of these incidents, one chemical more than any other was discussed as being the culprit; and for once, it was not a performance-enhancing drug. The chemical in question – so often touted as being responsible for all the fatigue and discomfort felt when exercising to the limit – was *lactic acid*.

There are many types of fatigue and the causes vary depending on the duration and intensity of the activity. Acute alterations to nerve and muscle function, to the metabolic environment in cells, to the availability of fuel for energy supply, and to hormonal levels, may all act to slow us down. The brain, too, plays its part in perceiving these signals and acting to protect the body from damaging overexertion. However, because lactic acid production increases with ever-heavier exercise, it has become the common scapegoat to explain declines in performance at the muscle level.

The bad boy of sport

The twentieth century was not a good era for lactic acid. In most fields of sports science, lactic acid was considered a useless (and detrimental) by-product of metabolism. Its build-up during exercise was not only responsible for making our muscles 'burn' and tire during a sporting performance, but lactic acid also led to aching muscles on the day following a big workout. In sum, lactic acid was considered no good to anybody. This perception of its evil nature has pervaded the sporting community to all scientific, professional, amateur and recreational levels.

Reports of lactic acid span back to 1808, when 'the muscles of hunted stags' were discovered to contain elevated levels of the molecule. In the early twentieth century, the oft-reported presence of lactic acid in exercising muscles was, in fact, thought to play a crucial role in normal function as a donor of energy to the working muscle. However, other discoveries quashed that hypothesis, but researchers were still fascinated by lactic acid, especially with its tight link to exercise – that is, as the intensity of exercise increased, so did the amount of lactic acid in the blood and muscles. It's little wonder that lactic acid was soon targeted as the molecule responsible for fatigue.

From this point, most thinking described lactic acid as a useless by-

A long day at the office

In a Greco-Roman semi-final at the 1912 Olympics, Estonian wrestler Martin Klein defeated Finland's Alfred Asikainen after grappling for 11 hours – however, Klein was too exhausted to contest his gold-medal match.

product that appeared when the body used carbohydrate as a fuel source and there was inadequate oxygen reaching working muscles. It was also believed that the presence of lactic acid, and the process of its removal, was responsible for the heavier-than-normal breathing experienced immediately after exercise. And of course, it was still the prime suspect for making muscles scream 'No more'.

The mobile molecule

However, since the 1970s, many researchers have risen to the defence of lactic acid by challenging many of the ideas perpetuated about its role within the body. Current evidence suggests that poor oxygen supply to the muscle is only one of many factors leading to lactic acid production during exercise. More importantly, the growing band of lactic acid supporters has generated convincing arguments through their research that lactic acid may, in fact, be a very beneficial molecule for exercise performance.

When lactic acid is generated in human cells, more than 99.9 per cent of it immediately separates into two components: (1) the *lactate* ion (La^-); and (2) a *hydrogen* ion (H^+), where a rising H^+ ion concentration reflects an increasing *acidosis*. These two components are often touted to inhibit the force and speed of muscle contraction, disrupt the ionic balance of the cells, and slow the work rate of the muscle's energy supplying pathways. Many studies have explored the impact that both lactate and acidosis have on muscle performance, and this work is now trumpeting the virtues of lactic acid.

It has been known for decades that La^- acts as a fuel source (somewhat like carbohydrate) within the body. Lactate that moves into the bloodstream from exercising muscle fibres can be taken up by the heart, by less active muscles, and even by neighbouring muscle fibres within the same muscle, to contribute to the energy needs of a cell. Called the 'lactate cell-to-cell shuttle', the mobile nature of lactate (as it is distributed around the body) is thought to be an important mechanism in coordinating whole-body metabolism. Some experiments have demonstrated that lactate may even become the fuel of choice for the heart during exercise, at times accounting for around 60 per cent of the fuel that it utilises. The brain, too, takes up lactate, particularly during intense exercise, demonstrating that lactate is not the negative by-product of metabolism that it is so often labelled; instead, it is actually a mobile fuel appreciated by other tissues.

Lactate is also taken up by the liver. Here, La⁻ is used as a precursor molecule for the eventual conversion to glucose in a process called *gluconeogenesis* ('the formation of new glucose'). The liver then may choose to retain the glucose for storage as glycogen or release it back into the bloodstream for other cells, like exercising muscle cells, to take up and use as a fuel source.

The bad boy turns good

So in truth, lactate is an indispensable intermediary molecule involved in many physiological processes, including a role in maintaining muscle force. In 2000/2001, Professor Graham Lamb's team at La Trobe University in Melbourne first established that lactate accumulation could not be responsible for the decline in force output exhibited by fatigued muscles, and more interestingly, have recently shown that lactate accumulation in fact helps muscle fibres maintain their 'excitability' (that is, the ability to stimulate muscle to contract) and work for longer than they would otherwise be able to in the absence of lactate. This is because the acidosis that accompanies lactate accumulation may block the movement of chloride across muscle fibre membranes – a mechanism that would enhance the excitability of the fibres.

Meanwhile, scientists at Aarhus University in Denmark demonstrated that lactic acidosis may even protect against potential losses in muscle excitability and in force output that can take place due to inevitable potassium escape from exercising muscle fibres. When muscles are stimulated to contract, especially during heavy exercise, potassium exits muscle fibres and progressively builds up outside of the cell. This elevated potassium outside of muscle cells is known to play a role in the onset of fatigue. By using rat muscles placed in chemical solutions that closely mimicked the normal bodily environment, the Danish researchers observed that rising H^+ levels (from lactic acid) in the contracting muscles actually protected against losses in muscle force and excitability that are usually brought on by rising external potassium.

Moving from these single muscle fibre experiments to regular exercise, the Medical School of Hannover in Germany recently reported that an induced acidosis did not negatively affect the contraction speed of muscles involved in handgrip exercise.

Moreover, a Swedish group has shown that some of the experiments that originally implicated acidosis in muscle fatigue (performed at a room temperature of 22 °C) do not hold true when these same trials are performed closer to body temperature (32 °C). Some scientists even suggest that lactate production actually operates to *decrease* muscle acidosis.

The accumulation of lactate in the muscle and blood during exercise may still be a good marker to indicate the onset of fatigue but this in no way declares that lactic acid *causes* muscle fatigue. There is now an overwhelming body of evidence from a myriad of experimental protocols expounding lactate as being not harmful to exercise performance, compared with limited evidence to the contrary; in fact, lactic acid production may even help muscles to work for longer during intense exercise than would occur if it were not present.

THE NEW HEART RATE MAXIMUM

One essential aspect of training sessions is the ability to monitor exercise intensity. This becomes especially important when training to improve endurance capacity by improving both aerobic fitness and resistance to fatigue. From the amateur to the elite level, many people will strap on a heart rate monitor so as to receive constant feedback regarding how hard they are working.

In many training programs, the intensity of each session will have been developed upon consideration of your theoretical maximal heart rate (HR_{max}). This parameter is used for several reasons. Firstly, when exercising at maximal exertion, your heart will also be pumping at its maximum rate in an attempt to supply as much blood flow, and hence oxygen and nutrients, to the working muscles. As such, the relative intensity of each training bout may be based on a percentage of your HR_{max}. Secondly, the ability to easily assess heart rate whilst training by wearing a commercial heart rate monitor provides exercisers of varied experience with accurate and immediate feedback to judge whether they are working too hard, too lightly, or just right.

A formula to make your heart skip a beat

A person's HR_{max} is usually estimated by a well-known predictive equation. The reason for predicting the value is that *direct* assessment of HR_{max} is impractical in most cases. It involves exercising progressively up to maximal exertion, which can be dangerous for some individuals, particularly without medical supervision. Furthermore, professional expertise and expensive equipment is often demanded as part of this accurate method of testing. Therefore, for decades, the following predictive equation has been used for estimating a person's theoretical HR_{max}:

$$HRmax = 220 - age \text{ bpm (beats per minute)}$$

For example, a 20-year-old person would have a theoretical HR_{max} of 200 bpm, whilst a 60-year-old would have a theoretical HR_{max} of 160 bpm. So how is this value used?

The ability to predict a person's theoretical HR_{max} is central to devising a training program to improve aerobic conditioning. One common application occurs following a *submaximal* aerobic exercise test (eg. on a bike), where the heart rate data obtained during the test can be extrapolated to the point of predicted HR_{max}. From this, the person's maximal aerobic fitness may be estimated. HR_{max} is also an important parameter used in other fields of exercise testing and prescription. In clinical settings across all ages, HR_{max} is used as an important basis for the provision of safe yet effective workouts that stress the cardiovascular system enough to produce significant aerobic training effects. Doctors will also use a percentage of the HR_{max} value as threshold for terminating exercise tests on patients when assessing their cardiovascular health. But just how accurate is *220 – age* for predicting the HR_{max}?

Despite this predictive equation becoming dogma in the physiological world, there is no published report that established this equation through rigorous scientific testing. In fact, it appears to have arisen from a limited amount of raw and averaged data – around ten studies in total – that was compiled into a loose *observed* estimation of maximum heart rate back in 1971. These studies also appear not to have included many individuals above 55 years of age, and may not have controlled for smokers or cardiac patients on medication, both of which affect heart rate. When researchers at the University of New Mexico delved into this paper and analysed the data statistically, the equation that surfaced was $HR_{max} = 215 - (0.9 \_ age)$ bpm !

Big Tex vs Big Mig

Lance Armstrong (aka Big Tex) won the Tour de France on seven successive occasions (1999-2005). Not long before that, the Tour was dominated by Miguel Indurain who won on five successive occasions (1991-1995). There is no doubt that both men reaped the benefits of having great teams around them, but their physiological make-up played a major role in filling their wardrobes with yellow jerseys.

An essential quality for any endurance athlete is the ability to efficiently transport oxygen from the air to the exercising muscles, by way of the lungs, heart and blood. Incredibly, at maximal exertion, Indurain's heart could pump near 50 litres of blood per minute! This is twice that of a normal male, and significantly greater than the majority of his Tour rivals. What this means is that with more blood circulating about the body every minute, more oxygen can be delivered to the muscles for energy production.

Perhaps of no surprise is that the amount of oxygen that the muscles of both Indurain and Armstrong actually used when riding at top intensities was very similar. The bigger Mig (weighing 81 kilograms) used 6.4 litres of oxygen per minute whilst Lance (72 kilograms) used 6.1 litres of oxygen per minute. This incredible efficiency for using oxygen was reflected by smaller amounts of lactic acid being produced by Armstrong's muscles – he produced 30-40 per cent less lactate than other professional cyclists when pedalling at maximum power.

When both riders were at peak fitness, their maximum oxygen use per minute translated to about 85-88 millilitres per kilogram of their body weight. Most other Tour riders would likely score in the high 70s to low 80s, whilst amateur male athletes would be near the 55-60 mark.

New formulae are hard to beat

Wading into the debate came a paper in 2001, published in the *Journal of the American College of Cardiology*, by researchers from the University of Colorado. The researchers not only wanted to examine the validity of the 220 – age predictive equation, but they also wanted to examine whether gender and physical activity levels affected HR_{max}. In contrast to the development of the original HR_{max} equation, these researchers reviewed 351 previous research studies, involving 18,712 subjects. The participants in these studies were all healthy, non-smoking, unmedicated adults free of cardiovascular disease. The maximal heart rate data from these studies was all determined *directly* – that is, all participants exercised to maximal effort so that their HR_{max} was actually monitored in the laboratory (not predicted by an equation).

What they found upon accumulating the data from these 351 well-controlled studies was that their analysis did not support the use of the 220 – age equation for predicting HR_{max}. Their findings elucidated a new equation, that of *208 – (0.7 _ age)* bpm. Therefore, our 20-year-old would now have a theoretical HR_{max} of 194 bpm, whereas our 60-year-old would have a HR_{max} of 166 bpm. Upon further analysis, the new findings highlighted that the original equation overestimated HR_{max} in younger individuals and underestimated HR_{max} in people above 40 years of age. Therefore, if you have a training program with workloads or target heart rates devised around the original equation, you may be overworking (if below 40 years old) or underworking (if over 40 years).

The research team did not stop there, though. To validate their new equation of *208 – (0.7 _ age)*, they tested 514 healthy, non-smoking participants of varying fitness levels, aged between 18 and 81 years, to see whether their new theoretical predictive equation stood up under practical conditions. The resulting equation from the practical laboratory testing was virtually identical to the theoretical equation generated from their review of 351 research studies. Of further interest was that age was still an excellent determinant for predicting HR_{max}, whilst gender and habitual physical activity levels had no significant impact on the value.

Subsequently, the researchers at the University of New Mexico pooled data from 30 well-controlled studies to recalculate a predictive equation for HR_{max}. The equation which they derived was similar to that of the researchers above, this time being: HR_{max} = *209 – (0.7 _ age)* bpm.

Evidence since the inception of the 220 – age formula highlights that a great deal of error exists in its use, particularly when testing across the entire population. Unfortunately, because all such equations are only estimating (and not directly testing) HR_{max}, there is always going to be some degree of error when testing individual people. That is, no one equation can accurately suit everybody. Overall, a predictive equation published in 1994 reports the lowest degree of variability across all studies of maximal heart rate. It was derived from testing over 1400 healthy women and men between the ages of 20 and 70 years. The resulting equation is: $HR_{max} = 206 – (0.7 \_ age)$ bpm.

The third, fourth and fifth equations in the table all provide similar estimations of HR_{max} for all age groups. The degree of error inherent in these three equations is likely low enough to provide enough accuracy for the design of training zones. However, if using HR_{max} in the estimation of maximal aerobic power (VO_{2max}) from cycling or walking tests (as often occurs in gyms, fitness clubs and sports teams), the associated error in any equation available in the literature is likely to be too great for the predicted VO_{2max} score to be trusted.

Various formulae for estimating maximal heart rate (HR_{max})					
Author/s	HRmax formula	16 years	25 years	45 years	60 years
Fox et al. (1971)	220 – age bpm	204 bpm	195 bpm	175 bpm	160 bpm
*Robinson (1938)	212 – (0.77 _ age) bpm	200 bpm	193 bpm	177 bpm	166 bpm
Inbar et al. (1994)	206 – (0.7 _ age) bpm	195 bpm	188 bpm	175 bpm	164 bpm
Tanaka et al. (2001)	208 – (0.7 _ age) bpm	197 bpm	190 bpm	177 bpm	166 bpm
Robergs & Landwehr(2002)	209 – (0.7 _ age) bpm	198 bpm	191 bpm	178 bpm	169 bpm

*Cited in Robergs & Landwehr (2002).

Did You Know?

The average number of heartbeats for a
human in a lifetime is 2.5 billion.

TOUR DE FRANCE: A MEASURE
OF TRUE INTENSITY

The Tour de France is a physiological battle that has the capacity to reveal much about human endurance. But despite the Tour's century-long history, science has kept its distance. Only in the last few years have research papers emerged in the sports science literature that focus on the demands of cycling's most-famed event.

These days, the Tour de France usually covers between 3500–4000 kilometres, meaning that the riders will again spend close to 100 hours in the saddle. Since the introduction of modern cycling equipment some twenty years ago, the average speed over the race's 21 days of pedalling sits around 39 km/h. However, on the flat, speeds are much greater. For example, in 2000, Lance Armstrong completed a 58.5-km time trial with an average speed of 53.99 km/h. At a glance, these numbers clearly demonstrate that professional road cyclists perform their jobs at immense intensities.

But now, with most riders donning a heart rate monitor on race day, a more accurate chart of their work rate is now available. Despite some limitations, heart rate responses can function as a valid indicator of exercise intensity – that is, the greater the heart rate, the harder the body is working.

In 1997, researchers used data obtained in the lab as an indicator of the work intensities performed by Tour riders during the actual three-week event. Intensities were divided into three zones. Zone 1 was termed 'light intensity', where heart rate values stayed below those observed at an exercise intensity of 70 per cent of the cyclist's maximal aerobic power (also known as VO_{2max}). Zone 2 was termed 'moderate intensity', where heart rate responses hovered between those occurring at work rates of 70 per cent to 90 per cent VO_{2max}. And zone 3 referred to 'high intensity' cycling, where heart rates neared levels seen at near maximal efforts (work rates above 90 per cent VO_{2max}).

When this technique was applied to the race itself, the relative time spent in zones 1, 2 and 3 was 70 per cent, 23 per cent and 7 per cent, respectively. These results suggested that riders were coasting most of the time! In flat stages where the 200-strong peloton remains largely intact, much of a rider's time is spent within the massive rolling group, thereby being shielded from the greatest impairment to forward motion – air resistance. This can reduce the energy requirements (and hence, exercise intensity) for a given speed by as much as 40 per cent.

However, in a time trial setting where riders approach and exceed average speeds of 50 km/h on the open road, air resistance accounts for over 90 per cent of the overall slowing force. This combination of high speed and high resistance demands that cyclists spend a great proportion of their time in zone 3. The winner of the 65-kilometre time trial in 1997 spent 75 consecutive minutes at intensities above 90 per cent VO_{2mzx}. It is little wonder that time trial specialists like LeMond, Indurain, Ulrich and Armstrong have accepted the yellow jersey in Paris on 13 of the last 15 occasions.

Five-plus time winners of the Tour de France		
Rider	Country	Years
Jacques Anquetil	France	1957, 1961-1964
Eddy Merckx	Belgium	1969-1972, 1974
Bernard Hinault	France	1978, 1979, 1981, 1982, 1985
Miguel Indurain	Spain	1991-1995
Lance Armstrong	USA	1999-2005

BREAKING AWAY WITH MATHEMATICAL MEASUREMENT

The mathematical modelling of cycling has also been used to examine those components thought to influence the success of a 'breakaway' group of riders as they chance their arm and take off ahead of the main racing group. When the peloton allows a breakaway group to ride off, they must be very wary of the distance that opens up before they must start working together to reel the breakaway back in. The dynamics of the chasing group and that of the group breaking away both impact on the success or failure of road cycling's version of cat-and-mouse.

Research conducted at the University of South Australia mathematically modelled a breakaway group of five riders being chased by a 10-rider peloton over 20 kilometres of flat terrain. To make the calculations easier, it was assumed that all the riders had similar aerobic fitness levels. Then, by altering the number of riders in each group, the spacing of the riders within the group for aerodynamic purposes, and the terrain at which the chase is undertaken, the likelihood of a successful breakaway could be better understood.

Firstly, and not surprisingly, the larger the number of riders in the breakaway, the smaller the lead that is needed to hold off the peloton. Conversely, the bigger the peloton, the larger the lead that the breakaway group requires for success. This has much to do with the sharing of the workload during the ride and, more importantly, the reductions in air resistance of a bigger group.

With respect to the aerodynamics of the group, the wheel spacing between successive riders impacts greatly on the breakaway's success. In fact, the closer that cyclists sit behind each other, the smaller the breakaway lead needed to hold off the chase. The arrangement of the riders can also alter the drag effects on the group. One study reported that a cyclist sitting directly behind the lead rider has a 44 per cent reduction in drag, whereas a cyclist drafting in a lateral position will have drag reductions of 0–30 per cent, depending on the angle at which they sit off the hip of the lead rider.

And a breakaway has its best chance to finish ahead of the main group if the riders undertake it in the hills and mountains during an ascent. This once again has its basis in the drag experienced by the smaller breakaway group. The pace generated when pushing up the slopes is slower and therefore air resistance will have a lesser effect on hindering the progress of the breakaway.

It follows that the critical lead a breakaway requires for a successful challenge is determined mainly by the chasing group's ability to reduce the overall air resistance compared to the group out in front. When air resistance plays a greater role in the day's racing, such as with headwinds or with high speeds during a mountain descent, the more risky is a breakaway attempt. However, a larger breakaway group, a tighter formation, and an uphill battle, together with still air conditions and a slower race pace, all act to lower the relative importance of air resistance, thereby giving the brave front-runners more chance of success.

THE EVOLUTION OF TRAINING
AND COACHING: SO MUCH FOR
THE GOOD OLD DAYS

While the evolution of athletic technique and playing equipment is obvious to the naked eye, more subtle, but equally influential in how the game is played, are changes in the training, injury management and coaching approaches employed. The evolution of 100 years of Australian Rules football provides an excellent case study to illustrate how approaches to training and performance have changed.

In the early 1890s, players who were holding full-time jobs were struggling to combine work and football. This limited their training to gym work, with little emphasis on ball skills and teamwork. Fitzroy Football Club's first premiership in 1895 was attributed to its rigorous training program; they also had appointed specialist trainers around the same time. Similarly, Geelong Football Club was considered a pioneer of innovative training approaches. As highlighted by football historian Robin Grow, it was reported in the *Australasian* on 20 July 1895 that 'for a couple of hours each Tuesday and Thursday the players could be seen "running round and round the ground...like so many lunatics, kicking and knocking the ball to one another whilst they run"', after which they had their 'muscles, tendons and joints massaged'. Seemingly, not much has changed!

The old days

100 x 100s
Philosophy: More-or-less a 'survival of the fittest' test, the challenge being as much about the physical as about the mental.

Modern Wisdom: The completion of one hundred 100-metre sprints has little relevance to the physical demands of a football game and has greater potential to disrupt the pre-season conditioning of the players than facilitate performance.

Don't bring the balls out before Christmas
Philosophy: Ensure that a quality fitness regimen is completed for the establishment of a solid fitness base in all players.

Modern Wisdom: Numerous studies are now revealing that basic fitness characteristics can be developed equally as well by performing game-based training involving football skills. Ironically, most players also say that they work harder when a ball is involved in training drills.

No drinking of fluids during training

Philosophy: Like the '100 x 100s', this rule likely stemmed from the idea that doing it tough at training would make the demands of match day easier.

Modern Wisdom: Again, there is little science to back up the rationale. Modern wisdom tells that regular, regimented fluid intake is essential for optimal performance.

One size fits all

Philosophy: If you train as a team, you'll play as a team. Therefore, from ruckman to rover, all players underwent the same training program.

Modern Wisdom: This approach could never maximise player and team potential because positional demands differ, players vary in their strengths and weaknesses, and those carrying injuries are not capable of performing all drills.

The modern era

Bring in the athletics trainers

Trainers from the world of athletics are now called upon during preseason to focus on speed/endurance qualities with an emphasis on improving running technique (akin to a sprinter). The idea is that players will improve their movement efficiency and economy. However, the motions required by the game don't necessarily mean that players need to run like sprinters.

Individualised programs

Senior players and those who have played most games throughout the season are given lower training loads in order to maximise recovery and avoid accumulated fatigue. Young recruits, too, often undertake a lower training stress to provide them the opportunity over time to adapt to the demands of the professional game.

Players who regularly work off the bench or those who have had

> ### The old one-tutu
>
> The Tranmere Rovers' fitness coach has in the past had his team practise their moves with ballet dancers. He has now taken it one step further and got the team to wear tutus during practice. He said, 'I showed them how the bits should best be worn and, to be honest, they've all been very open to the idea. They're interested in new ways and ideas and will try anything that helps them.'

interrupted seasons due to injury will do more on the track with the objective of maintaining match fitness. The dropping of regular bench players to the secondary competitions such as the VFL, SANFL or WAFL is also a method of developing match fitness, as well as instilling confidence.

Refined measurement/recording of player performance

State-of-the-art techniques for assessing the work output of players during training sessions have allowed fitness advisers to quantify training loads to the kilometre. For example, it is rare to see a player in preseason without a heart rate monitor. Training volumes and intensities have increased as a result. The advent of player tracking during games has meant that conditioning coaches now better understand the positional demands and the distances and intensities covered out on the ground. For example, in the 2003 AFL season the West Coast Eagles used a tracking program called *TrakPerformance* to monitor the movements of three of their players over 10 games. Data collated from such an exercise included:

- total distance run (per game and quarter)
- total distance run at high intensities (per game and quarter)
- percentage of high-intensity running distance to total distance
- contests (player within 2 metres of the ball) and possessions
- the number of unrewarded runs.

Similarly, training sessions can also be tracked to determine how closely they match the demands of competition. For example, the following data was used to establish what the different demands were for each training drill in a session:

- work-to-rest ratio
- distance run per minute
- the number of high-intensity running bursts per minute
- possessions per minute
- the effect of drill distance and player numbers on work rate in a drill
- the effect of player position in a drill (looking at work rate).

Developments continue to occur in player tracking, with many clubs now using Global Positioning System (GPS) technology to monitor player work rates.

Tapering

Professor Frank Cotton (see page 175) was definitely on to something when he coined the term 'tapering'. All athletes now taper their training when approaching a major competition in an attempt to achieve peak performance. This *taper* period involves decreasing the *volume* of training, increasing rest/recovery, ensuring appropriate nutrition, and importantly, maintaining the *intensity* of training segments. Tapering is standard practice in sports like running, swimming and cycling where major events happen only a few times a year. Two to three days is usually needed to maximise carbohydrate stores in the body, whilst a week-long taper is often adequate for overcoming the minor damage and soreness that *normally* accompanies heavy training. Consequently,

Game-day preparation

A recent poll asked 3000 men about their superstitions when it came to watching football. The survey found that over a third of male football fans avoid sex the night before a big match. It also found 45 per cent wear a lucky shirt, and 4 per cent don't wash it if there has been a win. One man was even planning on wearing the same underpants for the duration of the World Cup. A further 10 per cent said they would eat the same breakfast every day. Other superstitions included not speaking to anyone the day of the game, and watching the TV with the volume down.

most athletes tend to taper for a week to ten days. However, in team sports like football, where big games are a weekly proposition and ladder position is vital, the optimal length and style of the taper is a challenge for any coaching staff. As such, season-long training schedules differ greatly from club to club.

Programmed recovery (post-game and post-training)

The ability of modern players to complete greater total training loads has much to do with the inception of immediate, programmed recovery. *Recovery* is a basic training principle adhered to by all professional clubs. The objective of its strategic programming is to schedule adequate time for players to both adapt to and recover from a training stimulus. Physiological recovery includes: (1) the adaptation of muscle and the physiological systems to new training stresses; (2) the regeneration of damaged tissue (a *normal* part of the adaptation process); and (3) fuel replacement (fluid, carbohydrate, protein). Skill-learning and psychological recovery/adaptation also takes place. These days, recovery is thought of as being as important as the training itself.

Ice baths, massage, hot showers alternated with cold baths, active recovery (such as swimming, light jogging, cycling) and passive rest are some of the more popular techniques used to enhance the rate of recovery. Players are also directed towards appropriate fluid (for example, water and sports drinks) and food consumption (carbohydrate replenishment via sports drinks and high glycaemic index foods) to replenish lost energy stores as rapidly as possible. After the initial 1–2 hours post-game/training, low glycaemic index foods become the preferred form of carbohydrate, whilst sufficient protein intake is readily monitored. In sum, programmed recovery translates to players engaging in more training sooner.

Recovery does not only entail the immediate post-game and post-training protocols aimed at resting, replenishing and regenerating. The philosophy of recovery also involves the inclusion of specifically designed training phases of low volume and intensity, 'built in' to a season-long regimen to help players avoid accumulated fatigue.

Japanese idol

In preparation for the 1992 Olympics, Japanese marksman Rhyohei Kobe not only gave up drinking, but also karaoke singing – he won the bronze medal.

Ball tracking

Chilean artist Antonio Becerro has persuaded
Colo Colo football player Francisco Huaiquipan to
help him with an art exhibition with a difference.
Antonio will defend penalty shots from Francisco,
the ball will be covered in paint and the goals will
be a white canvas.

Video analysis and review

In the early 1970s, Ron Barassi became the first Australian Rules coach
to use video sessions to assist in the preparation of his players. Now in
the twenty-first century, a typical football coaching panel will contain
at least one performance analyst responsible for integrating broadcast
vision from the game, with coding software that allows any facets of a
match to be labelled in real time. This process then allows coaches to
immediately retrieve any moment from a game they wish to review, and
similarly, provide a customised 'highlights package' of an individual
player's possessions. Additionally, sports statistics companies such as
Champion Data in Melbourne provide all manner of statistics to AFL
clubs on a weekly basis, with matched vision of the game events.

Sports medicine innovations used by the Brisbane Lions

- Use of intravenous drips to replenish fluids at half-time (subsequently banned by the AFL)
- Hypoxicators to simulate training in an oxygen-deprived environment
- The chartered flight that transported the team to Melbourne for the 2003 Grand Final travelled at lower than normal altitudes to reduce cabin pressure
- Use of a coolroom at the 2001 Grand Final and a mobile refrigerated van at the Gabba
- Hyperbaric chamber available at the club for injury recovery

UPDATE FROM THE LAB: TO STAY ON TOP, STAY ON THE PARK

In *Run Like You Stole Something*, we included a full chapter on injuries in sport. Here we provide an update to that work, relaying some interesting new sidelines to the field of sports injury management.

Football historian Robin Grow reported that back in the early days, the major causes of injury were rough play and leg injuries due to players slipping on the grass (some things never change). Boot spikes caused lacerations to players' hands and legs, and lace-up guernseys caused serious finger injuries when opponents' fingers became caught in the lacework. The risk of life-threatening infection from tetanus or rheumatic fever was also present.

One hundred years on, it's still a long-held belief that injuries can make or break a team's season, particularly in the football codes where aggressive physical contact is a major ingredient. Recently, a unique study examined the relationship between injuries and team performance across an entire elite sporting season. The records of all injuries and the days spent on the disabled list for each player in 17 of the top 20 teams in the two highest levels of Icelandic soccer were examined.

The study reported a relationship between the total number of days players spent injured per team and the team's final ladder position. What surfaced was that the teams that finished in the top four positions in both the elite and first division leagues, in general, had fewer injury days across the season. This trend was most significant in the elite league.

This finding carries more weight when considering that the researchers also reported that, overall, fitness differences between clubs (often assumed to be strongly correlated with team success) had no effect on the final league standings.

One practical implication of this work is that injury prevention is a key to, and a potential strong predictor of, a team's success. Intuitively, perhaps this is nothing

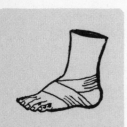

Loose aim
American marksman Sidney Hinds shot a perfect 50 at the 1924 Olympics despite being injured part-way through the event – he was shot in the foot when another competitor dropped his rifle during an argument with officials.

new, but at least now there is scientific evidence to substantiate such claims. So what can clubs do to limit the havoc that injuries may wreak on their upcoming season?

A great deal of research suggests that the number one predictor of injury is fitness level (that is, lower fitness, greater chance of injury). However, at the elite level, most players will be at or near peak fitness. Therefore, for professional athletes, previous injury has been suggested as the most significant risk factor for injury. So, expect recurrent injuries to take their toll if adequate rehabilitation is not addressed prior to putting players back on the ground.

A study that assessed injury risk in English Premier League soccer matches reported that the first and last 15 minutes of a game were most dangerous for players; the first 15 minutes contain the most vigorous intensity of play whilst in the latter stages of a game players are competing under the stress of fatigue. The greatest number of actions with a high risk of injury also occurred in the attacking/defending zones of the ground – in the vicinity of the goals – where players' desperation to score or defend was reflected in a higher number of tackles and physical contact.

Although the idea of a life as a professional athlete seems appealing, the occupational health and safety risks may convince you otherwise. The risk of acute injury in professional soccer, for example, has been reported to be three times higher than in industries such as construction and manufacturing.

A game that could cost you your head

A game played in Scotland, which has Viking origins, has been scrutinised for being too rough. The inhabitants of Kirkwall on Scotland's north coast have been celebrating the New Year for thousands of years with the game commonly known as 'Ba'; a game that originated when there were mad scrambles for the severed head of an enemy warrior. A leathery ball has now replaced the head. The players still get cracked ribs, dislocated fingers and broken noses when the two 200-member teams chase the ball down Kirkwall's stone streets.

ENDNOTES

CHAPTER 1:
THEY DON'T PLAY LIKE THEY USED TO

Anderson, I. (1996). Let's go surfin'. *New Scientist,* 27 July, 26–27.

Asai, T., Akatsuka, T., & Haake, S. (1998). The physics of football. *Physics World,* June, 25–27.

Australian Football League. (1996). *100 Years of Australian Football.* Penguin Books.

Baker, J. & Ball, K. (1993). *Technique Considerations of the Drop Punt.* Research report to the Australian Sports Commission.

Barilotti, S. (2003). Pounds per square inch. *Surfer Magazine,* Vol. 43(9).

Black, K. (2000). Department of Earth Sciences, University of Waikato, New Zealand. 3RRR-FM Radio, 15 April.

Blount Jr, R. (1969). Being backward gets results. *Sports Illustrated.*

Brasch, R. (1995). *How Did Sports Begin?* Angus & Robertson.

Bunyan, N. (2000). *Computer hits on the secret of Bradman's style.* 27 April. Telegraph Group Ltd, London.

Dapena, J. (2000). The high jump (Chap. 14) In: Zatsiorsky, V.M. (ed.), *Biomechanics in Sport: Performance Enhancement and Injury Prevention.* (Volume IX of the Encyclopaedia of Sports Medicine). Blackwell Sciences, Oxford.

de Mestre, N. *The Mathematics and Physics of Body Surfing.* Bond University research report. <http://www.bond.edu.au/it/staff/neville.html>

Dennis, R. (2003). Australian Cricket Board National Fast Bowling Workload and Injury Study 2000–2002. In: Stretch, R.A. (ed.), *Second World Congress of Science and Medicine in Cricket,* Cape Town, 81–82.

Doherty, K. (1980) *Track and Field Omnibook (3rd edn).* Tafnews Press, Los Altos, CA.

Elliott, B.C. (2000). Back injuries and the fast bowler in cricket. *Journal of Sports Sciences,* 18, 983–991.

Foster, D., John, D., Elliott, B.C., Ackland, T., & Fitch, K. (1989). Back injuries to fast bowlers in cricket: A prospective study. *British Journal of Sports Medicine*, 23, 150–154.

Happell, C. (1999). Famous roosts in Australian football history. *The Age*.

Hay, J.G. (1993). *The Biomechanics of Sports Techniques (4th edn)*. Prentice-Hall.

Hess, R., & Stewart, B. (1998). *More Than a Game*. Melbourne University Press, Melbourne.

Jackson, R.C. (2003). Pre-performance routine consistency: temporal analysis of goal kicking in the Rugby Union World Cup. *Journal of Sports Sciences*, 21(10), 803–814.

Komi, P.V., & Virmavirta, M. (2000). Determinants of successful ski-jumping performance (Chap. 17). In: Zatsiorsky, V.M. (ed.), *Biomechanics in Sport: Performance Enhancement and Injury Prevention*. (Volume IX of the Encyclopaedia of Sports Medicine). Blackwell Sciences, Oxford.

Lawson, G. (1997). *World Record Breakers in Track & Field Athletics*. Human Kinetics, Champaign, IL.

Lyttle. Start Right – a biomechanical review of dive start performance.

Marcus, B. From Polynesia, with love. The history of surfing from Captain Cook to present.

Mehta, R.B. (1985). Aerodynamics of sports balls. *Annual Review of Fluid Mechanics*, 17, 151–189.

Orchard, J. & James, T. (2003). *Cricket Australia Injury Report 2003*. October.

Orchard, J., James, T., Alcott, E., Carter, S., & Farhart, P. (2002). Injuries in Australian cricket at first class level 1995/96 to 2000/01. *British Journal of Sports Medicine*, 36, 270–275.

Parkin, D., Smith, R., & Schokman, P. (1984). *Premiership Football*. Hargreen Publishing.

Pruett, M. & Towery, C. (2002). Technology of the now. *Eastern Surf Magazine*, May.

Rath, D. (2000). *Biomechanics of kicking*. Research report to the Australian Sports Commission.

Sloan, S. The evolution of the surfboard.
<http://www.blackmagic.com/ses/surf/papers/boardessy.html>

Surfing for Life. <http://www.surfingforlife.com/history.html>

Thornley, M. & Dante, V. (1998). *Surfing Australia*. Periplus Editions.

Wallechinsky, D. (2001). *The Complete Book of the Winter Olympics (2002 Edition)*. The Overlook Press, Woodstock.

Wallechinsky, D. (2004). *The Complete Book of the Olympics (2004 Edition)*. Aurum Press, London.

Wikipedia: The Free Encyclopaedia. <http://en.wikipedia.org/wiki/High_jump>

Wulf, G., McNevin, N.H., Fuchs, T., Rittner, F., & Toole, T. (2000). Attentional focus in complex skill learning. *Research Quarterly for Exercise in Sport*, 71(3), 229–239.

CHAPTER 2:
NEW BALLS PLEASE

Adair, Robert. (1990) *The Physics of Baseball*. HarperCollins, New York

Arthur, C. (1992). Anyone for slower tennis? *New Scientist*, 2 May, 24–28.

Bahill, T., & Karnavas, W. (1991). The ideal baseball bat. *New Scientist*, 6 April, 24–29.

Bartonietz, K. (2000). Javelin throwing: an approach to performance development (Chap. 20). In: Zatsiorsky, V.M. (ed.), *Biomechanics In Sport: Performance Enhancement and Injury Prevention*. (Volume IX of the Encyclopaedia of Sports Medicine). Blackwell Sciences, Oxford.

BBC Beyond The Broadcast. (2005). Making history: Overarm bowling. BBC Home. <http://www.bbc.co.uk/education/beyond/factsheets/makhist/makhist8_prog5b.shtm l> (January).

Blackwell, J. & Knudson, D. (2002). Effect of Type 3 (Oversize) tennis ball on serve performance and upper extremity muscle activity. *Sports Biomechanics*, 1(2), 187–191.

Brancazio, P. J. (1983). *Sportscience*. Simon & Schuster, New York.

Brasch, R. (1995). *How Did Sports Begin?* Angus & Robertson.

Briggs, L.J. (1959). Effect of spin and speed on the lateral deflection (curve) of a baseball; and the Magnus effect for smooth spheres. *American Journal of Physics*, 27, 589–596.

Brody, H. (1990). Models of baseball bats. *American Journal of Physics*, 58(8), 756–758.

Brody, H. Racquet technology and tennis strokes. Coaches' infoservice: Sports science information for coaches. <http://coachesinfo.com/>

Cassidy, J. (1989). *The Aerobie Book: An inquiry into the world's ultimate flying mini-machine*. Klutz Press, Palo Alto, CA.

Cooper, J. An evolutionary history of tennis racquets. <http://tennis.about.com/od/racqetsballsstringing/a/evolmodracquet.htm>

Cropper, G., Simpson, E., Burton, A., & Hornby, P. (). *The Giant Book of Fantastic Facts*. Peter Haddock Ltd, Beidington, Eng.

Davies, J.M. (1949). The aerodynamics of golf balls. *Journal of Applied Physics*, 20(9), 821–828.

Doherty, K. (1980). *Track and Field Omnibook (3rd Edition)*. Tafnews Press, Los Altos, CA.

Elliott, B.C., Alderson, J., Reid, S., & Foster, D. (2004). Bowling report on Muttiah Muralitharan. *Research Report to the Sri Lankan Cricket Board*. <http://www1.cricket.indiatimes.com/articleshow/685040.cms>

Fischetti, M. (2001). Flight control. *Scientific American*, 284(6), 80–81.

Fox, D. (2003). Lethal impact. *New Scientist*, 179 (2410), 38–39.

Gelberg, J.N. (1998). Tradition, talent, and technology: The ambiguous relationship between sports and innovation. In: Busch, A. (ed.), *Design for Sport*. Princeton Architectural Press, New York.

Greenman, C. (2001). A tennis umpire that never blinks. *The New York Times*, August 31.

Hammond, T. (1988). *Collins Eyewitness Guides: Sport*. Collins Publishers Australia.

Happell, C. (2001). Great balls of fire. *The Age* (Sports), 28 March, 6.

Hecht, J. (2000). Livelier balls are flying further. *New Scientist*, 168(2264), 28.

Hummel, S. (1997). Frisbee flight simulation and throw biomechanics. Master's thesis, University of Missouri.

Hummel, S.A. & Hubbard, M. (2001). A musculoskeletal model for backhand Frisbee throws. *8th International Symposium on Computer Simulation in Biomechanics*. Politecnico di Milano, Milan, Italy, 5–6 July.

Jarichar. History of biomechanics and kinesiology. <http://www.usd.edu/~jarichar/HIST.html>

Martin, B.R. (1999). A genealogy of biomechanics. *Presidential lecture presented at the 23rd Annual Conference of the American Society of Biomechanics*, University of Pittsburgh.

Lawson, G. (1997). *World Record Breakers in Track & Field Athletics*. Human Kinetics, Champaign, IL.

Llewelyn Nichols, R. (2002). Danger at the plate. *Campus Review,* 12(34), 12–13.

Maskin, A. (2004). A hole in what? Understanding golf technology. *Harvard Science Review*, February.

Mehta, R.B. (1985). Aerodynamics of sports balls. *Annual Review of Fluid Mechanics*, 17, 151–189.

Mehta, R.B., & Pallis, J.M. (2001). Sports balls aerodynamics: effects of velocity, spin and surface roughness. In: Froes, F.H., & Haake, S.J. (eds), *Materials and Science in Sports*. The Minerals, Metals & Materials Society, Warrendale, PA, 185–197.

Miah, A. (2000). 'New balls please': Tennis, technology, and the changing game. In: Haake, S., and Coe, A.O. (eds), *Tennis Science and Technology*. Blackwell Science, London, 285–292.

National Institute of Standards and Technology. (2001). A real corker. <http://www.100.nist.gov/battampering.htm> (May).

O'Donoghue, P., & Ingram, B. (2001). A notational analysis of elite tennis strategy. *Journal of Sports Sciences*, 19, 107–115.

O'Donoghue, P., & Liddle, S.D. (1998). A notational analysis of time factors of elite men's and ladies singles tennis on clay and grass surfaces. In: Lees, A., Maynard, I., Hughes, M., & Reilly, T. (eds), *Science and Racket Sports II*. E & FN Spon, London, 247–253.

Pallis, J.M., Mehta, R., Pandya, S., Roetert, P., Lutz, A., Knudson, D. & Brody, H. (1997–2000). *Tennis aerodynamics*. <http://wings.avkids.com/Tennis/Project/index.html>

Roberts, M. (2004). About technology, Bruce Elliott & the doosra. Is technology misleading? <http://www.cricket-online.org/news.php?sid=4044>

Sawicki, G.S., Hubbard, M., & Stronge, W.J. (2003). How to hit home runs:

Optimum baseball bat swing parameters for maximum range trajectories. *American Journal of Physics,* 71, 1152–1162.

Stewart, I. (1997). Crystallography of a golf ball. *Scientific American*, February, 96–97.

Wallechinsky, D. (2004). *The Complete Book of the Olympics (2004 Edition).* Aurum Press, London.

CHAPTER 3:
EQUIPPED FOR SUCCESS

Allinger, T. (1998). Clapskates at Nagano: World records tumble in speed sprinting. *Sportscience*, 2, <http://www.sportsci.org/news/news9803/clapnagano.html> (Mar–Apr).

Bassett, D.R., Kyle, C.R., Passfield, L., Broker, J.P., & Burke, E.R. (1999). Comparing cycling world hour records, 1967–1996: modeling with empirical data. *Medicine and Science in Sports and Exercise,* 31(11), 1665–1676.

Brasch, R. (1995). *How did sports begin?* Angus & Robertson.

Brearley, M.B., & Finn, J.P. (2003). Pre-cooling for performance in the tropics. *Sportscience,* 7. <http://sportsci.org/> (December).

Clapp, A.J., & Bishop, P.A. (1996). Effect of the Breathe Right external nasal dilator during light to moderate exercise. *Medicine and Science in Sports and Exercise*, 28(5), S88.

De Koning, J.J. (1997). Background to the slapskate: Fifteen years of slapskate history, biomechanical backgrounds, first results and recent developments (Slapskate Extra). *Sportscience*, 1. <http://www.sportsci.org/news/news9703/slapxtra.htm> (Mar–Apr).

De Lucas, R.D., Balikian, P., Neiva, C.M., Greco, C.C., & Denadai, B.S. (2000). The effects of wetsuits on physiological and biomechanical indices during swimming. *Journal of Science and Medicine in Sport*, 3(1), 1–8.

di Prampero, P.E. (2000). Cycling on Earth, in space, on the moon. *European Journal of Applied Physiology*, 82, 345–360.

Doherty, K. (1980). *Track and Field Omnibook (3rd Edition).* Tafnews Press, Los Altos, CA.

Duffield, R., Dawson, B., Bishop, D., Fitzsimons, M., & Lawrence, S. (2003). Effect of wearing an ice cooling jacket on repeat sprint performance in warm/humid conditions. *British Journal of Sports Medicine*, 37, 164–169.

Faria, E.W., Foster, C., & Faria, I.E. (2000). Effect of exercise and nasal splinting on static and dynamic measures of nasal airflow. *Journal of Sports Sciences*, 18, 255–261.

Formula One Administration (2004). Understanding the sport. *The Official Formula 1 Website.* <http://www.formula1.com/> (December).

Garside, I., & Doran, D.A. (2000). Effects of bicycle frame ergonomics on triathlon 10-km running performance. *Journal of Sports Sciences*, 18, 825–833.

Gregor, R.J., Conconi, F., & Broker, J.P. (2000). Biomechanics of Road Cycling. In: Gregor, R.J., & Conconi, F. (eds), *Road Cycling*. Blackwell Science, Oxford, 18–39.

Hatfield, F.C. (1997). Breathe Right nasal strips: Not for most athletes. *Sportscience*, 1. <http://sportsci.org/> (March).

Huffman, M.S., Huffman, M.T., Brown, D.D., Quindry, J.C., & Thomas, D.Q. (1996). Exercise responses using the Breathe Right external nasal dilator. *Medicine and Science in Sports and Exercise*, 28(5), S70.

Ingen Schenau, G.J. Van, De Groot, G., Scheurs, A.W., & De Koning, J.J. (1996). A new skate allowing powerful plantar flexions improves performance. *Medicine and Science in Sports and Exercise*, 28, 531–535.

Jeukendrup, A.E., & Martin, J. (2001). Improving cycling performance: how should we spend our time and money. *Sports Medicine*, 31, 559–569.

Kruszelnicki, K. (2004). Rocket science and brain power. *The Age,* 4 March, Drive, 8–9.

Lane, T. (1996). Push to the limit. *The Australian Way*, November, 84–87.

Lawson, G. (1997). *World Record Breakers in Track & Field Athletics*. Human Kinetics, Champaign, IL.

Lloyd's Register Marine Services. (2005). The history of international yachting and the America's Cup. *Lloyd's Register.* <http://www.lr.org/services_overview/shipping_information/is005america_cup.htm#rules> (January).

Lowdon, B.J., McKenzie, D., & Ridge, B.R. (1992). Effects of clothing and water temperature on swim performance. *Australian Journal of Science and Medicine in Sport*, 24(2), 33–38.

Lunt, G. (2005). From Windcheetah to Superbike. *Welcome to ChrisBoardman.com*. <http://www.chrisboardman.com/> (January).

Mackenzie, D. (2004). The speed freaks of Battle Mountain. *New Scientist*, 184 (2476), 36-41.

Manishin, G.B. (2004) Formula One history. *Formula One: Art & Genius*. <http://www.f1-grandprix.com/> (March).

Marks, A. (1987). *Quest for the Cup: The America's Cup Challenges 1851–1987*. Australian Broadcasting Corporation, Sydney.

Martin, D.T., Hahn, A.G., Ryan-Tanner, R., Yates, K., Lee, H., & Smith, J.A. (1998). Ice jackets are cool. *Sportscience*, 2. <http://sportsci.org/> (December).

Millet, G.P., Millet, G.Y., & Candau, R.B. (2001). Duration and seriousness of running mechanics alterations after maximal cycling in triathletes. *Journal of Sports Medicine and Physical Fitness*, 41, 147–153.

Minetti, A.E., Pinkerton, J., & Zamparo, P. (2001). From bipedalism to bicyclism: evolution in energetics and biomechanics of historic bicycles. *Proceedings of the Royal Society (London)*, B268, 1351–1360.

Olds, T. (2001). Modelling human locomotion: applications to cycling. *Sports Medicine*, 31, 497–509.

Olds, T., Norton, K., & Craig, N. (1996). *Optimising cycling performance.*

Australian Sports Commission, Canberra, 1–16.

Padilla, S., Mujika, I., Angulo, F., & Goiriena, J.J. (2000). Scientific approach to the 1-h cycling world record: a case study. *Journal of Applied Physiology*, 89,1522–1527.

Paine, L.P. (1997). *Ships of the World: An Historical Encyclopedia*. Houghton Mifflin, New York, 47–48.

Papanek, P.E., Young, C.C., Kellner, N.A., Lachacz, J.G., & Sprado, A. (1996). The effects of an external nasal dilator (Breathe-Right) on anaerobic sprint performance. *Medicine and Science in Sports and Exercise*, 28(5), S182.

Quindry, J.C., Brown, D.D., Huffman, M.S., Huffman, M.T., & Thomas, D.Q. (1996). Exercise recovery responses using the Breathe Right nasal dilator. *Medicine and Science in Sports and Exercise*, 28(5), S70.

Rushall, B. (2001). Why flotation bodysuits are unfair. *Swimming Science Journal*, 27 March. <http://www-rohan.sdsu.edu/dept/coachsci/swimming/bodysuit/unfair.htm>

Rushall, B.S. (2000). The serious threat to the very nature of competitive swimming or not? *Swimming Science Journal*, 26 April.

<http://www-rohan.sdsu.edu/dept/coachsci/swimming/index.htm>

Ryan, M. (2004). View from the driver's seat. *The Sunday Age*, 7 March, Sport, 13.

Sanders, R., Rushall, B., Toussaint, H., Stager, J., & Takagi, H. (2001). Bodysuit yourself: But first think about it. *Swimming Science Journal*, 24 April.

<http://www-rohan.sdsu.edu/dept/coachsci/swimming/bodysuit/fiveauth.htm>

Sargeant, A.J., & Jones, D.A. (1995). The significance of motor unit variability in sustaining mechanical output of muscle (Chap. 24). In: Gandevia, S.C. (ed.), *Fatigue*. Plenum Press, New York.

Seiler, S. (1997). The new Dutch 'slapskates': Will they revolutionize speed skating technique? *Sportscience*, 1, (Mar–Apr).
<http://www.sportsci.org/news/9703/slapskat.htm.>

Sharp, R.L., & Costill, D.L. Shaving a little time. *Medicine and Science in Sports and Exercise*, 22(5), 576–580.

Slooff, J.W. (1984). On wings and keels. *International Shipbuilding Progress*, 31 (357), 94–104.

Spadaccini, J. (2005). Science of cycling. *The Exploratorium*.
<http://www.exploratorium.edu/cycling/> (January).

Toussaint, H.M., Truijens, M., Elzinga, M.J., van de Ven, A., de Best, H., Snabel, B., & de Groot, G. (2002). Effect of a Fast-skin 'body' suit on drag during front crawl swimming. *Sports Biomechanics*, 1, 1–10.

Van Manen, J. D., & Rijken, H. (1975). Dynamic measurement techniques on swimming bodies at the Netherlands Ship Model Basin. In: Lewillie, L., & Clarys, J.P. (eds), *Swimming II*. University Park Press, Baltimore, 70–77.

Wallechinsky, D. (2001) *The Complete Book of the Winter Olympics (2002 Edition)*. The Overlook Press, Woodstock.

Wallechinsky, D. (2004). *The Complete Book of the Olympics (2004 Edition)*. Aurum Press, London.

White, M.D., & Cabanac, M. (1995). Physical dilatation of the nostrils lowers the thermal strain of exercising humans. *European Journal of Applied Physiology*, 70, 200–206.

Wright, P. (2001). *Formula 1 Technology*. Society of Automotive Engineers, Warrendale, PA.

CHAPTER 4:
THE TALE OF THE TAPE

Ainsworth, C. (2004). Built to win. *New Scientist*, 30 October, 50–53.

Anon. (1998). Having a short Achilles tendon may be an athlete's Achilles heel. *Peak Performance*, 100 (February), 19.

Ashcroft, F. (2001) *Life At The Extremes: The Science of Survival*. London: HarperCollins.

Atkinson, G., Storrow, M., & Cable, N.T. (2001). Eating habits and body mass control methods in flat race and National Hunt jockeys.

Bam, J., Noakes, T.D., Juritz, J., & Dennis, S.C. (1997). Could women outrun men in ultramarathon races? *Medicine and Science in Sports and Exercise*, 29(2), 244–247.

Bergh, U., Thorstensson, A., Sjödin, B., Hulten, B., Piehl, K., & Karlsson, J. (1978) Maximal oxygen uptake and muscle fiber types in trained and untrained humans. *Medicine and Science in Sports*, 10, 151–154.

Bramble, D.M., & Lieberman, D.E. (2004). Endurance running and the evolution of Homo. *Nature*, 432 (18 November), 345–352.

Budiansky, S. (1996). Don't bet on faster horses. *New Scientist, August 10,* 29-31.

Camhi, J.M., & Johnson, E.N. (1999). High-frequency steering maneuvers mediated by tactile cues: antennal wall-following in the cockroach. *Journal of Experimental Biology*, 202, 631–643.

Clarke, D.H. (1986). Sex differences in strength and fatigability. *Research Quarterly for Exercise and Sport*, 57, 144–149.

Costill, D.L., Daniels, J., Evans, W., Fink, W., Krahenbuhl, G., & Saltin, B. (1976). Skeletal muscle enzymes and fiber composition in male and female track athletes. *Journal of Applied Physiology*, 40, 149–154.

Craig, N.P., & Norton, K.I. (2001). Characteristics of track cycling. *Sports Medicine*, 31, 457–468.

Dawson, T.J. (1977). Kangaroos. *Scientific American*, 237(2), 78–89.

Evans, D.L., Harris, R.C., & Snow, D.H. (1993). Correlation of racing performance with blood lactate and heart rate after exercise in Thoroughbred horses. *Equine Veterinary Journal*, 25, 441–445.

Evans, D.L., & Rose, R.J. (1988). Cardiovascular and respiratory responses to submaximal exercise training in the thoroughbred horse. *Pflugers Archive*.

Farrow, D., & Kemp, J. (2003). *Run Like You Stole Something*. Allen & Unwin, Sydney.

Gelfi, C., de Palma, S., Ripamonti, M., Eberini, I., Wait, R., Bajracharya, A.,

Marconi, C., Schneider, A., Hoppeler, H., & Cerretelli, P. (2004). New aspects of altitude adaptation in Tibetans: a proteomic approach. *FASEB Journal*, 18, 612–614.

Graham, S. (2002). Scientists discover new adaptation to oxygen-poor air at high altitudes. *Scientific American.com*, 3 December. <http://www.sciam.com>

Hall, M. (1997). *The Big Book of Sumo*. Stone Bridge Press, Berkeley, CA.

Hill, C.A., O'Connor, H.T., Hooper, M., & White, B. (1999). Energy intake and resting metabolic rate of professional jockeys. *Proceedings of the 5th IOC World Congress on Sport Sciences*.

Hill, C.A., & O'Connor, H.T. (2000) Professional jockeys (Chap. 6). In: Norton, K., Olds, T., & Dollman, J. (eds), *Kinanthropometry VI: Proceedings of the 6th Scientific Conference of the International Society for the Advancement of Kinanthropometry*.International Society for the Advancement of Kinanthropometry, Underdale, South Australia.

Kanehisa, H., Kondo, M., Ikegawa, S., & Fukunaga, T. (1997.) Characteristics of body composition and muscle strength in college sumo wrestlers. *International Journal of Sports Medicine*, 18, 510–515.

King, M.B., & Mezey, G. (1987). Eating behaviour of male racing jockeys. *Psychological Medicine*, 17, 249–253.

Kram, R., & Taylor, C.R. (1990). Energetics of running: a new perspective. *Nature*, 346, 265–267.

Kumagai, K., Abe, T., Brechue, W.F., Ryushi, T., Takano, S., & Mizuno, M. (2000). Sprint performance is related to muscle fascicle length in male 100-m sprinters. *Journal of Applied Physiology*, 88, 811–816.

Labadarios, D., Kotze, J., Momberg, D., & Kotze, T.J.W. (1993). Jockeys and their practices in South Africa. In: *Nutrition and Fitness for Athletes. World Rev. Nutr. Diet. Vol. 71*. Karger, Basel, 97–114.

Lindstedt, S.L., Hokanson, J.F., Wells, D.J., Swain, S.D., Hoppeler, H., & Navarro, V. (1991). Running energetics in the pronghorn antelope. *Nature*, 353 (24 October), 748–750.

Lucía, A., Hoyos, J., & Chicharro, J.L. (2001). Physiology of professional road cycling. *Sports Medicine, 31*, 325–337.

McIlroy, E. (2003). Leaping bug is new high-jump champion. *NewScientist.com*, 3 July. <http://www.newscientist.com>

McKee, M. (2004). Astronomers pinpoint date of first marathon. *NewScientist.com*, 4 July. <http://www.newscientist.com>

Marconi, C., Marzorati, M., Grassi, B., Basnyat, B., Colombini, A., Kayser, B., & Cerretelli, P. (2004). Second generation Tibetan lowlanders acclimatize to high altitude more quickly than Caucasians. *Journal of Physiology, 556*, 661–671.

Martin, D.T., McLean, B., Trewin, C., Lee, H., Victor, J., & Hahn, A.G. (2001). Physiological characteristics of nationally competitive female road cyclists and demands of competition. *Sports Medicine*, 31, 469–477.

Martino, M., Gledhill, N., & Jamnik, V. (2002). High VO2max with no history of training is primarily due to high blood volume. *Medicine and Science in Sports and*

Exercise, 34(6), 966–971.

Misner, J.E., Massey, B.H., Going, S.B., Bemben, M.G., & Ball, T.E. (1990). Sex differences in static strength and fatigability in three different muscle groups. *Research Quarterly for Exercise and Sport*, 61, 238–242.

Mujika, I., & Padilla, S. (2001). Physiological and performance characteristics of male professional road cyclists. *Sports Medicine*, 31, 479–487.

Nihon Sumo Kyokai (Japan Sumo Association). (1997). *The Power and the Glory! Australian Grand Sumo Tournaments*. Nihon Sumo Kyokai.

Nishida, Y., Akaoka, I., Hayashi, E., & Miyamoto, T. (1983). Elevated erythrocyte phosphoribosylpyrophosphate and ATP concentrations in Japanese sumo wrestlers. *British Journal of Nutrition*, 49, 3–7.

Nishizawa, T., Akaoka, I., Nishida, Y., Kawaguchi, Y., Hayashi, E., & Yoshimura, T. (1976). Some factors related to obesity in the Japanese sumo wrestler. *American Journal of Clinical Nutrition*, 29, 1167–1174.

Norton, K., Olds, T., Olive, S., & Dank, S. (1994). Will the real Ken and Barbie please stand up. In: *Proceedings of the International Conference of Science and Medicine in Sport*. Sports Medicine Australia, 248–249.

Nowak, R. (2004) Exercise doesn't work for all of us. *New Scientist, 184* (2476), 15.

Phillips, S.M., Atkinson, S.A., Tarnopolsky, M.A., & MacDougall, J.D. (1993). Gender differences in leucine kinetics and nitrogen balance in endurance athletes. *Journal of Applied Physiology*, 75, 2134–2141.

Postman, A., & Stone, L. (1990). *The Ultimate Book of Sports Lists*. Bantam Books, New York.

Proske, U. (1996). Hopping mad. *Nature Australia*, Spring, 57–63.

Pyne, D. (1993). Is there a gender difference in running economy? *Sport Health*, 11(2), 45–46.

Radford, P. (1984). The nature and nurture of a sprinter. *New Scientist*, 2 August, 13–15.

Randerson, J. (2003). Big hearted horses are first past the post. *NewScientist.com*, 9 January. <http://www.newscientist.com>

Rose, R.J., Hodgson, D.R., Kelso, T.B., McCutcheon, L.J., Reid, T.-A., Bayly, W.M., & Gollnick, P.D. (1988). Maximum O_2 uptake, O_2 debt and deficit, and muscle metabolites in Thoroughbred horses. *Journal of Applied Physiology*, 64, 781–788.

Sharp, C. (1984). Physiology and the woman athlete. *New Scientist*, 2 August, 22–24.

Speechly, D.P., Taylor, S.R., & Rogers, G.G. (1996). Differences in ultra-endurance exercise in performance-matched male and female runners. *Medicine and Science in Sports and Exercise*, 28, 359–365.

Steen, S.N. (1989). Nutritional concerns of athletes who must reduce body weight. *Sports Science Exchange*, 2(10), SSE#20.

Stupka, N., Lowther, S., Chorneyko, K., Bourgeois, J.M., Hogben, C., & Tarnopolsky, M.A. (2000). Gender differences in muscle inflammation after eccentric exercise. *Journal of Applied Physiology*, 89, 2325–2332.

Tarnopolsky, L.J., MacDougall, J.D., Atkinson, S.A., Tarnopolsky, M.A., & Sutton, J.R. (1990). Gender differences in substrate for endurance exercise. *Journal of Applied Physiology*, 68, 302–308.

Tarnopolsky, M.A. (2000). Gender differences in metabolism: nutrition and supplements. *Journal of Science and Medicine in Sport*, 3, 287–298.

Tarnopolsky, M.A. (2000). Gender differences in substrate metabolism during endurance exercise. *Canadian Journal of Applied Physiology*, 25, 312–327.

Wallechinsky, D. (2004). *The Complete Book of the Olympics (2004 Edition)*. Aurum Press, London.

Wheeler, M. (1996). Welcome to the animal Olympics. *Herald Sun*, 15 September, 72.

Whipp, B.J., & Ward, S.A. (1992). Will women soon outrun men? *Nature*, 355 (2 January), 25.

CHAPTER 5:
BEATING THE CHEATS

Anderson, J.L., Schjerling, P., & Saltin, B. (2000). Muscle, genes and athletic performance. *Scientific American*, 283(3), 48–55.

Aschwanden, C. (2000). Gene cheats. *New Scientist*, 15 January, 25–29.

Ashcroft, F. (2001). *Life At The Extremes: The Science of Survival*. HarperCollins, London.

Ashley, S. (2004). Doping by design. *Scientific American.com*, January. <http://www.sciam.com>

Australian Sports Doping Agency. (2005). History of drugs in sport. *Australian Sports Doping Agency*. <http://www.asda.org.au/media/history.htm> (January).

Australian Sports Doping Agency. (2005). Drug testing procedure. *Australian Sports Doping Agency*. <http://www.asda.org.au/athletes/testing.htm> (January).

Australian Sports Doping Agency. (2005). Substance fact sheets. *Australian Sports Doping Agency*. <http://www.asda.org.au/athletes/sub_fact.htm> (January).

Australian Sports Drug Agency. (2005). Prohibited substances and methods. *Australian Sports Drug Agency*. <http://www.asda.org.au/athletes/banned.htm> (January).

Bridge, M.W., Weller, A.S., Rayson, D., & Jones, D.A. (2003). Responses to exercise in the heat related to measures of hypothalamic serotonergic and dopaminergic function. *Journal of Applied Physiology*, 89, 451–459.

Brooks, G.A., Fahey, T.D., White, T.P., & Baldwin, K.M. (2001). *Exercise Physiology: Human Bioenergetics and its Applications (3rd edn)*. McGraw-Hill, New York.

Cohen, D. (2004). Steroids boost performance in just weeks. *New Scientist*, 183(2460), 6–7.

Davis, J.M., & Bailey, S.P. (1997). Possible mechanisms of central nervous system fatigue during exercise. *Medicine and Science in Sports and Exercise*, 29, 45–57.

Eichner, E.R. (1992). Better dead than second. *Journal of Laboratory & Clinical Medicine*, 120, 359–360.

Ekblom, B., & Berglund, B. (1991). Effect of erythropoietin administration on maximal aerobic power. *Scandinavian Journal of Medicine and Science in Sports*, 1, 88–93.

Gaudard, A., Varlet-Marie, E., Bressolle, F., & Audran, M. (2003). Drugs for increasing oxygen transport and their potential use in doping. *Sports Medicine*, 33(3), 187–212.

Gayagay, G., Yu, B., Hambly, B., Boston, T., Hahn, A., Celermajer, D.S., & Trent, R.J. (1998). Elite endurance athletes and the ACE I allele – the role of genes in athletic performance. *Human Genetics*, 103, 48–50.

Graham, T.E., & Spriet, L.L. (1996). Caffeine and exercise performance. *Sports Science Exchange*, 9(1), #60.

Hasegawa, H., Watson, P., Roelands, B., Looverie, R., Buyse, L., De Schutter, G., Piacentini, M.F., & Meeusen, R. (2004). Time trial performance in the heat is influenced by a dopamine/noradrenaline reuptake inhibitor. *Proceedings of the 9th Annual Congress of the European College of Sport Science*, 179.

Kutscher, E.C., Lund, B.C., & Perry, P.J. (2002). Anabolic steroids: A review for the clinician. *Sports Medicine*, 32, 285–296.

Lasne, F., & de Ceaurriz, J. (2000). Recombinant erythropoietin in urine. *Nature*, 405, 8 June 8, 635.

Lawson, G. (1997). *World Record Breakers in Track & Field Athletics*. Human Kinetics, Champaign, IL.

Lee, S-J., & McPherron, A.C. (2001). Regulation of myostatin activity and muscle growth. *Proceedings of the National Academy of Science*, 98(16), 9306–9311.

Linderman, J.K., & Gosselink, K.L. (1994). The effects of sodium bicarbonate ingestion on exercise performance. *Sports Medicine*, 18, 75–80.

Lucia, A., Earnest, C., & Arribas, C. (2003). The Tour de France: a physiological review. *Scandinavian Journal of Medicine & Science in Sports*, 13, 275–283.

Martinek, V., Fu, F.H., & Huard, J. (2000). Gene therapy and tissue engineering in sports medicine. *Physician and Sportsmedicine*, 28(2), 34–51.

Marx, J.J.M., & Vergouwen, P.C.J. (1998). Packed-cell volume in elite athletes, *Lancet*, 352, 451.

Montgomery, H.E., Marshall, R., Hemingway, H., Myerson, S., Clarkson, P., Dollery, C., Hayward, M., Holliman, D.E., Jubb, M., World, M., Thomas, E.I., Brynes, A.E., Saeed, N., Barnard, M., Bell, J.D., Prasad, K., Rayson, M., Talmud, P.J., & Humphries, S.E. (1998). Human gene for physical performance. *Nature*, 393, 221–222.

Nelson, M., Popp, H., Sharpe, K., & Ashenden, M. (2003). Proof of homologous blood transfusion through quantification of blood group antigens. *Haematologica*, 88, 1284–1295.

Nielsen, B., & Nybo, L. (2003). Cerebral changes during exercise in the heat. *Sports Medicine*, 33, 1–11.

Noakes, T.D., St Clair Gibson, A., & Lambert, E.V. (2004). From catastrophe to complexity: a novel model of integrative central neural regulation of effort and fatigue during exercise in humans. *British Journal of Sports Medicine*, 38, 511–514.

Nybo, L., Nielsen, B., Blomstrand, E., Møller, K., & Secher, N. (2003). Neurohumoral responses during prolonged exercise in humans. *Journal of Applied Physiology*, 95, 1125–1131.

Nybo, L., Nielsen, B., Pedersen, B.K., Møller, K., & Secher, N,H. (2002). Interleukin-6 release from the human brain during prolonged exercise. *Journal of Physiology*, 542 (Pt 3), 991–995.

Parisotto, R., Gore, C.J., Emslie, K.R., Ashenden, M.J., Brugnara, C., Howe, C., Martin, D.T., Trout, G.J., & Hahn, A.G. (2000). A novel method utilizing markers of altered erythropoiesis for the detection of recombinant human erythropoietin abuse in athletes. *Haematologica*, 85, 564–572.

Pärssinen, M., Kujala, U., Vartiainen, E., Sarna, S., & Seppälä. (2000). Increased premature mortality of competitive powerlifters suspected to have used anabolic agents. *International Journal of Sports Medicine*, 21, 225–227.

Pasman, W.J., van Baak, M.A., Jeukendrup, A.E., & de Haan, A. (1995). The effect of different dosages of caffeine on endurance performance time. *International Journal of Sports Medicine*, 16, 225–230.

Piacentini, M.F., Meeusen, R., Buyse, L., De Schutter, G., & De Meirleir, K. (2004). Hormonal responses during prolonged exercise are influenced by a selective DA/NA reuptake inhibitor. *British Journal of Sports Medicine*, 38, 129–133.

Powers, S.K., & Howley, E.T. (2004). *Exercise Physiology: Theory and Applications to Fitness and Performance (5th edn.)*. McGraw-Hill, New York.

Rankinen, T., Pérusse, L., Rauramaa, R., Rivera, M.A., Wolfarth, B., & Bouchard, C. (2004). The human gene map for performance and health-related fitness phenotypes: the 2003 update. *Medicine and Science in Sports and Exercise*, 36(9), 1451–69.

Rendell, M., & Cheetham, N. (eds). (2003). *The Official Tour de France Centennial 1903–2003*. Weidenfeld & Nicolson, London.

Robergs, R.A., & Roberts, S.O. (1997). *Exercise Physiology: Exercise, Performance, and Clinical Applications*. Mosby, St. Louis.

Robson-Ansley, P.J., de Milander L., Collins, M., & Noakes, T.D. (2004). Acute interleukin-6 administration impairs athletic performance in healthy, trained male runners. *Canadian Journal of Applied Physiology*, 29(4).

Saris, W.H.M., Senden, J.M.G., & Brouns, F. (1989). What is the normal red-blood cell mass for professional cyclists? *Lancet*, 352, 1758.

Schumacher, Y.O., & Ashenden, M. (2004). Doping with artificial oxygen carriers: an update. *Sports Medicine*, 34, 141–150.

Science and Industry Against Blood doping. (2004). Research: Blood transfusion. *Science and Industry Against Blood doping Research Consortium*. <http://www.siab.ws/research.htm> (November).

Sweeney, H.L. (2004). Gene doping. *Scientific American*, July, 37–43.

Taubes, G. (2000). Towards molecular talent scouting. *Scientific American (Quarterly)*, 11(3), 26–31.

VanHelder, W.P., Kofman, E., & Tremblay, M.S. (1991). Anabolic steroids in sport. *Canadian Journal of Sport Sciences*, 16, 248–257.

Wallechinsky, D. (1984). *The Complete Book of the Olympics*. Penguin Books, Middlesex.

Wallechinsky, D. (2004). *The Complete Book of the Olympics (2004 Edition)*. Aurum Press, London.

Williams, M.H. (1992). Bicarbonate loading. *Sports Science Exchange*, 5(1), #36.

World Anti-Doping Agency. (2004). A brief history of anti-doping. *World Anti-Doping Agency*. <http://www.wada-ama.org/en/dynamic.ch2?pageCategory_id=20>(December).

World Anti-Doping Agency. (2005). Prohibited list. *World Anti-Doping Agency*. <http://www.wada-ama.org/en/dynamic.ch2?pageCategory_id=47> (January).

Yang, N., MacArthur, D.G., Gulbin, J.P., Hahn, A.G., Beggs, A.H., Easteal, S., & North, K. (2003). ACTN3 genotype is associated with human elite athletic performance. *American Journal of Human Genetics*, 73, 627–631.

CHAPTER 6:
IN THE LAB

Abernethy, B., Côté, J. & Baker, J. (2002). *Expert decision-making in team sports*. Research report to the Australian Sports Commission, Canberra.

American College of Sports Medicine. (1995). *ACSM's Guidelines for Exercise Testing and Prescription*. Williams & Wilkins, Baltimore.

Arnason, A., Sigurdsson, S.B., Gudmundsson, A., Holme, I., Engebretsen, L., & Bahr, R. (2004). Physical fitness, injuries, and team performance in soccer. *Medicine and Science in Sports and Exercise*, 36, 278–285.

Australian Institute of Sport. *National Talent Search Program – What is it?* <http://www.ais.org.au/talent/index.asp>

Bishop, D. (2004). *Professor Frank Cotton: 'Father of sport science'*. Presentation at the AAESS National Conference, Brisbane, Australia.

Brooks, G.A. (1992). Blood lactic acid: Sports 'bad boy' turns good. *Gatorade Sports Science Exchange*, 2.

Chad, K. & Steele, J. (1990). *Relationship between Physical Requirements and Physiological Responses to Match Play and Training in Skilled Netball Players: Basis of Tailor-Made Training Programs*. A report presented to the Australian Sports Commission's Applied Sports Research Program. Australian Sports Commission, Canberra.

Coyle, E.F. (2005) Improved muscular efficiency displayed as Tour de France champion matures. *Journal of Applied Physiology*, 98, 2191-2196.

de Groot, A. (1965). *Thought and choice in chess*. Mouton, The Hague.

Draper, J.A. & Lancaster, M.G. (1985). The 505 test: a test for agility in the horizontal plane. *Australian Journal of Science and Medicine in Sport*, 17(1), 15–18.

Drawer, S., & Fuller, C.W. (2002). Evaluating the level of injury in English professional football using a risk based assessment process. *British Journal of Sports Medicine*, 36, 446–451.

Dutka, T.L., & Lamb, G.D. (2000). Effect of lactate on depolarization-induced Ca2+ release in mechanically skinned skeletal muscle fibers. *American Journal of Physiology: Cell Physiology*, 278, C517–C525.

Farrow, D. (2003). Virtual netball…a new age in skill testing. *Australian Netballer*, 10, 18–19.

Farrow, D. (2004). Reading the play in team-sports: Yes it's trainable! *Sports Coach*, 27(3).

Farrow, D., Chivers, P., Hardingham, C., & Sachse, S. (1998). The effect of video-based perceptual training on the tennis return of serve. *International Journal of Sports Psychology*, 23, 231–242.

Farrow, D., Young, W., & Bruce, L. (in press). The development of a test of reactive agility for netball: A new methodology. *Journal of Science and Medicine in Sport*.

Fox III, S.M., Naughton, J.P., & Haskell, W.L. (1971). Physical activity and the prevention of coronary heart disease. *Annals of Clinical Research*, 3, 404–432.

Froelicher, V.F., & Myers, J.N. (2000). *Exercise and the Heart (4th edn.)*. WB Saunders Philadelphia.

Gladden, L.B. (2004). Lactate metabolism: a new paradigm for the third millennium. *Journal of Physiology*, 558, 5–30.

Gulbin, J. (2004). Paradigm shifts in talent identification (Abstract). *Conference Proceedings of the Pre-Olympic Congress*. Thessaloniki, Greece. 6–11 August.

Haskins, M. J. (1965). Development of a response recognition training film in tennis. *Perceptual and Motor Skills*, 21, 207–211.

Hilbert, M., Shushakov, V., Stuke, N., & Maassen, N. (2004). The influence of respiratory acid-base disturbances on performance during intermittent exercise of high intensity of a small muscle group. *Proceedings of the 9th Annual Congress of European College of Sport* Science, 259.

Hollmann, W. (2001). 42 years ago – development of the concepts of ventilatory and lactate threshold. *Sports Medicine*, 31, 315–320.

Inbar, O., Oten, A., Scheinowitz, M., Rotstein, A., Dlin, R., & Casaburi, R. (1994). Normal cardiopulmonary responses during incremental exercise in 20–70-yr-old men. *Medicine and Science in Sports and Exercise*, 26(5), 538–546.

Johnson, L. (2004). Brisbane medicos the key players. *The Age*, 24 September.

Lawson, G. (1997). *World Record Breakers in Track & Field Athletics*. Human Kinetics, Champaign, IL.

Lucia, A., Earnest, C., & Arribas, C. (2003). The Tour de France: a physiological review. *Scandinavian Journal of Medicine & Science in Sports*, 13, 275–283.

Lucia, A., Hoyos, J., Carvajal, A., & Chicharro, J.L. (1999). Heart rate responses to professional road cycling: the Tour de France. *International Journal of Sports Medicine*, 20, 167–172.

Nielsen, O.B., de Paoli, F., & Overgaard, K. (2001). Protective effects of lactic acid on force production in rat skeletal muscle. *Journal of Physiology*, 536, 161–166.

Olds, T. (1998). The mathematics of breaking away and chasing in cycling. *European Journal of Applied Physiology*, 77, 492–497.

Otago, L. (1983). A game analysis of the activity patterns of netball players. *Sports Coach*, 7(1), 24–28.

Padilla, S., Mujika, I., Angulo, F., & Goiriena, J.J. (2000). Scientific approach to the 1-h cycling world record: a case study. *Journal of Applied Physiology*, 89,1522–1527.

Pedersen, T.H. (2004). Arhus University. 3RRR-FM, 31 March.

Pedersen, T.H., Nielsen, O.B., Lamb, G.D., & Stephenson, D.G. (2004). Intracellular acidosis enhances the excitability of working muscle. *Science*, 305, 20 August, 1144–1147.

Phillips, M. *From Sidelines to Centrefield – A History of Sports Coaching in Australia*. UNSW Press, Sydney.

Posterino, G.S., Dutka, T.L., & Lamb, G.D. (2001). L(+)-lactate does not affect twitch and tetanic responses in mechanically skinned mammalian muscle fibres. *Pflügers Archives – European Journal of Physiology*, 442, 197–203.

Rahnama, N., Reilly, T., & Lees, A. (2002). Injury risk associated with playing actions during competitive soccer. *British Journal of Sports Medicine*, 36, 354–359.

Robergs, R.A., Ghiasvand, F., & Parker, D. (2004). Biochemistry of exercise-induced metabolic acidosis. *American Journal Regulatory Integrative Comparative Physiology*, 287, R502–R516.

Robergs, R.A., & Landwehr, R. (2002). The surprising history of the 'HRmax=220-age' equation. *Journal of Exercise Physiology online*, 5(2). <http://www.asep.org/jeponline/JEPhome.htm> (May).

Smith, A. (2002). The Science of Winning. ABC Radio National's *The Sports Factor*. <http://www.abc.net.au/rn/talks/8.30/sportsf/stories/s686461.htm>

Smith, A. (2002). The Whirlwind Ebony Trundler. ABC Radio National's *The Sports Factor*. <http://www.abc.net.au/rn/talks/8.30/sportsf/stories/s695690.htm>

Steele, J. & Chad, K. (1992). An analysis of the movement patterns of netball players during matchplay: Implications for designing training programs. *Sports Coach*, 15(1), 21–28.

Tanaka, H., Monahan, K.D., & Seals, D.R. (2001). Age-predicted maximal heart rate revisited. *Journal of the American College of Cardiology*, 37, 153–156.

The Times Athletics Correspondent. (1954). Stepping-stones to the four minute mile. *Times Online*. <http://www.timesonline.co.uk/article/0,,13849-1097264,00.html> (6 May 2004).

Torrey, L. (1985). *Stretching The Limits: Breakthroughs In Sports Science That Create Superathletes*. Dodd, Mead & Company, New York.

TrakPerformance Software. *An Eagle View of Trak Performance*. <http://www.sportstecinternational.com/index.html>

UK Athletics. (2004). First four minute mile – 50th celebrations. *International Association of Athletics Federations*. <http://www.iaaf.org/news/Kind=2/newsld=23993.html> (February).

University of Michigan. *The Virtual Football Trainer*.
<http://www-vrl.unimich.edu/project/football/>

Westerblad, H. (1999). The role of pH and inorganic phosphate ions in skeletal muscle fatigue (Chap. 12). In: Hargreaves, M., & Thompson, M. (eds), *Biochemistry of Exercise X*. Human Kinetics, Champaign, IL.

Westerblad, H., Bruton, J.D., & Lännergren, J. (1997). The effect of intracellular pH on contractile function of intact, single fibres of mouse declines with increasing temperature. *Journal of Physiology*.

Wilson, C. (2003). Raise you 50. *New Scientist*, 180(2426), 64.

Woolford, S., & Angove, M. (1991). A comparison of training techniques and game intensities for national level netball players. *Sports Coach*, 14(4), 18–21.

For exhibitions relating to sport visit:

Powerhouse Museum

500 Harris Street, Ultimo, Sydney, New South Wales, Australia

Ph +612 9217 0111

<www.phm.gov.au>

Scienceworks Museum & the Melbourne Planetarium

2 Booker Street, Spotswood, Victoria, Australia

Ph +613 9392 4800

<scienceworks.museum.vic.gov.au>

Australian Gallery of Sport and Olympic Museum (AGSOM)

MCG, Melbourne

Ph +613 96578879

PHOTOGRAPHIC CREDITS

Cover
Front cover: Image of Dick Fosbury, courtesy of Getty Images; background image from 1968 Mexico Olympics, unknown source. Back cover: Author photo: Kemp (left) and Farrow (right), courtesy of Natalie Cursio

Text
Pages (i), 31, 63, 109, 141 and 173: courtesy of Natalie Cursio
Page 1: courtesy of Felicity Pearson

Illustrated section
Figures A to K: courtesy of Powerhouse Museum. Images are from the 'Sport: more than heroes and legends' exhibition, touring Australia, organised by the Powerhouse Museum in association with the Australian Gallery of Sport and Olympic Museum at the MCG in Melbourne. Photography by Paul Rovere.
Figure L: courtesy of the Australian Institute of Sport

ACKNOWLEDGEMENTS

Justin and Damian would like to acknowledge and thank the following runners and stables for their assistance during the 2006 Book Production Carnival.

Race 1   The *Why Dick Flopped* Stakes   3200m
(Three-Year-Olds & Upwards. Open. Apprentices can claim)

No. Form	Runner	Jockey	Trainer	Barrier	Weight	Price
1 – 518s	GREAT DANES	Niels Ørtenblad	Thomas Pedersen	(10)	60.5	15.00
2 – 541s	SNAP HAPPY	Natalie Cursio	Paul Rovere	(3)	58.5	15.00
3 – 73s0	PAPER BOY	John Harms	Peter Hanlon	(12)	57.5	21.00
4 – 3121	LAB RAT	Craig Goodman	Brett O'Connell	(13)	57	17.00
5 – 9460	FACE FOR RADIO	Jason Agosta	Jesse Fyfe	(5)	56.5	5.00
6 – s00	BINAURAL HEAD	Richard Pike	Nik Tripp	(8)	55.5	4.50
7 – 6421	GOAL SNEAK	Ted Hopkins	Morgan Williams	(14)	54.5	9.00
8 – 4367	BIG EARS	Andrea Farrow	Oliver Scott	(11)	54	15.00
9 – s095	FRANK EINSTEIN	Aleks Subic	Travis Dutka	(6)	54	9.00
10 – 7909	SECOND CHANCE	Sue Hines	Andrea McNamara	(2)	54	4.50
11 – 2311	DEWEY DECIMAL	Greg Blood	Tim Byrne	(1)	53	41.00
12 – 2152	FOOT IN MOUTH	David Rath	John Baker	(7)	53	13.00
13 – 4014	BURGER BOY	Tony Rice	Marc Portus	(9)	52.5	21.00
14 – 1s14	HAIRLESS	Inigo Mujika	Jason Gulbin	(4)	52	6.00

STABLES FEATURED IN THIS RACE:
Australian Institute of Sport
National Sport Information Centre, Australian Sports Commission
School of Exercise Science (Vic), Australian Catholic University
Raheen Library, Australian Catholic University
Muscle Cell Biochemistry Laboratory, Victoria University
Champion Data Pty. Ltd.
Scienceworks Museum
Allen & Unwin Book Publishers

LISTEN TO THE BIG RACE
In Melbourne   3RRR 102.7 FM – Saturday mornings 9-10am
Around Australia   http://rrr.org.au – LIVE on the Net

INDEX

Also by

DAMIAN FARROW & JUSTIN KEMP

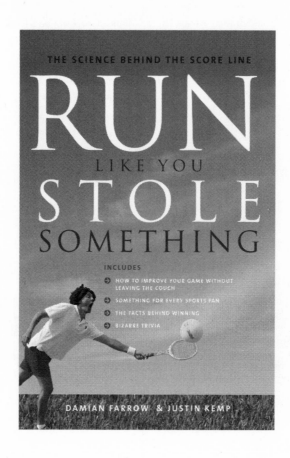